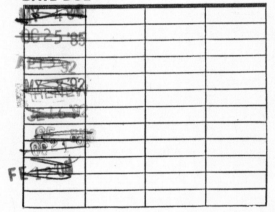

# BEALE BLACK & BLUE

# BEALE BLACK &BLUE

*Life and Music on Black America's Main Street*

Margaret McKee • Fred Chisenhall

Louisiana State University Press
Baton Rouge and London

DESIGNER: Patricia Douglas Crowder
TYPEFACE: Linotype Caledonia
TYPESETTER: Service Typesetting Co.

The authors wish to acknowledge the generosity of the National Endowment for the Arts for providing a grant that aided in research.

This book was written in cooperation with the Everett R. Cook Oral History Program of the Memphis and Shelby County Public Library and Information Center.

LIBRARY OF CONGRESS CATALOGING IN PUBLICATION DATA

McKee, Margaret.
  Beale black and blue.

  Bibliography: p.
  Includes index.
    1. Afro-Americans—Tennessee—Memphis—Music—History
and criticism. 2. Music—Tennessee—Memphis—History
and criticism. 3. Afro-American musicians—Tennessee—
Memphis—Interviews. 4. Memphis (Tenn.)—Social life
and customs. 5. Beale Street (Memphis, Tenn.)
6. Memphis (Tenn.)—Streets. I. Chisenhall, Fred.
II. Title.
ML3556.M117        781.7'296073076819        81-4995
ISBN 0-8071-0863-4        AACR2

*To Sam Bledsoe*

# Contents

# Illustrations

# Preface and Acknowledgments

We could not have started or completed this book without the help of friends—friends of the blues, of Beale Street, and of ours.

Not the least of our problems was our own self-doubt about our credentials. We were neither historians nor musicologists. We were journalists—white journalists, at that, one from the Mississippi Delta, the other from Arkansas on the other side of the river. Having grown up listening to Gene Autry, Tex Ritter, Roy Acuff, and Hank Williams, we had no particular knowledge of black blues. We were aware that our research into black history and the blues might be regarded as somewhat presumptuous.

But we undertook our research not as a study of the blues but of the blues musicians themselves. They were a dying breed, these wandering minstrels who had become the principal storytellers of their people; and many of their stories—as well as their expressive idioms, whose strength and beauty we believe to be unmatched—were dying with them. Several blues musicians who rightly belong in this book aren't in it, either because of death or, as with such important figures as Gus Cannon and Memphis Minnie McCoy, debilitating illness. Several whose stories are included have died since our interviews.

Originally we intended to base the book entirely on the oral history interviews with the blues musicians. The deeper we got into the project, however, the more we became aware that the emotional attachment of the blues people to Beale Street was a dominant part of their story (and also that Beale, as viewed by most white people, may well be the world's most misunderstood mile of real estate). We expanded our scope to include some of the history of Beale but immediately learned one of the hard lessons about black history: so much of it has gone unrecorded, so many documents have been mutilated, lost, or destroyed. Black newspapers, including the Memphis *World*, probably the leading black publication in the Memphis area, were not preserved. In several places we have quoted from private clippings of columns in these papers, which included neither date nor page number. White newspapers made little or no effort to record what was happening in the black community.

Our research, in fact, ran into so many brick walls that on more than one occasion we were on the verge of shucking the whole project. But each time someone stepped forth with a gentle nudge to get us going again.

The late Sam Bledsoe never doubted, even when we did, that we could do the job. His reminiscences of his days as a young newspaper reporter in Memphis gave us a look at the past nowhere else available.

The Memphis Public Library provided equipment, tapes, and secretarial help in transcribing the interviews. We're particularly indebted to Nat Josel, former director of the library's history department, who spent untold hours working with us and the tapes. He and his wife, Jackie, were steadfast in their encouragement and cooperation.

Thanks largely to the efforts of Congressman Jamie Whitten of Mississippi and former Congressman Wilbur Mills of Arkansas, we received financial assistance on the research with a grant from the National Endowment for the Arts.

Blues and jazz authority Harry Godwin was an invaluable ally in locating many of the old Beale Streeters and blues people. John B. McKee, Jr., gave generous aid in a number of ways. Bill Leaptrott and his camera contributed some unforgettable pictures. The Memphis *Press-Scimitar* allowed us access to its files. We owe special thanks to Paul Coppock, retired newspaperman and author of several books dealing with Memphis history, who read the final manuscript and offered valuable suggestions, and to Charles T. Traylor of Memphis State University, our cartographer.

We could have done nothing, of course, without the cooperation of the blues people and the Beale Streeters themselves. They were gracious, patient, and understanding and opened doors to us in more ways than one. Tapes of our interviews with them from 1972 through 1976 will be on permanent file at the Memphis library, with some of the tapes duplicated for the National Archives in Washington, D.C.

And then there was the most important ally of all, the man who loved Beale Street most, Nat D. Williams. At the time we met him, he was still recovering from a stroke that had forced him to retire from his teaching position and his radio news-music-history show. In no way did his illness affect what he called "a feel for Beale—the *real* Beale," nor his ability to bring the old street to life again as he sat for hours during our taping sessions. Much of the information from him in chapters four through seven came from these interviews at his home on February 2 and 9, 1973, and on Beale Street, October 19, 1973. In addition, thanks to his "Down on Beale" columns for the Memphis *World* and the Pittsburgh *Courier* from 1931 to 1970, he filled in many of the history gaps that had frustrated us. To him we owe an everlasting gratitude—not only for opening our eyes to the way it was, but for sharing his vision of the way it ought to be.

PART I

# BEALE

• "The white people of Memphis have never understood just what Beale Street really meant and means to my people."

> W. C. Handy, in an interview at his home in New York, Memphis *Press-Scimitar*, November 16, 1955.

• "It is the Main Street of Negro America, where the pulse of dark America beats highest, where richly dark red brown lovely women, hang-jawed country rubes mingle with spruce urban Negroes in an atmophere pungent with barbecued pig, alive with loud and plaintive music of those who sit around in the cafes trying to ease their souls with ready-made song."

> George W. Lee, insurance executive and author, in a speech before the Memphis Downtown Association, December 21, 1965.

• "The average person that went shopping back in those days, I don't care what part of the town they lived in, they going to come to Beale Street before they go home—the Christians, the hypocrites, and everybody else."

> Alex Sims, blues musician, in an interview at his home in Memphis, November 11, 1973.

• "Beale Street approaches more nearly an expression of the mass of American Negroes than any other place, including Harlem, for Beale is closer to the great bulk of the nation's colored population, and speaks more distinctly their traditional language of frustration, hope, struggle and slow advance."

> Walter P. Adkins, "Beale Street Goes to the Polls," M.A. thesis, Ohio State University, 1935.

• "Beale Street cuts a ragged gulch thru the toughest sector of Memphis. Day-time Beale Street runs up from the river and down to Hernando. Here are the pawn shops, the hand-me-downs fringing the sidewalk with bristling show racks, flapping suits and men who buy and sell. Night-time Beale Street lies between Fourth and Hernando, and, as midnight drifts past the street, pulls at its belt, tucks in its ragged shirt-tail, looks over its shoulder and waits for something to happen. Little time is spent in waiting."

Walter Stewart, *Press-Scimitar*, March 2, 1935.

• "I hope they can keep Beale Street like it is. It's going to be a controversial thing. But would it be Beale Street if it was remodeled up?"

Otto Lee, blues musician, in an interview by Jack Hurley, at Lee's home in Memphis on March 3, 1967, on file at Memphis State University Library.

• "Come what may, there will always be a Beale Street, because Beale Street is a spirit . . . Beale Street is a symbol . . . Beale Street is a way of life . . . Beale Street is a hope."

Nat D. Williams, Memphis *World*, November 30, 1945.

• "Beale Street is as dead as a dodo nowadays and hants walk the street like natural men."

Nat D. Williams, Memphis *Tri-State Defender*, September 26, 1970.

Nat D. Williams, the man who loved Beale Street most, standing in the
ruins of fabled Palace Theater, in 1973.
Courtesy of William Leaptrott

# 1· New Beale

The evening sun was going down on Beale. Nat D. Williams sat in the lengthening shadow of the W. C. Handy statue in the abandoned little park, alone with his hants. He watched an old man sorting out salvageable brick in the rubble of the Palace Theater. One wall of the Palace remained standing, a tombstone for the bones of Beale. Pieces of Nat D.'s own life lay buried beneath the splintered timber. He saw himself as a boy, looking on wide-eyed as his mother performed her shake dances on the Palace stage; he saw himself in middle age, marching on stage to open the Palace amateur shows, chanting Handy's song: "Take my advice, folks, and see Beale Street first. . . . I'd rather be there than any place I know." He wondered what kind of blues Handy would write about this new Beale.

He watched Robert Henry bring his folding chair to the sidewalk in front of his pool hall across from the ruins of the Palace. Nat D. smiled, remembering their last walk together on Beale. "Urban reNEWal," Mr. Henry had snorted. "What we need is some urban reOLDal. Why, Nat, I can remember when you couldn't walk down this street at midnight without saying ' 'Scuse me, let me by, please,' it was so crowded, don't you know. Now look at it."

He looked around now, counting the people on the street: Robert Henry, the old man working in the rubble, a woman going into Schwab's department store, two men sitting on a junked car on a corner lot, passing a bottle in a brown paper sack back and forth. And himself, Nat D. Williams, retired history teacher, newspaper columnist, master of ceremonies at the Palace Amateur Nights, disc jockey, and about-to-be-retired Beale Streeter. No. He was a Beale Streeter by upbringing and by inclination. He would remain one until death.

He looked again at the ruins of the Palace, at the old black man sifting through the debris, and reflected on the irony: black men had made Beale world famous under the watchful eyes of white men, and black men under the watchful eyes of white straw bosses had wielded the iron wrecking balls that tore down the framework of Beale, had manned the bulldozers that shoveled up the bones of their street.

The white man had said the black man couldn't go certain places, that Beale was the place for blacks; and the black man turned it around and said Beale was the *only* place to be. It was more than a collection of stores and saloons, pawnshops and lodge halls and church headquarters. Beale was Main Street and back alley and the Rialto and Courthouse Square; Christians, hypocrites, heathens, gamblers, the upright, and the uptight; harlots and mothers of the church; professional men in their black suits and dark ties; country folks in overalls and flour-sack dresses; easy riders in their boxback suits, stetson hats, and silk shirts, with diamond stickpins and gold chains, glittering symbols of Beale's glamorous wickedness; wandering minstrels singing their blues; itinerant preachers shouting a hell-fire-and-brimstone blues of their own; conjure men and con men; voodoo and hoodoo women. It was a melting pot of black America. Maybe he was guilty of overromanticizing, just as others overexaggerated the violence and unsavory aspects, but it was as blues man Booker White had said: "If ever there was a good time, so help me God, there was good times on Beale. But the good times are gone for good."

Where did the good times go? Another irony: integration itself had helped bring about the disintegration of Beale. As the civil rights movement gained momentum, as the Jim Crow's nests disappeared, as even newspapers in the South grudgingly began capitalizing the word *Negro* and using *Mrs.* instead of "the Jones woman" in referring to black women, blacks marched from the back of the bus to the front and onward and upward—away from Beale. "When integration came," Robert Henry had grumped, "the Beale Streeters went everywhere, and it kilt this place."

A third man with a brown bag of his own had joined the two serious drinkers in the vacant lot. One of them began beating out a rhythm on the hood of the battered old car, softly at first, then intensifying. Soon all three were jiving, clapping hands, hamboning, scatting—making music out of nothing. That's the way it has always been, he thought; give us a can or jug to blow on, a box to beat on, a bucket and a broom handle, a cigarette paper and a comb, and we'll make music. We got the lick. We got blues in our bones, and Beale brings them out. Beale didn't birth the blues, of course, any more than Handy fathered them, but it helped build them into an art form. Beale was a touchstone for the blues and a stepping-stone, just as it was for Handy and other blues people who came before and after him.

He began piecing together in his mind a compacted film history of Beale like the quickie documentary he had seen on television about Martin Luther King, a silent staccato of snapshots freezing at intervals on climactic events in his life, including the sanitation strike in Memphis, the march down Beale with him in its midst, the balcony of the Lorraine Motel, the rifle barrel protruding from the second-story window of a dingy flophouse, Dr. King falling, falling, falling, in slow motion. Nat D. would begin with an overview of the new Beale, ghost-town quiet, the skeletal remains strewn across the landscape, and dissolve into a tableau of the old Beale, boomtown boisterous, crowded with commerce and elbow-to-elbow aliveness. Next a quick click-click-click succession would trace Beale's early growth: Lincoln reading his Emancipation Proclamation; Negroes laying down their hoes, leaving the fields, and streaming to the city, freed people in search of freedom. The camera would zoom in on some of them looking up at a Beale Street marker, pan to one of the mansions

farther east on Beale in what was the most fashionable neighborhood in white Memphis, return to the growing, huddled black
masses, go back to the mansion, with the occupants moving out—
white flight in the first reconstruction of Beale—then back to the
overview of the clamorous, congested Beale that beckoned black
Everyman.

And then to the pleasure places of Beale: the Monarch, the
Midway, Pee Wee's Saloon, and the Hole in the Wall; the Palace
and Daisy theaters; the One-Minute Cafe; the riverfront area at
the foot of Beale with its carnival-like allure, its hucksters peddling fried fish, watermelon, and other fresh fruit, its hognose
restaurants offering barbecue, pigs' feet and, yes, chitlins, the
tantalizing odors attracting the riverboat roustabouts sweating
and swearing as they wrestled with crates of flapping, fractious
chickens weighing much less than the 500-pound bales of cotton
they skillfully hoisted.

And the games Beale Streeters played: all-hidey, kick the
can, coon-can, craps, cotch, and that strange, sometimes amus-
ing, sometimes deadly, name-calling pastime called the dozens.
(The memory of a New Year's Eve drinking party and of an old
acquaintance on Beale intruded on Nat D.'s mental camera work.
"I ain't gonna play the blues no more," the old fellow had re-
solved. "I ain't gonna play the policy, and I ain't especially gonna
play the dozens.")

And on to their music makers: Handy and his horn; Johnny
Dunn using an old tin can to originate the wah-wah sound on his
trumpet; Roosevelt Sykes, Sunnyland Slim, and Piano Red thump-
ing out barrelhouse blues on the piano; Big Bill Broonzy finishing
second in a Beale Street blues contest (but running off with the
first prize, a fifth of booze); Furry Lewis, Booker White, and
Sleepy John Estes with their street-corner guitars; Big Mama
Lillie Glover booming what she called the old-time, original, natural, everyday blues; Little Laura Dukes and her high-pitched
rendition of "Mr. Crump"; latter-day bluesmen like B. B. King,
Bobby Bland, and Muddy Waters; and then, for double-take

effect, Elvis Presley watching old Charlie Burse, "Ukulele Ike," twitching his knee, rocking his pelvis, and rolling his syllables during a show at a Beale Street honky-tonk (the style Elvis copied to launch the blue-suede blues).

And their dances: the trigger-toe, the shimmy-she-wobble, the black bottom, the bump, the funky chicken, the jitterbug, and the jubilee wham.

And heroes: Lincoln again and Handy; Frederick Douglass and Harriet Tubman; Booker T. Washington, George Washington Carver, and W. E. B. Du Bois; FDR and Eleanor; Joe Louis knocking out Schmelling, and pretty young black girls prancing and dancing down Beale singing "Joe Louis done did it again"; Jackie Robinson swinging, running, and sliding as a Brooklyn Dodger; and Branch Rickey of the Dodgers coming to Martin Stadium in Memphis, sitting behind home plate instead of in the section reserved for whites, and later that night signing Dan Bankhead of the Memphis Red Sox as the first black pitcher in the big leagues. And the unremembered but unforgotten heroes who in the 1950s stood up, sat in, and reached out for rights in Yassa Land. On to the martyred John F. Kennedy, Robert F. Kennedy, and Martin Luther King (pictures of them, singly or all three together, decorating more walls than Christ, even, in black households).

And then back to the picture of the rifle barrel and the fallen King, and finally to the fallen landmarks of Beale, to the overview of the desolate and deserted Beale of urban renewal, and perhaps to Nat D. himself sitting alone in this nondescript little park (where just seven years earlier he had come to hear congressmen and the secretary of the interior commemorate the Handy statue and declare the park a national shrine—hollow words followed soon by demolition crews clawing, smashing, defacing, erasing). The wrecking ball spared the park itself, but now it was used mainly by down-and-outers. He noticed that vandals had smeared blue paint on the Handy statue. Some shrine, he thought.

The three idlers had concluded their car concert and drifted away. Robert Henry had taken his folding chair back inside the poolroom, and the old man had finished his day's work in the debris of the Palace. Now, in the gathering dusk, the one remaining wall hovered like a ghostly sentinel standing guard over the fragmented monument of memories. Again Nat D. saw himself in his role as the emcee at Palace Amateur Nights, striding to center stage and chanting Handy's song: "If Beale Street could talk, if Beale Street *would* talk. . . ." He looked up at the blue-bronze statue of the man with the golden horn. "If Beale Street *could* talk, Mr. Handy," he said softly, "Beale Street would cry."

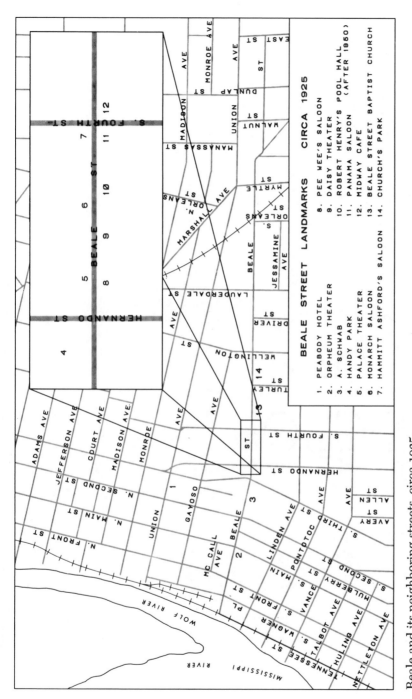

Beale and its neighboring streets, circa 1925.
Courtesy of Memphis State University, Cartographic Services Laboratory

W. C. Handy's Memphis home in 1912. Its address, 659 Jennette Place, is in the area known as Greasy Plank.
Courtesy of Memphis *Press-Scimitar*

# 2 · Old Beale

Near the turn of the century, Memphis had recovered from the devastating effects of the yellow fever epidemics of 1877 and 1878 to become one of the South's fastest-growing cities. Its population of 100,000 included 49,000 blacks. They had no parks, no playgrounds, no theaters or other recreational facilities. Then, in 1899, Church's Park opened on Beale Street. The $50,000 auditorium, seating 2,000 people, and six acres of landscaped grounds were all for blacks.[1]

The man behind the change was Robert Reed Church, Sr., black son of a white steamship captain. At age twelve he went aboard his father's riverboats as a cabin boy and advanced to the position of steward, in charge of buying food and liquor. When federal troops commandeered his father's boats, after a brief naval battle on the Mississippi River in 1862 put Memphis in the hands of the Union, young Church used his experience to get a job ashore in a saloon. He went on to accumulate a fortune in real estate and to become the wealthiest black man in Memphis, the first black millionaire in the South, and possibly the richest Negro in America.[2]

Much of the property Church accumulated came as a result of the flight of Memphis citizens from the yellow fever; he was able to purchase their property at bargain rates. Thousands died

1. Annette E. Church and Roberta Church, *The Robert R. Churches of Memphis* (Ann Arbor, 1974), 13.
2. *Ibid.*, 5–13.

during the epidemics and thousands more left, never to return. Whites were particularly vulnerable to the fever, especially recent immigrants from the British Isles and northern Europe, who had no natural immunity to tropical fevers. On the other hand, blacks seemed to have some resistance to the disease. Only 20,000 people remained in the city during the epidemic of 1878. Of the 14,000 blacks who stayed, 900 died; of the 6,000 whites who remained, 4,000 fell to the fever.[3]

Memphis, with its citizens fleeing and virtually no revenue coming in, had to give up its charter and submit to being governed as a taxing district of the state. There were warnings that the city would be forever plagued and even some demands to burn it to the ground. But Memphis cleaned up its filth and built sewers and, after twelve years as a taxing district, recouped enough to offer a bond issue as the first step toward regaining its charter. The first man to step forward to purchase a bond—at the full offering price of one thousand dollars—was Robert Reed Church.[4]

While Church was among the leaders of the black social circle, his close friends and intimates included some of the upper crust of white Memphis society. He dined with them in restaurants and rode with them in Pullman cars, despite Jim Crow laws. For his second wife, Anna Wright, a school principal described by the *Daily Memphis Avalanche* as a "belle in colored society," he built an elaborate thirteen-room house just off Beale in a silk-stocking neighborhood where most of the residents were white.[5]

By the time of Church's death in 1912, Church's Park had become the center of social life for most of the black people of Memphis. Graduations, dances, lodge gatherings, conventions, and church meetings were held there. For years it was the only spot where black entertainers could perform for black audiences. But gradually the situation changed, and theaters, vaudeville

3. Federal Writers' Project, *Tennessee: A Guide to the State* (New York, 1939), 211.
4. Church and Church, *The Robert R. Churches*, xii.
5. *Ibid.*, 40–42.

houses, and moving-picture shows opened on Beale. The Savoy, the Pastime, the Daisy, and the Grand theaters were owned and operated by a group of Italian families, the Zerillas, the Pacinis, and, most importantly, the Barrassos. Anselmo Barrasso, who later was to open the Palace Theater, the largest showhouse for blacks in the South, and his brother, F. A. Barrasso, had founded the Theater Owners' Booking Association in 1909. A circuit for black performers, TOBA eventually included more than forty theaters, among them the Howard in Washington, the Apollo in New York, and the Regal in Chicago. The initials were sometimes said to stand for "Tough on Black Asses" because of the low wages, poor working conditions, and substandard dressing rooms, but TOBA offered work for black artists when there otherwise might have been none.[6]

Things were tough all over for black people. The standard pay for manual labor was a dollar a day. Blacks lived in the worst possible housing, in back alleys and tenements. The pattern of black housing in Memphis followed the course of the bayous; land was cheaper on the banks of these muddy, polluted streams. Houses were crowded together, the tiny yards fouled with outdoor toilets, garbage heaps, and refuse dumps. W. C. Handy himself, though by then his band and his blues were winning wide recognition, lived with his wife and children in a section of town called Greasy Plank.

To Handy and untold other blacks, Beale became as much a symbol of escape from despair as had Harriet Tubman's underground railroad. On Beale you could find surcease from sorrow; on Beale you could forget for a shining moment the burden of being black and celebrate being black; on Beale you could be a man, your own man; on Beale you could be free.

This was the Beale that enthralled young Nat D. Williams when his grandfather moved him back into town from a farm near Raleigh, Tennessee, on the outskirts of Memphis. The street became a mile-long adventure that he explored from one end to

6. Paul Oliver, *The Story of the Blues* (New York, 1969), 69–71.

almost the other. Almost. Past Church's Park and east of the enormous mansions built by whites in a separate township named South Memphis but called Sodom by its neighbors because life there was so extravagant (South Memphians retaliated by referring to the adjoining area as Pinchgut or Pinch), Beale trailed off into a gloomy, swamplike area Nat D. was happy to steer clear of. It was here that Beale's mysterious voodoo practitioners thrived.

Nat D. soaked up everything he encountered on Beale—its minstrels, miseries, triumphs and tragedies, ironies and idiosyncrasies, color and character, as well as its colorful characters. In years to come, he would resent that most white people saw Beale only through its vice and violence, as the place where blacks converged for "living it up"; in reality, it was an extension of everyday living. Its patrons did their shopping for food and clothes there, saw their doctors, dentists, and lawyers there, paid their burial insurance there. Many a Beale Streeter lived out his life without setting foot in Beale's saloons and gambling dens. Still, early on, the sporting life in the tenderloin area held particular fascination for Nat D. His age kept him from being an active participant, of course, but neither that nor his grandmother's scoldings kept him from looking and listening and learning, storing away the memories of a life-style he was to recount later in his newspaper columns.

The Monarch Club, with its mirrored walls throughout the lobby, its black-cushioned seats built into the wall, and its brass-railed mahogany bar, was the classiest spot on the street. The Panama Club, gathering place of the racetrack set until Tennessee outlawed racing in 1905, still attracted the better sort of clientele. Joints like the Hole in the Wall—so named because of a back exit used frequently during times of trouble or police raids—drew the less affluent.

Well known at the gambling spots, both high and low, were such sharks as Slop Crowder, Casino Henry, and the top card handler of them all, Mac Harris. A tall man who wore his moustache twisted up at the ends, Harris preferred the English style of dress, including a frock coat, pinstriped trousers, Chesterfield topcoat, and Homburg hat. He matched his skill against all comers, both the local sports and imports like the sharpie from Baltimore he took for $2,000 in a four-day poker battle. He met the famous, cross-eyed gambler, Nine Tongue, in New Orleans and cleaned him of $10,000. He wasn't as lucky when one of Beale's saloonkeepers sent to New York for a big-time player; this round it was Harris on the losing end after a 36-hour duel. He vowed he would never play another game of cards—a vow he broke many times.[7]

Pee Wee's Saloon on Beale was the favorite hangout of musicians, including Handy, because Pee Wee, a short, stocky Italian named Vigello Maffei, and his partner and son-in-law, Lorenzo Pacini, were always willing to take messages on the phone at the cigar counter from promoters, committee chairmen, funeral directors, and anyone else booking musicians. Most of Beale Street's musicians checked in there daily, trying to find another night's work. The majority lived from one night to the next. While they were hanging around Pee Wee's, they could occupy their time rolling dice, playing cards, shooting pool, or betting on the policy game.

Pee Wee and other Italians had been latecomers to Beale, arriving on the wave of south European immigration around 1900, but they soon made a place for themselves. Italian proprietors were popular with their black patrons. The saying on Beale was that the Jews had the pawnshops and the dry goods stores, the Greeks had the restaurants, the Italians had the entertainment —the theaters, the saloons, the gambling—and the blacks were the customers.

One of the outstanding exceptions was Hammitt Ashford's saloon at Beale and Fourth. Ashford, a light-yellow mulatto who wore a diamond stickpin in his four-in-hand tie, ran one of the street's oldest and best saloons, with a mahogany bar, marble-

7. Memphis *World*, January 24, 1947, p. 1. Mac Harris died in poverty in 1947, reduced to peddling shoestrings to earn a living. By his bed when his body was found were a Chesterfield overcoat and a Homburg hat.

topped tables, and a lounging room upstairs. Beale Streeters still talked with anger and awe about the night at Ashford's place in 1908 when Wild Bill Latura, a white man, walked in brandishing a pistol and killed five blacks and seriously wounded two others. Latura, who owned a number of small hamburger stands and gambled frequently on Beale, had lost money at Ashford's and was looking for revenge. The *Commercial Appeal* quoted Latura as telling the police, "I just shot 'em and that's all there is to it." That's all there was to it. A jury acquitted him. The newspaper editorialized on December 12 that the killing of blacks without cause was "being overdone" and ought to be stopped because "those white men who kill negroes as a pastime . . . usually end up by killing white men."

Beale Streeters, of course, had long been accustomed to such white-against-black crime going unpunished. It was generally accepted that the injustice was part of being black and that no one could do anything about it. But when a white mob tried to punish, or at least intimidate, all of Beale Street following the rape and murder of a young white girl in 1917, the black outrage was so widespread that something, finally, was done about it. The mob seized Ell Persons, a young black man accused of the crime, burned him at the stake, and strewed his charred remains about Beale. Robert Church, Jr., who had inherited his father's fortune and by now was on the threshold of national power in Republican politics, and a number of other black businessmen launched a protest movement leading to a charter for the first Memphis chapter of the National Association for the Advancement of Colored People. There were fifty-three members on June 11, 1917, three weeks after the burning of Persons, and the membership grew into the hundreds in the next few months.[8]

Before then, one of the most outstanding persons in civil rights efforts in Memphis was Julia Britton Hooks, freeborn, Berea College educated. An accomplished musician, she offered private

---

8. Lester C. Lamon, "Negroes in Tennessee, 1900–1930" (Ph.D. dissertation, University of North Carolina, 1971), 330.

lessons after moving to Memphis near the turn of the century and at one time coached Handy on orchestration. Soon after Edward Hull Crump was elected mayor in 1909 (with the help of a campaign tune titled "Mr. Crump," written by Handy), she had marched into his office and demanded that a juvenile court be established for blacks. Crump agreed, and she and her husband became the first officers of the court. Among her duties was that of truant officer. Nat D. recalled her dashing into the street and chasing down many a young hooky player—himself included.

Mrs. Hooks later took her young son, Robert, to the Cossitt Library, trying to force the opening of the city's only library to blacks. Turned back, she raised such a fuss that the police were called to remove her from the building. (Nearly a half-century later, in 1959, her great-granddaughter, Carol Hooks, would be among the college students whose sit-ins finally succeeded in opening the Memphis libraries to black citizens. Among the attorneys fighting the students' court battles was her grandson, Miss Hooks' uncle, Benjamin Hooks, later to become a member of the Federal Communications Commission and the executive director of the NAACP.)

Although Mrs. Hooks failed with the library, she succeeded in attending a major cultural event at a white theater. Negroes were not permitted to see performances except from the topmost balcony, but Mrs. Hooks persuaded a white friend to buy her a box seat. She seated herself among the whites and, although the management tried to eject her, stood her ground and finally was permitted to stay.[9]

But even such small victories were rare. The rampant racism and injustice, the fear and frustration, helped make Memphis a part of the northward migration that put thousands of southern blacks on the move. The outbreak of World War I and the resulting shortage of labor for northern factories had prompted efforts to lure blacks northward. Labor agents came to the South to recruit workers. The flow to the north was heightened by the 1915

9. Interview with the late Robert Hooks, Julia Hooks' son, October 25, 1973.

floods and the onslaught of the boll weevil, which left planters in straitened circumstances, unable to employ as many workers as in the past. Credit was cut off, and the migration became more of an exodus. Mules were left hitched to plows, hoes were dropped in cotton rows, and fires were left burning in cookstoves. Thousands of acres were without tenants, stores without customers, schools without pupils, and churches without members.[10]

Memphis was the likeliest stop in the northward progression for country blacks from farther south, but many of Memphis' own were moving on. It was true that Memphis offered more in the way of jobs and higher pay than the rural areas; the city railroad yard, factories, sawmills, and lumber manufacturing plants provided work for blacks as laborers. Hundreds held jobs in the building crafts, though at lower wages than white union workers. They could dig ditches, lay railroad tracks, work at domestic jobs, yard jobs, odd jobs. But with his meager earnings, a black laborer struggled to feed, clothe, and provide heat for his family. If his wife cooked or washed for white people, his family had the advantage of food from the white man's kitchen and cast-off clothes to wear. Still, if trouble came—illness, court fines—there was no backlog of savings to draw on. Often the only way out was to go hat in hand to the "boss man" to ask for help.

As the black flight continued, white Memphis became more and more concerned and began a campaign to curb the migration. The efforts even included some attempts to arrest blacks at railroad stations. The Memphis Chamber of Commerce established the Industrial Welfare Committee for the purpose of keeping blacks in Memphis. Bankers and company presidents announced that blacks were one of Memphis' greatest assets and urged the city to initiate programs to keep blacks happy and contented and home. Whites lent their support to black conservative leaders to start social welfare programs.[11] The *Commercial Appeal* joined

10. T. O. Fuller, *Pictorial History of the American Negro* (Memphis, 1933), 191–92.
11. Lamon, "Negroes in Tennessee," 197–98.

the drive to deter the migrants. On October 24, 1916, the newspaper urged blacks, "Better stay down here, because when things get tight, every one of you knows the road to the back door of some white man's kitchen."

But the lure was too strong. The prospects of better jobs with higher wages, the promise of more freedom for themselves and greater opportunities for their children, continued to influence blacks to go "upcountry."

W. C. Handy was among them, though by then he was so swamped with engagements, mainly for white people, that he split his band into three groups and was booking not only for himself but for other musicians as well. He was playing at the most elegant dancing spot in town, the Alaskan Roof Gardens atop the Falls Building downtown, drawing top Memphis society; and upper-class blacks, after having snubbed him earlier, now were trying to hire him for their society balls and concerts. But he still was earning a penny-ante income and realized that many Memphis whites recognized him only as their pet black musician, not as an artist who happened to be dark skinned.[12]

Handy moved on to New York. Nat D. finished high school and—rare for a Beale Streeter of that era—moved on to college at Tennessee Agricultural and Industrial in Nashville. But Beale kept calling, and he came back after graduation, got a teaching job at the new Booker T. Washington High School, and became a columnist for the *Memphis World* and the voice of the Palace Theater. More than that, he became the voice of Beale Street itself—its most ardent advocate, defender, lover, and critic.

12. W. C. Handy, *Father of the Blues* (New York, 1941), 131.

Robert Henry, long-time promoter of entertainment events and Beale
Street, in 1973.
Courtesy of William Leaptrott

# 3 · The Beale Street Beat

Beale Streeters, knowing the scales of justice were weighed against them, tried to steer clear of the law and the courts when possible. They settled their own differences, often violently. Whites readily accepted this solution; they generally remained complacent toward violence among blacks as long as it did not affect whites. Paternalistic whites held that blacks were children, irresponsible and unaccountable. Less kindly disposed whites regarded the killing of a black by another black as good riddance. If the police did make an arrest in a black murder, white judges and juries levied minor penalties, usually no more than a few months in the workhouse.

The commonplace violence among blacks accounted for the highest percentage of homicides in Memphis each year and helped make the city known as the "murder capital of the world."[1] There were varied theories about the violence. Back in 1908, G. P. Hamilton, who at the time was principal of the only black high school in Memphis, set forth his ideas in his book, *The Bright Side of Memphis.*

It is doubtful just why the colored people as a whole have such a violent temper . . . we have given this matter very careful thought and we have come to the conclusion that the kind of meat most generally eaten by colored people has a great deal to do with their health and their tempers. It is a fact that can be substantiated by most dealers in meats that the colored people generally eat pork meat. The pork chop

1. Memphis *World*, July 15, 1932, p. 1.

is eaten plentifully to the exclusion of beef and mutton, which are considered more nutritious as food. The physiological effects of pork meat on the human system are dangerous in the extreme, and it is not at all surprising that the man whose system is charged with the elements from pork meat should feel like fighting even his best friend. So it is our belief that much of the crime committed by the colored may be attributed to pork meat.[2]

Others theorized that drug addiction heightened crime and violence. Cocaine caused problems intermittently on Beale, though never so many as in the years between 1900 and 1905. During that era, Lehman's Drug Store on Union near Fourth sold so much cocaine in dime boxes that a song was written about the store.

> I went to Mr. Lehman 'bout half past nine,
> Said to Mr. Lehman I've only got a dime
> To get my habits on, to get my habits on.
>
> I went to Mr. Lehman 'bout half past ten,
> Said to Mr. Lehman I'm back again,
> To get my habits on, to get my habits on.
>
> I went to Mr. Lehman 'bout half past leben,
> Said to Mr. Lehman, I'll never get to Heben,
> With my habits on, with my habits on.
>
> I went to Mr. Lehman 'bout half past twelve,
> Said to Mr. Lehman, I'm gonna go to hell,
> With my habits on, with my habits on.

Beale Street sang another ditty about cocaine.

> Sniff my cocaine, sniff it by the grain,
> Doctor said it'd kill me but he didn't say when,
> Hey, hey, honey, take a whiff on me.
>
> Buy my cocaine, buy it by the box,
> People said it's good for the old small pox,
> Hey, hey, honey, take a whiff on me.[3]

2. G. P. Hamilton, *The Bright Side of Memphis* (Memphis, 1908), 8–9.
3. Fred L. Hutchins, *What Happened in Memphis* (Kingsport, Tenn., 1965), 48–49.

Another verse added by some was:

> All people ought to be like me.
> Drink gin, let the cocaine be,
> Hey, hey, honey, take a whiff on me.

Beale Street told macabre stories of its callousness to violence: about a man's getting killed at a crap game and the other players dragging his body under the table and playing on top of him; about a killing in a night spot when the owners threw the body out the window; about a dive that provided a chute to the undertaker's; about an undertaker who sat on a dead gambler's body until his hearse came, so that he would be sure to get the funeral.

Battier's Drug Store on the corner of Third and Beale patched up many a sufferer. Early-opening shopkeepers would sometimes see a trail of blood leading into Battier's and maybe a second trail leading out, heading up the street on Third to a doctor's clinic.

Beale's vice and violence led to cleanup campaigns from time to time. Tennessee had approved prohibition in 1910, but Crump, backed by the majority of the city's business community and the newspapers, had made no attempt to enforce it, claiming it would cause more trouble than it would prevent. But Crump was ousted from office in 1916 and a spirit of reform swept the city, with the strongest swipe aimed at the saloons and bordellos of Beale.[4] Another cleanup movement came in 1919. The Citizens League, a group made up of some of the leading business and professional people, talked Rowlett Paine, a big, good-looking wholesale grocer, into running for mayor that year. Though active in civic clubs for years, Paine had never been in politics. But with the handsome figure he cut—and women were voting that year for the first time in Tennessee—and the prominent backing he enjoyed, he won by 2,700 votes.[5] The "good government" movement was in, and

---

4. William D. Miller, *Mr. Crump of Memphis* (Baton Rouge, 1964), 107–113.
5. *Ibid.*, 129–30.

Beale's free-swinging, big-money, wide-open days were out. To compound the situation, nationwide Prohibition came in 1920. The street was never to be quite the same again.

But, of course, drinking and gambling did not cease at the mayor's decree or at congressional action. Prohibition didn't moderate the sale of whisky, much less stop it. Beale sold its bootleg in all sizes—short, medicine-style bottles called "slabs"; half-pints; tall, thin, twelve-ounce bottles; little bottles called "austins." If made by experts, such as the Italian moonshiners who put their white lightning in barrels and buried it in order to age it, corn whisky could be excellent. If the moonshiners were of a lesser breed, those who allowed anything from frogs to old shoes in their distilling vats, the results were hardly drinkable. But it was drunk anyway.

The stills were located mainly on Presidents Island, a short boat ride from downtown, and the sellers were everywhere, in the backs of grocery stores, walking the streets, in garages and outhouses, and behind trees. The Hole in the Wall kept its supply in garbage cans outside the saloon, careful to take the cans in while the garbagemen made their collections.

One bootlegger named James Green, called 'Fessor, sold whisky out of the upper story of a building that housed the Palm Gardens. 'Fessor Green had a way of adding a final double e to most words, and his customers had picked up his manner of speech. The customer would shout up to the 'Fessor in the upstairs window, " 'Fessor Green-ee, yes, indeed-ee." And 'Fessor would say, "What you want-ee?" From down below would come the answer, "I want one-ee." He'd say, "Put your money in the bucket." He'd let a bucket down from the window, pull the bucket and the money back up, and send the whisky down a chute to the thirsty customer below.

Then the police found out about the 'Fessor's activities. One of the Beale Street patrolmen came up to the Palm Gardens. " 'Fessor Green-ee, throw me three-ee in the buck-ee," he shouted up. 'Fessor Green-ee looked down and said, "Hell-ee, no-ee, not for you-ee!"[6]

Although its surroundings were no longer so plush nor its participants so dapper, gambling, like drinking, defied the reformers' efforts to stamp it out. The gambler who came to public attention was Red Lawrence, known for his skill with dice, cards, and guns. Lawrence, thought by some to be the illegitimate son of a white saloonkeeper, looked nearly white, with very light skin and blond hair. He was said to have killed thirteen people in the years between 1915 and 1941. He was never convicted of any of the slayings.[7]

The Beale Street beat was a plum for policemen on the take. Robert Henry and other Beale Streeters said payoffs from saloons and gambling parlors were regular and ample. Henry recalled the story about the black man who had been arrested and was asked by the judge:

"Say, boy, where do you work?"

The man answered: "I work for Mr. ——" (one of the Beale Street beat patrolmen).

"What do you do for him?"

"I'm the butler."[8]

Although they were quick to inflict violence if given any trouble or "sassing" by blacks, Beale Street policemen generally had a live-and-let-live policy. Most blacks felt if they didn't bother policemen or give them any trouble, they wouldn't be bothered themselves.

Among the legendary police officers was Detective Sergeant Lee Quianthy. Sam Bledsoe, police reporter for the *Commercial Appeal* in the 1920s, said in his unpublished reminiscences of those days, "I don't know how many men Quianthy killed, several

6. Memphis *Commercial Appeal*, August 11, 1975, p. 17.

7. Interview with Thomas Pinkston, violinist for Handy and for the Palace Theater orchestra, October 31, 1973.

8. Interview with Robert Henry, October 15, 1973.

whites and more Negroes, but the latter didn't count for much on a man's record."

Cliff Davis, city judge at the time, was described by Bledsoe as a natural-born comedian and mimic who put on a courtroom show that always drew large audiences. One day a black man arrested by Quianthy appeared before Judge Davis and testified that the officer had fired at him but missed. "He shot at you?" asked the judge. The accused man nodded. "And he missed?" asked the incredulous Davis. "Yessir," said the prisoner. Quianthy nodded. "Case dismissed," the judge said. "Any man that Lee Quianthy shoots at and misses is entitled to go his way."

Bledsoe had a chance to see Quianthy in action more than once. He wrote about one time when he was a member of a posse that swept down on a black desperado, Two-Gun Charlie Pierce, in a South Memphis "ark," a Memphis name for a black dive.

In the spring of 1923 Two-Gun had shot a couple of policemen in a fight at the intersection of Trigg Street and Louisiana Avenue. He got his nickname on that occasion by using two weapons. He had several other brushes with officers and shot a couple more.

Two-Gun was a hero to the blacks. There was a ditty about him, rendered to the tune of "Casey Jones." Few dared sing it openly, but a drunken Negro in the jail one night defiantly yelled it until the jailer went back and silenced him with a blackjack. I remember one verse:

> Two-Gun Charlie is a mighty man.
> Mows down 'dem cops wherever he can.
> Got two pistols that sho' am fine.
> Gives 'dem bastards a hot old time.

One fine fall night in 1924, word came in that Two-Gun had been located in a South Memphis Negro ark. Quianthy and his partner, a man named Thompson, were in the station, waiting, as I later learned, for the call.

The makeshift posse, including Bledsoe, loaded up in a big Hudson with Quianthy driving. "The moon was bright and full and, holding my jaws together to keep my teeth from chattering, I wondered if I ever would see moonlight again," Bledsoe wrote.

The car stopped and the men rushed toward the honky-tonk. Quianthy flung open the door. The large room was filled with a crowd of blacks, men and women. "Smoke hung like a fog. As we went in, I had the sense of noise stopped suddenly as if one had moved into shelter from a steadily blowing wind," Bledsoe said. Then came a roar of shots, shouts and screams, and it was all over. The crowd was told to leave while the posse remained, along with two black men, one lying on his back with a gun near his hand, the other sitting on the floor with his hand over his groin. A policeman pointed to the prone figure and said: "Two-Gun. He's shot his last policeman."

Bledsoe continued:

As men often do after a violent death, the bad man looked puny. Some of the shots had been fired at such close range that his coat had caught on fire and smoldered. A thin flame arose and a policeman stamped it out with his foot, giving the body a kick in the bargain. Two-Gun's cap, a new one with bold red and black checks, had fallen off, revealing hair so kinky that it almost formed peppercorns. His shoes were yellow, sharp-pointed and freshly polished. His suit was a good one and he wore a big, blue bow tie. I had heard that he was a dandy and that the women ran after him. He could not have been more than twenty-five or twenty-six and, lying there, he seemed pitifully harmless. Markham, one of the policemen, threw back Two-Gun's coat and there, in a holster, was another pistol which the policeman confiscated and wore afterwards.

I was amazed to see Quianthy and another policeman helping the fallen Negro to his feet gently. He was a huge, lantern-jawed, red-skinned man and his treatment was accounted for by the fact that he was one of several stool pigeons assigned to help out with the campaign to destroy Two-Gun.

Although some of the police became well known—and reasonably kindly regarded—by the blacks on Beale, others made their reputations by their sadism, their free hand with their nightsticks, their roughing-up of handcuffed prisoners, and their verbal insults and contemptuous air. But nowhere were sadism and indifference to suffering more clearly demonstrated than in the treatment of dope addicts. The standard method of dealing with an addict was to arrest him, throw him into a cell, and leave him until the agonizing pangs of withdrawal were over. "Apparently, from their response, these pangs were like Apache tortures," Bledsoe said. He would hear high-pitched screams from the jail cell, continuing for hours, even days. A few died going through the tortures of cold-turkey withdrawal, but there were never any inquiries or changes in the way they were handled. Just another dopehead gone. If the prisoner survived, he was sentenced to a few weeks of hard labor at the county farm.

The police assigned two men to deal with the drug program, Bledsoe said—"a captain, a broad-shouldered, dour-faced man who never smiled," and his patrolman partner, "who had the countenance of a permanently unhappy sheep." The two made arrests for crimes other than violation of the drug laws and were greatly feared by the underworld and blacks. The patrolman was reputed to be the most skillful man on the force at punishing a man with the barrel of his gun. "The pair were not liked by the rest of the police force and Granny Heckle [a detective] told me that they took a sadistic pleasure in watching those who had come back from the county farm," Bledsoe said. "They waited, Granny said, until the unfortunate had once again become thoroughly saturated with drugs. Then they pounced on him. Back to the jail and screaming."

Alonzo Locke, the widely known headwaiter at Hotel Peabody, with 1946 Cotton Carnival King Vance Norfleet and Queen Phoebe Cook. Courtesy of Memphis *Press-Scimitar*

# 4 · The Complexion Complex

The short, round-faced, nearsighted, near-genius Nathaniel Dowd Williams represented, in some ways, the multifaceted character of Beale itself—its ambiguities and contradictions. He was a man torn between his attachment to his grandmother's religious teachings and his fondness for the blues, his schoolteacher respectability and his love for dancing and music, his affection for the street and his dislike for its vulgarity, his pride in his race and his scorn for its weaknesses, his loyalty to his town and his resentment of its faults.

Nowhere were the ambiguities of Beale expressed more than in its attitude toward the blues themselves. Although the blues were considered by whites to be the music of all black people, the music met heated opposition from within the black community. The leader in the battle against the blues was the church, which viewed the blues as the work of the devil. As no man could worship both God and mammon, no man could sing the blues and serve God, too.

Nat had encountered the conflict early in life. "My grandmother planned to make a preacher out of me, but she figured there was never going to be any hope for me because I liked the blues. She'd come up on me sometimes back in the yard singing the blues, which she considered devil music, and I'd catch the devil." Even later, after he had become a high school teacher and a respected citizen of the community, Nat ran into trouble with his love for the blues. His minister wanted to throw him out of the congregation for singing the "Beale Street Blues" as master of ceremonies of Amateur Night at the Palace Theater. Opposition to the blues came, in addition, from the educated classes. Because Nat liked the blues, some people would say to him: "With your education, you're misleading these people. You're going back to that old stuff we're trying to get away from, old blues and things."

The night spots on Beale reflected the conflict. One club would have nothing but the kind of music white people wrote for whites. Its customers would be blacks who were trying to put the blues and anything else Negroid behind them, blacks who felt the more they got away from being Negroid, the more chances they had to be free from the restrictions placed on their people. In contrast were the places for the average workingman, where the musicians created their music as they played. Many of the songs didn't have titles, and the crowd would call out, "Play the boogie blues," "Play the honky-tonk blues." Even when the band played the white man's music, they changed it, making it blacker, with a stronger beat, and with more of the blues.

The dancing on Beale also demonstrated its own kind of black distinctiveness. "At the first part of the dance, it would be just like the dances that white people gave," Nat recalled. "But when the hour got a little later and the drink got to hitting just right, then people would do the type of dancing that suited them. You did what the spirit told you. If it said, 'Jump up and kick,' you jumped up and kicked. If it said, 'Turn around,' you'd turn around. The polite movements of white people's creation—Negroes could do them. But when they got to the place where they felt they could relax, just go on and enjoy themselves, they'd give a show."

When upper-class black people went to Beale, they were not expected to choose the more boisterous spots. "If you had a good-type education," Nat recalled, "you were supposed to be educated beyond that. Sometimes if you took a notion to go native, though, you'd be there jumping to yourself and look over in the corner and there's another friend over there doing the same thing."

In general, the upper class looked down on Beale, particularly as the years passed, for many of the business and professional people moved their offices off the street and the more elegant establishments deteriorated. "Many of my friends were trying to put Beale and all it stood for behind them," Nat said. "Those who stayed on Beale Street—stayed with the old-time way—were different, we felt, than those of us who had gone on further. The big difference was what you thought of yourself. You felt that you had some education and could use pretty good English and didn't want to be classed as an ordinary 'nigger,' as we call it. We call another Negro of a certain class 'niggers' with as much animosity as a white person would call them—and more." Going beyond Beale meant more than just going beyond the lower element that frequented the street. It meant also an attempt to go beyond the white man's stereotype of a black man.

Southern whites used Jim Crow laws, the Ku Klux Klan, night riders, and Judge Lynch to maintain dominance over blacks. Living as a black man in a white man's world was like walking a tightrope with a noose hanging above one end. And whites exercised other weapons as well—contempt, degradation, disparagement. Blacks were told they were childish, volatile, vulgar, dirty, smelly, disease ridden, violent, lazy, and inept. Whites insisted that blacks use titles of respect and say "Sir" or "Ma'am" at all times when speaking to any white person. On the other side of the coin, no black was ever to be addressed as Mister, Mrs., or Miss, though he might be called Parson, Uncle, or Boy.

In a study of black life in the 1930s in Indianola, Mississippi, a black woman is quoted as saying: "We know we're Negroes but when we're alone we sometimes forget it. But white people never let you forget it; they always make you stay in your place."[1]

1. Hortense Powdermaker, *After Freedom* (New York, 1939), 340.

Whites made it clear, time and time again, that that place was at the very lowest level. Blacks had to struggle to overcome not only the disadvantages imposed on them by whites but also the undermining of their own pride of racial identity and self-esteem. Nat wrote, "I feel that no matter how much the white folk study us scientifically and no matter what they write, they can only know 'about' us but can never 'know' us. Why, we don't know ourselves." Indeed, the white man had taught the black man to dislike himself and his fellow blacks. Nat cited the "antagonism, hatred and just plain malice with which the average Negro 'cusses' another when he's riled up." Blacks were the only group to play the dozens, the exchange of vulgar remarks about a man's female relatives. "Look how light-skinned Negroes scuffle to keep darker Negroes out of their families (unless the hapless blackamoor happens to have some cash or other negotiable possibilities).... Look how Negroes laugh at each other's misfortunes.... Look at the number of Negro 'stool-pigeons' who openly ply their wares among us."[2]

Blacks disliked being blacks so much, he said, that they didn't even worship a God who was black. "All other races make their Gods look like themselves," he wrote. When Nat's children reached Sunday school age, he decided not to send them because he thought they might be confused and alienated by a God with whom they could not identify. "All the 'good' folks in the Christian religion, Christ and all the saints, are pictured as white," he wrote. "So how can a colored child feel that anything black, brown or beige can be good."

Not only did blacks not want their God to look like them, they didn't even want their children to look like them, he wrote. "I have long had a sneaking suspicion that the average Negro woman finds it impossible to really love a Negro man ... the average Negro woman does not want her children to be born looking like Negroes.... It is a commonplace occurrence for a Negro girl to tell her boy friend that she would marry him but she had to think

2. Memphis *World*, October 14, 1932, p. 8; January 28, 1947, p. 6.

in terms of how her children will look."[3] Skin lighteners and hair straighteners were sold to every level of society, with promises to "whiten skin seven shades in seven nights" and to make hair silky smooth, straight, and easy to manage. Products like Dr. Fred Palmer's Skin Whitener, Golden Peacock Bleach Cream, and Black and White Hair Dressing attracted wistful yearners after the epitome of fashion, nearly white skin and straight hair.

White standards of beauty were even prerequisites for acceptance as a dancer or chorus girl, and Nat complained in more than one column about the lack of a single black woman in a black show. Of one particular show he wrote: "As to be expected, there wasn't a really dark woman in the whole she-bang. . . . You can't tell me that a chorus of more nearly Negro women wouldn't look just as well up behind the footlights. There's one thing certain, there'd surely be more color on the occasion." At times he wasn't as lighthearted about catering to the standards of the white race. "We will go downtown to see white shows," he wrote about Irving Miller's Brown Skin Models. "So, show us brown girls, Mr. Miller."[4]

The prestige and favored status that went along with light skin began with schoolchildren, the fair ones being most often selected as class representatives. "It's a helluva thing to be born a Negro boy," Nat wrote. "I know what it means to play with a bunch of kids, white, black and varied colored, and then have yourself singled out one day and be designated 'Nigger.' I know what it means to be a Negro boy."[5]

Light-skinned blacks found it easier to get and keep jobs; the darker a man was, generally the harder the economic struggle. The saying went: "If you're white, you're right. If you're brown, stick around. If you're black, get back, get back."

Whites started the so-called coon songs in minstrel shows, but

3. *Ibid.*, September 23, 1947, p. 6.
4. *Ibid.*, November 18, 1932, p. 8; March 4, 1932, p. 7.
5. *Ibid.*, January 14, 1949, p. 8.

blacks picked them up and in the minstrel and medicine shows sang songs like:

> Coon, coon, coon, I wish my color would fade,
> Coon, coon, coon, I'd like a different shade,
> From morning, night and noon, coon, coon, coon,
> I wish I was a white man instead of a coon.

Nat usually was understanding about this desire to be light-skinned, but occasionally he became sarcastic. In one column he chastised "lamp-black white folk, guys and gals who would give their eye teeth to escape from being Negroes. They are the ones who make the hair straightening business one of the best in the Negro business field. They keep the skin-whitener hoaxers lousy with dough.... They grin—invariably grin—when their pictures are snapped with white folks. They seem anything but flattered when circumstances force them to pose with other Negroes unless the other Negroes bear the unmistakable sign of having been smeared with a pale paint brush."[6]

Because of the low position of the man with a black skin, Nat's status both as teacher and columnist took on added significance. His accomplishments lent the lie to the theory that a dark-skinned Negro did not have the ambition, intellect, or talent that his lighter-skinned brother—who had some measure of white blood—possessed. "I'm black, Jack," Nat wrote of himself, "black as a hundred midnights in a cypress swamp. But, may I remind you, I ain't mad about it. This black I've got is all right with me. It hasn't cost me a dime. I pay only for my ignorance ... not my blackness."

While others tried to change, Nat did not. "I found a terrific amount of enjoyment from just being black," he said. "You just want to be yourself and want people to accept you for what you are. Why should I straighten my hair and put a whole lot of bleach on my skin and put on a lot of peculiar manners which

6. *Ibid.*, April 12, 1946, p. 8.

are foreign to me just to get somebody to say 'he's a good guy'? I just want to be me."

Nat understood his people and defended them. He understood that the black man, faced with scorn and self-doubts, liked to brag about his achievements, to revel in his successes. And he understood that those who had achieved, who had fought and won the battle for accomplishment, were supersensitive about their own importance. Their position was tenuous, and their tenure recent, and they took themselves seriously in their efforts to gain and maintain their dignity. In doing so they often lost their sense of humor. Poke fun at the president or the Supreme Court justices, Nat said, but "don't laugh at Mr. Big Sam."

With all his understanding, Nat still was embarrassed by the vulgar or insensitive among his race. He wrote of them more than once. In August of 1932, he took a trip to Kansas City, Missouri. On part of the return journey, there were no Jim Crow regulations, and whites and blacks were seated in the same car. Even without Jim Crow, the whites took over the front and the blacks gravitated to the rear, without complaint.

In fact the cullud folk waxed merry and made me want more than ever to save my race, when they began talking loud enough to wake the dead; laughing long and open-mouthed belly-laughs that would have done justice to a full-grown mule. And when they began taking off their shoes, and not having any house-slippers, allowing the aroma of their nether portions to clutter the close air of the car, I commenced wondering how the "Crow laws" got started. The answer seemed to be pretty close at hand whenever I pulled my head in out of the window. Only a few of the folks went "back to nature" and got loud, careless and aromatic. But that was enough. From the knowing looks cast in our direction by the ones up front, I could see that we were all classified as birds of a feather—black owls.[7]

Once the train got to Springfield, the Jim Crow system went into effect, and the blacks were jammed into an inferior coach, where the doors slammed every time the train stopped, letting in the

7. *Ibid.*, August 5, 1932, p. 6.

cold wind and frightening the sleepers with the noise. Even with the packed car, certain seats could not be used because the trainmen supposedly had to keep their tools in them.

In a column titled "Nigger! Nigger! Nigger!" Nat summed up the contempt the white man had induced blacks to feel for themselves and their race.

Heard a white man observe the other day that he had passed corners down on Beale Street where he had heard any number of colored men refer to other colored men as "niggers." . . . Of course, he didn't understand why most of them showed resentment when a white person called them "niggers."

Well, Mister, it's like this. The darker brother is a victim of his environment. One book holds that when two diverse groups of people are thrown into contact in the same locality, the weaker group tends to conform to the standards of the stronger one. Now as a matter of necessity the sons of Ham have studied the white man's standards. The results of that study some folk call imitation, others call it adjustment, and still others say it's just a blind rush to accept the other man's standards without figuring out some of our own. Be that as it may, the fact remains that all "God's chillun" who don't have wings, want them. Let's look at some of these wings.

Nature gave the white man straight hair; so the black man uses a hot comb and grease; Nature gave one a pale skin; so the other uses skin whitener; years of dominance gave the former a sense of contempt towards the other which feeling was summed up in the one word, "nigger." But note, this same sense of contempt towards things black is one of those "wings" I spoke about—you know—one of those standards that the apparently stronger group as a whole maintains. Of course, Ham's sons, in their role of weak travellers in a strange land, do all in their power to adopt the rules of the mighty. To most white men the Negro is only a two-legged household pet and invariably an object of contempt. Hence, their affectionate or disdainful use of the word "nigger." As a result of Mr. Charlie's standard, there is no contempt like that which one black man holds for another black man. And so, is there any wonder that we employ the term "nigger" also? . . . It does seem inconsistent on the surface that Negroes resent being called "niggers" by other groups and yet call themselves that, but it's really a matter of group response to a standard set by their slave masters. A lot of us know better, but habit, you know, is a strong chain. Then, too, a lot of us really feel badly about our hair and skin and all, and there's nothing more enjoyable than to see greater misery than our own. And with white folk seemingly enjoying their standard of beauty so much, and hinting to us that we might have a measure of that pleasure by adopting a similar standard, why how can you blame us for straightening our hair, whitening our skin, and calling each other "nigger"? I'll bet the pot gets a world of satisfaction out of calling the kettle black even if the kettle can retaliate.[8]

8. *Ibid.*, July 12, 1932, p. 8.

*Left*, E. H. Crump in the 1940s. His manipulation of black voters cemented his iron-fisted control over Memphis for half a century. *Right*, Blair Hunt in 1968. A leading accommodationist, he was the black community's liaison with Boss Crump for many years.
Courtesy of Memphis *Press-Scimitar*

# 5 · Mr. Crump and the Accommodationists

The inferiority complex so carefully cultivated by whites in blacks also gained advocates within the black community itself, men like the Reverend Sutton E. Griggs. Ironically, Griggs started out as a militant—and unsuccessful—novelist. When his books didn't sell, he changed his tactics and enlisted the white man as an ally. Griggs proclaimed the social Darwinist theory that blacks had lagged behind other races in their social evolution and therefore were an inherently inferior race. According to this philosophy, blacks had developed more slowly because they lacked certain racial traits, the so-called Anglo-Saxon traits of honesty, reliability, tolerance, patience, courtesy, tact, and self-control. Griggs used his Tabernacle Baptist Church to hold a home economics class to teach black women to be better cooks for white people. He took part in a city-wide, anticrime campaign to urge blacks to uphold the law, to stop being idle, to avoid whisky, to stay away from bad company, and not to carry dangerous weapons. Black children, he declared, should receive "socialization" rather than Anglo-Saxon education, so that they might be taught to resemble other races. Called an Uncle Tom or a "white folks' nigger" by blacks, he found support among whites who underwrote his programs with substantial contributions.[1] The *Commercial Appeal* editorialized on August 17, 1925, "If the Negroes had more leaders with the vision of Sutton Griggs and T. O. Fuller . . .

1. David M. Tucker, *Lieutenant Lee of Beale Street* (Nashville, 1971), 60–62.

it would not be long before there was a great change for the better in every way among the members of the race."

The Reverend T. O. Fuller dramatically opposed Griggs' theory about the capabilities of the black man, but he also advocated accommodation with white people as the best way to advance the race. A former legislator from North Carolina, Fuller came to Memphis as president of Howe Institute in 1902. Although an accommodationist, Fuller did not accept the theory of racial inferiority. He considered the Negro race more Christian and more forgiving than the white and took pride in being a pure black member of it. Nothing in the Bible or in the black man's appearance indicated that he could not measure up to the white man, Fuller said. "I hope and pray that the Anti-Kink and Anti-Black which wily schemers of the country are now dumping on the market will fail to destroy the identity of the race and make us ashamed that we are Negroes," he wrote in his *Twenty Years in Public Life*. "I rejoice . . . that I am a Negro."[2]

When he talked to whites, he stressed the programs at Howe to train blacks for jobs, but he failed to mention that they were a small part of the curriculum that included such courses as Greek and psychology. He organized the Inter-Racial League, which led the anticrime campaign and sponsored playgrounds for black children, drawing support from whites and attacks from militant blacks. Through C. P. J. Mooney, editor of the *Commercial Appeal* and more of a liberal than most Memphis whites, he gained a forum in the press for his ideas on peace and goodwill, which he hoped would help deter the violence and repressiveness of whites. His goal was not integration, but separatism directed by Christian ideals. Using his personal influence and contacts with men like Mooney and Crump, he became one of the most respected black leaders advocating accommodation.

It was natural for ministers such as Griggs and Fuller as well as the Reverend Blair Hunt—who also was the principal, and Nat

2. David M. Tucker, *Black Pastors and Leaders: Memphis 1819–1972* (Memphis, 1975), 58–59.

D.'s boss, at Booker T. Washington High School—to take leadership roles in the black community. Ministers were the traditional leaders of the black people. The early 1890s produced such militant pastors as the Reverend Taylor Nightingale, who published the weekly *Free Speech* in his Beale Street Baptist Church and encouraged Ida B. Wells, the associate editor, in her fiery anti-lynching editorials that caused her to be run out of Memphis in 1892.[3] Then came ministers with accommodationist tactics, who cooperated with the white power elite to obtain financial and social aid for their people.

The power of the ministers indicated the importance of religion in black life. The church offered hope and comfort in a world where despair and misery were all too prevalent. In addition, it afforded blacks a training ground for leadership—training difficult to obtain when only menial positions were open to the black man in business. The church gave blacks a place to assemble without arousing either suspicion or antagonism from whites. It provided music and an outlet for emotion, a relief from the hardships of the present in the contemplation of the rewards of heaven.

Through black ministers such as Fuller, Griggs, and others who drew on white support, the greatest social progress in Memphis was made. Black pride advocates such as insurance executive George Lee opposed the accommodationists and said the way to advance the cause of the race was to achieve economically. But the black middle class in Memphis was too small and the need too great for their efforts to succeed.

Men like Griggs, Fuller, and Hunt used their ability to understand and manipulate the white man as a tool to gain support and thousands of dollars for their causes. The black man, though repressed in many ways, had learned in the school of hard knocks how to use the white man while being used by him. With the restraint, hostility, and mistreatment of the day, a certain measure of manipulation was necessary merely for survival. Some blacks

3. *Ibid.*, 45–46, 60–64.

became masters of the art, achieving their ends by playing on the weaknesses, prejudices, guilty consciences, and gullibility of the white man. While some used the art for the betterment of their fellows, others lined their own pockets.

Nat had no doubts that bilking the white man out of his money or talking him into supporting some "worthy cause" that would enrich some black con man was quite a simple accomplishment. How could there be such a thing as white supremacy, he asked, if the con men could hoodwink whites out of so much money so easily? Nat wrote that "all a 'smart' Negro . . . has to do is put on a clean shirt, buy himself a briefcase, learn one or two big words, and take off his hat and say, 'yes, sir,' at the right times and nine cases out of ten he will walk out of the man's office with the check and with the man's estimation that: 'Now, there's the kind of Negro we need here in the South. I wonder why there aren't more like him.' "[4]

Whereas whites referred to the black man who talked back to them as a "smart" Negro, Nat said really smart blacks didn't "sass" white folks. They knew that the right amount of obsequiousness would pay off. "Now, it's not 'Uncle Tomming' in the usual sense of the word, it's a kind of 'graduated' Uncle Tom-ism. The kind that old-time Negro college presidents used when they were begging money for their educational rackets . . . at one time called 'colleges' and 'universities.' "[5]

One technique used by the black con artist involved a spiel about the "white man's burden," about how he was misunderstood and the majority of blacks didn't appreciate what was being done for them. "The average white man likes that," Nat said. "It salves his conscience."[6]

Nat had a basic mistrust of out-of-town blacks who started spouting off about what the local blacks ought to do and feel. Most times the outsiders planned a short stay and fast departure

4. Memphis *World*, July 1, 1947, p. 2.
5. *Ibid.*
6. *Ibid.*

with money in their pockets. If they cussed the town and called the local blacks cowards, the con scheme was on blacks. If they praised the town and called the Memphis blacks ingrates, they were planning a fast play at some white man's bank account.

The ordinary black man, with no intention of liberating the white man's money or bettering social conditions, developed his own techniques of handling white people, which proved successful over decades. And the success of the techniques—not dignity, pride, or honor—was the key point. All the pride and honor in the world would be of little worth to the man who didn't survive to enjoy them, and the fate of many a "sassy" black in the South was extinction. So the clever man placated whites with subservience and watched for the moment to obtain his own ends.

The black man learned to lie skillfully to the white, to agree with him on every subject, to tell him what he wanted to hear. So successfully did the black man accomplish his goals that many whites lived in a dream world in which they believed that all blacks had naturally happy, childlike dispositions, were contented with their lot in life, had no aspirations beyond their achievements, and loved the white man. For the most part, white people, particularly upper-class whites, saw few blacks except in a servant-employer relationship, and a virtual conspiracy among black household workers kept their bosses both happy and ignorant.

Equally accomplished at manipulation were waiters and bellhops at first-class establishments. Not only did they attend to their duties with professional skill, they also made their customers so satisfied and content that many of them became fairly well-to-do on tips. Much of the achievement lay in reading the character of the customer, deciding how to handle him, being totally and completely discreet about any lapses in the customer's behavior, and giving him a sense of well-being. The talent also paid off in valuable white connections—so valuable that head bellhops and headwaiters often became local race spokesmen and were among the most respected men in the black community.

Alonzo Locke, headwaiter at the Gayoso Hotel and later at the

Peabody Hotel when it succeeded the Gayoso as Memphis' finest, reigned as one of the city's acknowledged black leaders. A small, dapper man known for his impeccable dress and military carriage, Alonzo ruled the Peabody's many dining rooms with the grace of a courtier and the iron hand of a benevolent dictator. In the heyday of the Peabody, the "showplace of the South," he held waiters' school every afternoon for the hundred waiters and seven captains to make certain they could pronounce and properly describe the items on the menu. It was considered a point of prestige to be greeted by name by Alonzo, and he could call the names of hundreds of the hotel's patrons.[7]

Many a black man found boosting the white man's ego profitable. A master of the technique was Vernon "Preacher" Cash, long-time locker room attendant at the Memphis University Club. Preacher often was called upon to fill in on the handball court when another player wasn't available. An excellent player who could beat almost any member of the club, Preacher never won a game. As one member groused after a match: "Damn that Preacher! He could beat me with one hand tied behind him and he just barely let me win. That'll cost me a five-dollar tip for sure."

Many blacks did not feel degraded by using various methods to get along with the white man. Instead, they felt they had the last laugh because they reaped the profits. As Rufus Thomas, the singer who introduced the funky chicken and other dances, recalled about his days as a waiter in the 1920s in Nashville: "During that time, the white fellow was quite boastful, if he's out with his woman. Man, he was something. And he'd say all these things. But he'd pay well, pay well. At the end of the night, I had the money. I won't say he was broke, but he splurged and I had the money. And so you ask yourself: 'Hell, who's the fool or who's stupid?' Because I had the money at the end of the night and that was what I was working for."[8]

7. Shields McIlwaine, *Memphis Down in Dixie* (New York, 1948), 316–18.
8. Interview with Rufus Thomas, October 9, 1973.

A position of service to the rich, aristocratic, and powerful was valued and respected. The rank of the person employed derived from the rank of the employer or the prestige of the hotel or club where he worked. And the respect achieved by becoming one of the top echelon of service personnel was of no little worth in a society where the black man was awarded scant respect by any white man for anything.

The elevated status achieved by men who were essentially servants to white people galled some blacks, among them—for a time—Nat D. He had received an invitation in 1932 to a dance at the Hotel Men's Improvement Club, formed in 1924 by a group of hotel employees, including Alonzo Locke. The invitation recalled his resentment on first coming home from college and realizing that this was the club where the swankiest affairs of black Memphis were held.

I remembered the thoughts I had when first I learned that Memphis was still a typical antebellum town of the Old South where the cullud folks continued to learn their social manners and customs from the men who placed food in the faces of the patrons of the downtown hotels for the white folks. I thought of the "big-house" of the old plantation days when the sons and daughters of Hagar, who served the white folks and were around them most constantly, were the rulers of the cullud social whirl. . . . In the first radical reactions of my youthful inexperience I resented the fact that the social world of colored Memphis was dictated to by men who worked in hotels, despite the fact that I knew that ever since Emancipation the most cultured and refined group of men in the race were, on the whole, just those self-same men who earned their livelihood by slinging hash.[9]

About the same time, Thomas E. Young, writing in the *World*, named the Negro employees of the Tennessee Club "catering to the white rich and prominent class." These men "have worked so long serving rich men that you would think they are rich by their nice street appearance." Also that year the Chauffeurs' Service Club was about to celebrate its first anniversary and was gener-

9. Memphis *World*, December 2, 1932, p. 8.

ally accepted as being stronger than any other club in the city.

The caste system operated among the cooks and maids as it did among the butlers, chauffeurs, and hotelmen. Social prestige aside, the practical aspects of working as a cook or maid for a white family, particularly a well-to-do and generous family, were not to be ignored. Often a black family was held together not only by the salary but also by the food from the house where the mother worked. Nat wrote, "I guess that's why we have that line of a Negro blues song which said, 'I don't have to work so hard, / 'cause I got a gal in the white folks' yard.' "[10]

Maids and cooks were sought after by the young men for the same reason. "The young fellows would be sure to have association with a girl who was a cook with a white family because that guaranteed you good food," Nat said. "Of course, you'd go with a girl who was a school teacher and she was all right, nice to be seen with. But you spent more time with the one who was providing us meals."

Whatever their circumstances, as servants or ministers, the spokesmen for blacks to whites were, with rare exceptions, men with "suitable" views; that is, they were not outwardly militant or belligerent about the black man's status. They had "proper" manners—in other words, they paid respect to anyone with white skin, and had cultivated speech and accommodating ways. And because these men gained acceptance from whites, they also had influence in the black community.

Nat, in a column about black leaders in the August 9, 1946, *World*, wrote:

Down on Beale Street the other day one guy was heard to say, "The Negroes about here who are called leaders are hand-picked . . . hand-picked by the white folks." And it must be admitted that he may have something there. But on the other hand, wonder if that fellow has ever stopped to observe that unless a Negro is approved by white folk in the United States, he never gains any real distinction or acceptance

10. *Ibid.*, January 28, 1949, p. 8.

as a leader. . . . Sad as it may be, it is a fact that no Negro ever rises, as a rule, among his fellow colored brethren until some white man or organization has recognized him. Then the other Negroes accept him. True, most of our churches have their preachers and deacons . . . but said preachers aren't really "ready" until they are able to boast of and prove their white connections. Who are our Memphis Negro leaders? Well, you know, don't you. They're the ones who know the "right white folks" best. You name 'em.

The first name to come to anyone's mind in Memphis was that of Blair Hunt, principal of Booker T. Washington High School and minister of Mississippi Avenue Christian Church, one of the wealthiest black congregations in the city. Hunt was hand-picked by E. H. Crump as his contact with the black community. Light-skinned, courteous, intelligent, soft-spoken, and statesman-like, Hunt represented Crump's idea of what a black leader should be. Although limited by Crump's authoritarianism and strong be-lief in white supremacy, Hunt's influence was more long-lasting than that of perhaps any black man in the community with the exception of Robert Church, Jr.

Hunt had no illusions about Crump's attitude toward blacks. "He didn't have any animosity toward blacks; he was just a strict segregationist," Hunt said. "This is a paternalistic view."[11] Hunt dealt with Crump under the terms of the era in which both were reared—terms of courtesy to each other but of a definite barrier between the races. They were men of the same time and generally of the same upbringing—Hunt's social status was as high among blacks as Crump's among whites—and both had been imbued with the concepts of southern gentility. While they could not have been considered friends, they maintained a relationship ade-quate for their purposes.

Crump ran Memphis with a firm hand; he did not accept in-subordination from whites, and he was certainly not about to accept it from blacks. Hunt recognized Crump's strong feelings

11. Interview with Blair Hunt, February 6, 1973.

and worked to keep conditions calm. He knew well the tenuous position in which he and his people lived and the violence that could erupt against them at a moment's notice.[12]

Crump made use of the Negro vote almost from the time he broke into politics as a young reformer in 1905. One of his main lieutenants, Frank Rice, was influential in getting the black vote by gaining the support of a number of the owners of Beale Street saloons and gambling houses and thereby the black votes they controlled.[13] Black supporters were given their poll tax and registration receipts by the ward heelers and told how to vote. They were taken in trucks from poll to poll for repeated voting.[14]

Robert Henry, a ward lieutenant for Church and for his right-hand man, Lieutenant George Lee, recalled the elections of that era. "The colored people, they voted plenty, all they wanted to vote," he said. "And nobody bothered them when they went in to vote either. With two different kinds of hats, different coats, and things like that, people'd vote four and five times. Get a dollar, dollar and a half."[15]

Along with Crump's manipulation of the black vote came further black support through his alliance with Robert Church, Jr., the acknowledged black political leader. Church distributed the patronage for the Republican party in West Tennessee and influenced the entire state, and Crump wanted to be on good terms with such officials as federal judges and district attorneys. On his side, Church was able to obtain some concessions for his people, as well as recourse when there were difficulties with the police or the local courts.

---

12. When black children were being jailed in Birmingham, Alabama, in the 1960s during protests over school desegregation, a friend complained to Hunt, "Isn't that a shame to do that to those children?" Hunt replied, "I've seen the time they'd have been shot right on the street." As he told the story during a 1973 interview, he added: "I've seen the time that you couldn't do those things and the black man knew it, as a matter of survival—and that's one of the first laws of nature, survival. And we survived. We used other tactics."

13. Miller, *Mr. Crump*, 103.

14. Walter P. Adkins, "Beale Street Goes to the Polls" (M.A. thesis, Ohio State University, 1935), 20–22.

15. Interview with Robert Henry, October 15, 1973.

The uneasy alliance between Crump and Church had first shown its muscle during the 1923 reelection campaign for Mayor Rowlett Paine. It came in the midst of the resurgence of the Ku Klux Klan in Memphis. Support for the Klan was so strong that several men, including the city coroner, battled publicly for its leadership. A full slate of KKK candidates filed for the November election.

Race was hardly an issue. The Memphis Klan opposed non-Protestants but did not speak out against blacks. In fact, the Klan held a rally in Church's Park, asking for black support and stressing the fact that blacks and Klansmen should be allied because both were native-born Americans and Protestants. The principal speaker pleaded for the purity of both races and denied that Klansmen hated blacks. The Klan even suggested that blacks form a Klan of their own. It was a strange spectacle, with flaming crosses and robed and hooded Klansmen speaking to curious rather than frightened black faces and asking for support. The two hundred blacks at the rally listened, but that was all. Cliff Davis, running for city judge, was the only one of the Klan candidates elected.[16]

The Klan had strength in numbers, but its members and leaders hardly qualified as the outstanding men in the city. The *News Scimitar* on November 5, 1923, pointed out the mediocrity of the membership. "One thing that can be said for the klan ticket is that the mask of the klansmen which they wear serves little purpose. No one in Memphis would recognize them if they saw them."

Church and other blacks were concerned enough about the Klan's strength to lend their support to Paine, in spite of the few improvements he had made for blacks during his first term. In addition, Paine was generally recognized as a better-than-average mayor, an honest man who had made great strides in improving the physical welfare of the city, particularly the water and sewage systems. The city had been in bad condition, with typhoid rampant, before he pushed through the improvements.

16. Adkins, "Beale Street," 39.

Sixteen black business and professional leaders endorsed Paine and his fellow candidates, saying that the Paine group would complete the $300,000 black high school, put in bright lights and good streets all over the city, and see to it that white and black were treated fairly, and—most of all—that they were not Ku Kluxers.[17]

With the black vote and Crump's last-minute support, Paine and his cohorts took every office but the city judgeship won by Cliff Davis. But the majority was narrow and the black vote small —not what Paine had expected. The size of the vote seemed to convince him that he did not have to live up to his campaign promises. On the contrary, it was as though he developed a hostility to blacks. He did complete the new black high school, but only after protest was he persuaded to name it Booker T. Washington High School rather than Negro Industrial School. He located the city incinerator near three of the largest black public schools and one of the best black residential sections, and no amount of complaint—not even a court suit brought by black leaders—caused him to move the site.[18]

The 1927 election found blacks determined to retaliate. Church, using George Lee as his front man, organized the West Tennessee Civic and Political League. Lee, an executive in an insurance firm, set up the organization as if he were selling insurance, appointing a chairman to each voting ward, a captain to each street within the ward, and a representative to each block on the street. Six thousand blacks registered and paid their poll taxes. The injustices of the Paine regime were trumpeted: unpaved and unlighted black streets in contrast to three million dollars spent on white streets; inadequate playgrounds, parks and hospitals; school funding of thirty-two dollars a child for whites and a third of that for blacks; no black policemen or firemen.[19]

The league was supposed to be nonpartisan, but there had

17. Tucker, *Lieutenant Lee*, 80.
18. Adkins, "Beale Street," 42.
19. Tucker, *Lieutenant Lee*, 92.

been a secret alliance made with Crump to support Watkins Overton in return for promises for improved conditions. Paine criticized the Crump candidates for having black support and declared that as long as he was in office, there would be no black policemen, no black firemen, and no admission of blacks to the white parks of the city. In turn, Crump criticized Paine in the *Press-Scimitar*, saying Paine had "so unfairly dealt with the Negro people after begging them for their votes in 1923." Blacks turned out to help give Overton a three-to-one victory and put the Crump regime back in control of city government. The voter turnout in the black wards was 80 percent against Paine, even though conservatives like Sutton Griggs opposed the league as "laying the foundation of a race riot."[20]

The alliance between Church and Crump came under fire in the governor's race of 1928. Crump supported Hill McAlister in his campaign against Henry Horton, speaker of the Senate, who had served as interim governor after Governor Austin Peay's death in office. Backing Horton was Colonel Luke Lea, owner of the *Commercial Appeal*. Also supporting Horton was Clarence Saunders, grocery store tycoon who had founded the Piggly Wiggly stores and then lost them in a battle with Wall Street. Saunders had started another group of grocery stores he called "Clarence Saunders, Sole Owner of My Name." Saunders ran newspaper ads connecting Crump with Church and accusing Church of being fifty thousand dollars in arrears on his taxes. Crump countered with full-page ads of his own criticizing Saunders.

On August 2, 1928, Saunders took out an ad in the *Commercial Appeal*, imploring:

Show to the world that the white men and white women of Shelby County will not stand for Negroes to be called to the polls in a Democratic primary—show your white blood of resentment at the insult to your race. . . . The Bob Church-Crump gang must go down in defeat by the votes of strong-hearted white men and white women of Memphis and Shelby County or they must acknowledge that they

20. Lamon, "Negroes in Tennessee," 378.

are weaklings and the political serfs of Bob Church and Ed Crump . . .
Does not the thought of this bring shame to your face and anguish
to your heart? If it does not then there is no strong back bone to hold
you up as a fearless and unterrified white man.

Generally, black newspapers in Memphis stayed out of local
issues, partly because their revenues depended largely on white
advertisers and additionally because bold political policies were
considered unwise. But this time the Memphis *Triangle* made an
exception. It ran a lead editorial, starting on page one, under the
caption, "We Know You, Mr. Saunders."

The colored people of Memphis are conscious of their friends and
their enemies among the white people of this city. It has been their
wonted endeavor to support their friends and laud them to the highest
in their prayers and in their patronage.

Our enemies we have tried to remember and avoid as well as ignore.
But we keep a catalogue of whom they are. At the head of the list
we are now ready to place the name of Mr. Clarence Saunders. Mr.
Saunders is a groceryman who has stepped outside of the realm of his
business into a field where he is at a loss. He insults us in the public
press.

We merely wish to remind you, Mr. Saunders, that hams and
turnip greens can be purchased some other place than just your
Clarence Saunders stores. When the colored housewives of this community find it necessary to make the turnstiles click, they will remember that "We Know You."[21]

The *Commercial Appeal* got into the act on July 29, 1928,
editorializing against the Negro vote in the white primary and
urging the chairman of the Shelby County primary board to ex-
clude Negroes from voting on the grounds that the "Democratic
party is the white man's party in the South." The newspaper said
that "white domination in the South is dependent upon keeping
negroes out of Democratic primaries. If the practice in Shelby
should extend to other Southern states where the negro is in majority, they would be able to control politics and the offices of the

21. Adkins, "Beale Street," 98.

South." The chairman, William Stanton, a Crump man, said Shelby had no rule barring Negroes.

In spite of the newspaper and Mr. Saunders, McAlister won an overwhelming victory in Shelby County, but not enough to give him the win statewide. After the election, Saunders inserted a paragraph over his grocery ad, saying he wasn't mad at anybody and that he had the best bargains in town.

Crump continued to be challenged and continued to win, as much through his personality as his machine. Brandishing his flamboyance like the gold-headed cane he carried, he captivated the city of Memphis, black as well as white. No person was too unimportant for him to remember; he greeted hundreds by name in his daily walks. Almost every organization in the city felt it had a friend in Mr. Crump, someone to whom it could turn for help. He was adept at awarding small favors, minor jobs, little courtesies, assistance in difficulties, handouts—and with evoking the loyalty of the recipients. Black and white shared in his generosity.

Black support for Crump was understandable for, throughout his political career, he worked to improve the quality of life for Memphis blacks, particularly in housing, health, and education. He saw no reason that blacks should not share in the improvements he wanted for his city—though at a slower pace and to a lesser degree. In 1920, when Mayor Paine raised white teachers' salaries, Crump complained that the raise had no provision for black teachers and no suggestion of improved black school buildings. The black teachers, Crump was quoted as saying in the *News Scimitar* on April 15, "are entitled to better pay on account of the greatly increased cost of living which has not been confined to a single race."

Crump spoke out for the black man's position on many occasions. He would tell a meeting of city officials not to forget the Negroes, that they were citizens, too.[22] Nat D., in a number of

22. Interview with Blair Hunt, February 6, 1973.

columns, quoted black leaders as saying that Memphis had better schools, housing projects, recreation sites, streets, and sidewalks in black areas than any other southern city, that Memphis was in a class by itself. Crump spoke up for the blacks when his was one of the few voices to be heard. In the Klan years of the 1920s, he seemed almost a southern liberal. But Crump's generosity toward the black community had well-defined boundaries. He provided only as he saw fit and his patience with "uppity" behavior was short.

Hunt recalled going to see Crump with another black leader, J. L. Campbell, after an election, the traditional time to ask for favors in return for black support at the polls. They asked first for a golf course. Crump said Negroes didn't play golf. Hunt replied that it was because they had no place. Crump promised them a course. Then they asked about postal employees. Crump told them the ratio of black employees to white at the post office was about the same as the population ratio and if it got any worse to let him know. "Another thing, Mr. Crump," Hunt said. "We would like to have Negro police officers." The meeting developed an icy chill. "You've got to go to somebody else to see about that, not here," Crump said coldly. "There's no place else to go, Mr. Crump, except here," Campbell said. "I've got nothing to do with that," Crump snapped and stood up to indicate that the meeting was over. Campbell and Hunt left and, going down in the elevator, Campbell said, "We made a big mistake today, didn't we, asking for Negro cops?" Hunt agreed, "Looks like it."[23] It wasn't until 1948, after Crump had suffered a major political defeat in the state elections, that the administration finally gave in and hired black policemen.

23. *Ibid.*

Beale Street in 1968—still alive, but fading.
Courtesy of Memphis *Press-Scimitar*

George W. Lee—political leader, silver-tongued orator, and author, in 1969.
Courtesy of Memphis *Press-Scimitar*

# 6 · Harder Times

Depression came to Beale Street more than a year before the crash of 1929 was to echo across the country. And, ironically, the hard times interrupted Beale's greatest business boom and shattered dreams of making Beale the greatest economic center of black America.

Hopes were high for the new enterprises: Wayman Wilkerson, funeral-home owner and one of the founders of the Fraternal Savings Bank, started the Tri-State Casket Company in 1920, with a group of associates; Bert Roddy, cashier of the Solvent Savings Bank, organized a chain of grocery stores; Dr. J. B. Martin added rental apartments and a black baseball team to his thriving drug business; the Fraternal Savings Bank established the Citizens' Mercantile Company to build a new department store on Beale and the American Home Investment Company to buy and build cheap rental property for blacks coming into Memphis.[1]

Black businessmen considered themselves the real leaders of the race, the examples that would dispute white claims that the black could not achieve. Economic advancement was the way to get the white man to respect the black, said the Negro Business League and the Negro press, and black business would arouse black pride. It was the businessmen who challenged the accommodationist tactics of the ministers and encouraged the black man to stand up for himself and show what he could do.[2]

1. Lamon, "Negroes in Tennessee," 222–23, 237.
2. George W. Lee, *Beale Street: Where the Blues Began* (College Park, Md., 1934), 168–70.

Then came disaster. The Solvent Savings Bank and the Fraternal Savings Bank both hit financial difficulties. A merger of the two in late 1927 did not help the situation, and in December, when the Christmas rush caused a run on funds, the joint bank closed its doors. State bank examiners found corruption and mismanagement rampant, with large, unsecured loans to most of the bank officials. Bank president A. F. Ward, a former boilermaker and piano hauler, had promised he would bring wealth to Beale. The examiners found most of the wealth had gone to Ward—$170,000 in unsecured loans. He and others were jailed. Depositors received only fifteen cents on the dollar and more than twenty thousand depositors and some fifty black-owned businesses were hard hit by the closing. A majority of Beale's most successful businessmen were officials and directors of the banks, and they were discredited in both the black and the white communities.[3]

Even the NAACP suffered from the general atmosphere of defeat and discouragement. The president of the Memphis branch, Mrs. Wayman Wilkerson, wrote the national office in April of 1928: "We have had a hard time since the bank closed. Our leading men are being attacked on every hand and everything possible is being done to intimidate the colored people. For that reason we are trying to be as quiet as possible to avoid trouble. I don't think it wise to work just now for the NAACP."[4]

Beale Street had not recovered from the setback of the bank closing when the depression came. Hotels closed, three Negro newspapers shut down, the Memphis Black Devils baseball team went out of existence, building and loan companies lost business. Even the recording sessions of black blues artists, held at the auditorium or the Peabody Hotel during the twenties, ended as the depression virtually wiped out the market for "race records."

There were some people, though, including the Reverend Blair Hunt, who felt the depression hit the white man harder than the black. "They had more to lose," Hunt said; "their living standards

3. Tucker, *Lieutenant Lee*, 57–58.
4. Lamon, "Negroes in Tennessee," 241.

were higher. And ours were always just by the skin of our teeth. We had soup kitchens on Beale during the depression, the street was still active, but money was just scarce."[5]

Most people, though, were not speculating on whether the blacks or whites suffered more. They were scuffling to keep themselves and their families fed. In the spring of 1932, Nat D. wrote about an incident he observed at the garbage heap at Booker T. Washington High School. The school's cafeteria was nonprofit and very little food was wasted, he explained. About five o'clock one afternoon he was shocked to see "a ragged, ash-colored, little Negro boy of about seven digging into some of the containers. He had a paper box at his side and in it he was very carefully placing pieces of old bread and other particles he had found. He was very meticulous about the pieces he chose, taking time to wipe each piece against his dusty trouser leg before depositing it."[6] In December of the same year, Nat wrote in the Memphis World, "When the aristocrats among Ham's sons—the preachers, teachers, mail men, doctors, insurance men and waiters—commence worrying about bread and things, you may conclude that things economic aren't so sporty."

Along with the decrease in income for the black ministers, the depression also dealt a blow to their influence. The ministers were criticized for talking too much about rewards to come through passivity and trust in God's grace for his "chosen people," while doing little to help those in misery on earth. Nat wrote about the declining reputation of the preachers.

The leading colored papers take delight in pointing out and playing up the weaknesses and shortcomings of particular preachers and declaring that they apply to the group generally. The modern trend seems to be toward unhorsing the black preacher from his traditional seat of racial leadership. But a still, small voice should caution that the vanguard of a race should include some preachers along with the rest. The men up front should not all be businessmen, nor should all be preachers. Anybody who has anything to contribute should be there.

5. Interview with Blair Hunt, February 6, 1973.
6. Memphis World, April 19, 1932, p. 6.

But—the sheep should learn that no preacher is "a little piece of God broke off."[7]

The depression saw bread lines stretched blocks long on Beale. Jim Mulcahy set up a free soup kitchen that gave away thousands of meals. Asked why he opened the soup kitchen, Mulcahy, who had owned several nightclubs on Beale, including the Panama, explained that blacks had spent their money with him when they had work and he couldn't stand to see them hungry.[8]

In spite of the bread lines, the people out of work, the men and women who would battle each other for the right to pick over the loads taken to the garbage dump, Beale Street didn't lose its ability to laugh. It told jokes about times being so hard that rats broke their necks falling into the flour barrel and that mice were eating onions and crying like babies. And Nat got a sardonic satisfaction from white men coming to ask black men for a handout. Black panhandlers didn't often show up on Beale, he said. That was the street where blacks were supposed to strut and it was a blow to the pride to acknowledge dire need on the avenue. He wrote in the December 30, 1932, Memphis *World*:

Ever so often you see one of the proud Nordics standing around speculating on a hand-out. Isn't it strange that a certain type of white man seeks Negro districts when he's down and out? Oh, well, maybe they're seeking the line of least resistance. Then too they say this is a "white man's country," so he can be expected to work and beg wherever his conscience leads him. Also you've got to consider that little tinge of superiority and pride most of us feel whenever we find one of the masters of this land needing something and asking us for it.

Despite the general lack of money, many of the saloons and gambling dives hung on. By and large, Beale was where the action was for big-time gamblers and hustlers. The true gamblers

7. *Ibid.*, September 6, 1932, p. 8.
8. At Mulcahy's death on September 6, 1940, the *Commercial Appeal*, p. 9, said, "His name was a conjure word among Beale Street negroes and among politicians who wanted the vote in that part of town." A man who had made fortunes and given them away, Mulcahy was being sued by the city for back taxes when he died.

on Beale shot craps and played poker. But the gambling that was the passion of the man on the street was the numbers game, policy. A dime, a quarter or a half-dollar was enough to play; if the three numbers selected were chosen in the drawing, the payoff could run from fifty to five hundred dollars. Policy was sold from every grocery store, saloon, liquor store, delicatessen, even some Chinese laundries, and up and down the street, by door-to-door salesmen. The policy writers, who sold on commission, would give their customers a ticket showing the name of the policy house plus the time and place of the drawings. Lottery drawings always drew large crowds of hopefuls. Even though the customers could watch the numbered balls being pulled out of a sack to select the winning numbers, there were ways to make certain the most popular numbers didn't come up. One way was to freeze the balls that were not to be chosen. Then the person drawing the balls out of the sack could avoid the cold ones and draw only from the others.

Some people played a favorite series of three numbers over and over; others would consult the "dream books" to find out which numbers to play. In these books, sold in the dry goods stores and drugstores along Beale, dreams and symbols were translated into number series.[9] Dream of a black man and play 14-41-70, of flying and play 10-69-70. The number 4-11-44 was known as the policy roll. Robert Henry recalled that once, following an automobile wreck on Beale, as the victims lay bleeding on the sidewalks, policy players rushed to the nearest policy writer to play the numbers for blood, 11-19-40. The numbers came up—the game was straight that day—and the policy writer was cleaned out. He fled, but returned later and paid off.

The Palace and its entertainers remained a drawing card for Beale during the thirties. When talking pictures had come in a

9. Interview with Leo Schwab, October 11, 1973. A. Schwab's, one of the few remaining businesses on Beale, still sells dream books, with business particularly brisk during the months when the greyhounds are running at the racetrack in West Memphis, Arkansas.

few years earlier, stage shows suffered a setback, and the Palace booked only a few engagements with stage performers. Even the famed Palace orchestra had been disbanded. But the newness wore off the talkies, and Anselmo Barrasso brought back stage shows. Even though the receipts didn't always cover the cost and he had to make up the difference out of his own pocket, Barrasso continued to have the shows. Nat D. recalled that Barrasso was also known as a soft touch for a little kid who wanted to go to the movies and didn't have a dime. Sometimes he even supplied the popcorn.

But the feature that drew the biggest crowds to the Palace regularly was Amateur Night, a revival of the amateur shows that the old minstrel men held years before on Beale. At eight o'clock on Tuesday nights, the houselights would be lowered, the big curtain would be slowly drawn, and the spotlight would center on a "short, shiny-faced black master of ceremonies, whose gleaming teeth in a grinning mouth rivalled his thick, double-lensed eyeglasses as points of reference," Nat wrote about himself. He would start: "It's Amateur Night on Beale Street . . . where the blues began . . . and the stuff is here."[10] The orchestra would play the "Beale Street Blues" as lines of ambitious amateurs packed the stage wings. The theater too was usually packed, while others listened to the broadcast at home over WNBR radio.

The amateurs competing for the five-, three-, and two-dollar prizes ranged from three-year-old tots to oldsters so creaky they could hardly climb the stairs to the stage. In front of footlights might be a man doing a dance on his fingers, a harmonica player, or a character with a snake he had taught to wiggle to a drum beat. There were tire-blowing contests, one-legged dancers, and the blues sung by all ages. If the audience didn't like the performer, it threw paper bags in winter, tomatoes in summer. If he was booed and still wouldn't leave the stage, the audience set up an uproar until the "Lord High Executioner" jumped from behind

10. Memphis *Tri-State Defender*, November 4, 1970, p. 4.

the wings and shot him with a pearl-handled revolver loaded with blanks. Usually one shot was sufficient, but sometimes the executioner would empty his gun before the performer would reluctantly leave the stage.

The Palace was best known to white Memphis through the Midnight Rambles, weekly shows for whites who came in throngs to see such top black entertainers as Duke Ellington, Count Basie, and Ella Fitzgerald. Attractions of another sort were the girlie shows—the Brown Skin Models or the Vampin' Baby Show—with their lines of shapely chorus girls, most of them the color of coffee heavily laced with cream. Barrasso at times had trouble keeping the white men off the stage during the shows. One prominent and wealthy man was thrown out of the theater more than once because he would get drunk and climb onto the stage after the girls.[11] The tone of the show was raucous, the jokes bawdy, the dances often vulgar, and the audience predominantly male. The management would put a halt to an enthusiastic dancer who started to strip, but virtually anything else went. Bootleg whisky flowed freely from pint bottles and pocket flasks, and the Rambles rambled on.

The Palace had competition as the spot for top performers. Earl Hines played for a Chauffeur's Service Club dance, King Oliver and his orchestra played at the Hotel Men's Club as well as at the Casino ballroom at the Fairgrounds for whites. Church's Park, with the old auditorium torn down and replaced by a smaller city community center in 1929, featured big-time jazz bands of the likes of Basie, Ellington, Louis Jordan, and Chick Webb. White spectators were allowed to sit through the concert in a special section, then go into the bleacher seats on the side when the dancing started. It became the fashion for young men around town to attend the shows with their society girl friends, the girls in fashionable frocks and wearing leghorn picture hats with long

11. Interview with Mrs. Anselmo Barrasso, widow of the Palace Theater owner, September 4, 1973.

streamers. One night, when a fight broke out in the auditorium, the society swains hustled their dates out the side door.

A breakthrough for Memphis came when Negro bands occasionally were booked to play for whites at the Casino ballroom. But even this custom received a setback in the 1930s when Cab Calloway's band played for a packed house. Calloway, light-skinned and sophisticated, drew more feminine attention than white southern male egos thought proper. The antagonism came to a head when a white woman went up to the bandstand to request a song. Her escort took exception, a fight broke out, and Calloway and his group were ordered out of town. After the incident, black bands playing for whites in any public place, even restaurants, were discouraged by the city administration.[12]

Beale Street had little enough to celebrate during the depression, but the whole street turned out for the big event of the decade, the dedication of Handy Park. The city razed the old Market House at the corner of Hernando and Beale in 1931 and built a small park there, with the intention of naming it Beale Park. Lieutenant George Lee finally persuaded Boss Crump to name it for Handy. On Sunday, March 29, 1931, Lee and Handy rode down Beale in Lee's black LaSalle at the head of a two-mile procession of fraternal orders, marching clubs, vocal societies, and uniformed bands. The Knights of Pythias, the Negro Masons, the Tribes of Canaan, the chauffeurs and barbers clubs marched to the "Beale Street Blues" before a crowd of ten thousand.[13] Beale Street took the pocket-sized patch of land to heart. Preachers preached there, musicians played there, Beale Streeters relaxed there.

Crump's decision to allow the park to be named for Handy was due at least partly to Bob Church's backing of the idea. The Republicans were still in power and Church's influence was strong. But times were about to change in national politics. Already there were rumblings of discontent in the black community

12. Interview with Robert Henry, October 15, 1973.
13. Tucker, *Lieutenant Lee*, 102–103.

about President Hoover and his turn to the lily-white factions in the South rather than to the black leaders.

When Hoover continued to ignore the blacks, Church wrote him that "a policy that excludes from the authority and responsibility of government twelve million citizens solely because they do not resemble others in face and feature is dangerous." In the letter, Church said the only recognition extended by the Hoover administration had been to ask for half a million dollars from Negroes to erect a memorial to dead black soldiers. "The dead are safe and their memory is as secure as the story of our nation, but the living are with us to contend for recognition as citizens." Continuance of such a policy, he said, will "leave the Republican Party a wreck upon the shores of the political ocean, but a memory to those who once loved it and a chapter in the history of government. Mr. President, the Negro, having stood the scorn of time, can stand the indifference and neglect of even so good a man as you are, but I, with millions of men, many white men of sober judgment, doubt that our country can afford to issue so open an invitation to the designs of oppression."[14]

Because of Hoover's attitude, many blacks were indifferent to his campaign and deserted the Republican party for the Democratic. Kelly Miller wrote in the Memphis *World* in 1931: "Once to call a Negro a Democrat was equivalent to stamping him with a brand of infamy. Now . . . no Negro can certainly take any pride in the fact that he is a Republican, nor need he feel ashamed to be called a Democrat." Even Church himself was not particularly interested in Hoover's reelection, although he maintained his support for the party and his belief that, in spite of the defections, the Negro was fundamentally a Republican and would return to the GOP.[15]

Most of the black community felt that the outcome of the election would make little difference in their lives. As Nat D. put it in his column just after the election: "It's true that a few of the

14. Church and Church, *The Robert R. Churches*, 264–65.
15. Adkins, "Beale Street," 103.

'favored of the Gods of Politics' who happened to know the right string to pull once upon a time are now, or soon will be, on the outside looking in; but dismiss a comparatively small number of post-office jobs and two or three bones thrown in the direction of the bigger dogs, and you'll find that the vast majority of the cullud folks around won't be able to tell whether a donkey was pulling the cart or an elephant was pushing it."

Franklin D. Roosevelt's election all but ended the political clout Church had enjoyed on the national level, but Church's personal influence was still great with the black electorate in Memphis and he retained his political alliance with Crump.

Church's connections enabled him to obtain concessions from the machine for blacks, gaining more for his people than all his influence with the Republican party ever did. But there were things even he could not achieve. One was a relaxing of the restrictions about the separation of the races. Crump felt he knew where Memphis wanted the color line drawn. He did allow the Midnight Rambles and white attendance at some Negro events, but that was no more than would have been accepted back in Holly Springs, Mississippi, when he was a boy. Whites had always attended black gatherings, churches, funerals, and socials, sometimes out of courtesy, sometimes out of curiosity. What he could not allow was for whites and blacks to assemble on equal terms— particularly sitting down.

So, when the American Legion held its state convention in Memphis in 1932, black delegates were sent to the balcony of Ellis Auditorium. The year before, when the convention was at Nashville, an attempt had been made at segregation. The blacks, who protested by seating themselves in the main hall in windows, chairs, and on the floor, finally were allowed to take their seats with the white members. Part of the reason for the permissiveness could have been that the Negro unit, the Autress Russell Post, with seventy-two votes—the third largest post in the state—held the balance of power at the convention. That factor did not alter the Memphis situation, however; even the black marchers and drum and bugle corps were ordered to march separately from the whites, whereas in Nashville the year before the Memphis units had marched together. Some of the white Memphis legionnaires showed their objections to the segregation by going to the balcony to sit with the blacks.[16]

Even with the restrictions in the Memphis convention, the legion was an outstanding exception to segregation. George Lee became an executive committeeman of the state legion. Dr. R. Q. Venson, a Memphis dentist, served as the only Negro member of the Tennessee State Hospital Committee of the legion. It was largely through his influence that a study was made on complaints about the United States Veterans Hospital in Memphis. The study found that blacks received inferior treatment. So that the white nurse would not have to use the same toilet as the black maid, one toilet and washroom were provided for all the Negro patients on a ward where there were provisions for three. Certain types of treatment were refused the black patients; some doctors indicated that prescribed hospital treatment was too good for a black man. Nurses made black patients come to them for temperature and pulse rate checks instead of their going to the patients. Whites were provided recreational facilities, but blacks were not.[17]

Along with the attitude that such treatment was all blacks deserved was the feeling that it was no more than they expected. The NAACP complained in 1932 about the treatment of Negroes working in War Department levee camps in Mississippi. They told Major General Lytle Brown, the official in charge of the levee work, about the unsatisfactory housing conditions; the work schedule of fourteen to sixteen hours a day for twenty cents an hour, with no overtime; the workers' being forced to buy food from the camp commissary at prices double and triple those outside the camps; and the beatings and mistreatment. Brown re-

16. Memphis *World*, August 26, 1932, p. 1.
17. *Ibid.*, September 25, 1931, p. 1.

plied to the complaints, as reported in the *World*, "Isn't that what Negroes are accustomed to?"[18]

Accompanying the whites' condoning of such situations was the opinion that Negroes would continue to accept them docilely. The Jackson, Mississippi, *Daily News* editorialized in 1932 that the Negro "will never become a dangerous agitator because there is very little lawlessness or hysteria in his heart. The Negro has a marvelous capacity for suffering in silence. Depression has dealt the race a much harder blow than it has the whites and the poverty prevalent among them in some sections is hardly short of appalling, but you rarely hear a Negro making a complaint." The editorial stated flatly that white supremacy would last forever and that all northern white friends of the Negro were social equality advocates.[19]

Social equality—the very words caused most whites to shudder. Fear of racial mixing had defeated the merger of Howe Institute with Roger Williams College, a black Baptist school in Nashville, in 1928. The two schools planned to build a new facility in Memphis with help from northern money. But white civic clubs banded together in opposition, saying that the school would bring in educated blacks from the North with their ideas on social equality. The City Commission backed the civic clubs and refused permission for construction.[20]

Blacks tried to dissuade whites from this fear by statements that they wanted justice between the races, not social equality. "The Negro does not seek social equality," Dr. Venson wrote in a letter to the editor of the *World* on June 17, 1932. "He is satisfied with his own race and desires most to be let alone. Equal opportunity is what he seeks."

The schools, which might have served to narrow the gap between black and white, were a part of it. In the Shelby County schools, many located in rural areas, the opening and closing

18. *Ibid.*, October 25, 1932, p. 8.
19. Jackson (Miss.) *Daily News*, quoted in the Memphis *World*, October 25, 1932, p. 2.
20. Tucker, *Lieutenant Lee*, 66–67.

schedules were timed to allow the black children to work in the fields. School closed in the early spring to plant and then to culti-vate the crops. Classes resumed during the summer months after the crops were laid by, with the children trying to study in stuffy, sweltering schoolrooms where daytime temperatures averaged in the high eighties and the nineties. The session shut down again about the middle of September when the cotton started to open, and resumed after the crop was gathered. Many youngsters at-tended classes no more than two to three months a year, if that long.

Negro schools in the city of Memphis operated on a standard schedule, but facilities, equipment, and teachers' salaries suffered in comparison with those for whites. Admittedly, improvements were made through the years, particularly under Superintendent R. L. Jones. When he took over as head of the school system in 1923, only a hundred black children went from elementary schools to the one black high school. By 1932, about a thousand black children were going to Booker T. Washington and to the new Manassas High School.[21] Buildings were built for both white and black, with the larger and more expensive ones for whites, as usual.

The depression brought more problems to the schools. Black teachers, already receiving lower wages than whites, were asked to take a pay cut. Eventually the city began paying salaries with scrip. Teachers could use the scrip to buy food, and certain loan offices would discount it; but it was a poor substitute for money.

Even so, teachers were so much better off than most other blacks that they were considered among the elite. Most of them shared what they had with the students, lending them nickels for school lunches, even though they knew they would never be repaid.

In 1932 schools closed because of a hard snow, but Nat hardly thought the black children were enjoying their holiday. "I have a

21. Memphis *World*, August 5, 1932, p. 1.

sneaking suspicion that the guy who can see enough beauty in snow to write poetry about it is the possessor of a nice, warm room, wears heavy clothing, and doesn't have to worry about a job, money, or the next meal, and he's not a poor cullud man in Memfus. Even the children realize that you can keep warmer in a steam-heated room—even in an over-crowded cullud school-house—than you can in a place where you hug the corner of a partially filled grate or iron heater."[22]

Migration to the North slowed dramatically during the depression; during the 1930s, the black population of Memphis climbed from 96,000 to 121,000 while the number of whites only rose from 156,000 to 171,000. Many blacks found it easier to get along in familiar surroundings than to try to make their way in northern cities already glutted with jobless, unskilled laborers. Some reverse migration took place as blacks returned to the South when city living grew too hard and winters too cold. Migration northward was further discouraged by spokesmen from various organizations such as the Rural Industrial Association; they toured the South, telling blacks to remain on the farms, that they were better off than their city brothers.

In a column in the *World* on September 18, 1931, Kelly Miller claimed the Negro had found no place in American industry outside the cotton belt. "Give any Negro forty acres and a mule and he can succeed in raising a crop of cotton," Miller wrote. "There is no other industry in which the colored man is deemed indispensable unless he considers the comparatively small field of Pullman porter. In these two fields the black man is irreplaceable. . . . Notwithstanding the ugly face of things agricultural, the Negro's future will be mainly found on the farm and largely in the cotton industry."

The economy of Memphis depended heavily on the success of the cotton crop. Memphis cotton merchants underwrote expenses for many farmers and sold their crops to the textile mills

22. *Ibid.*, December 20, 1932, p. 6.

on the eastern seaboard. Memphis stores relied on purchases by the rural dwellers, both black and white. Many Memphis fortunes were founded on cotton plantations. So the city in 1931 decided to prime the economy and honor the region's major money-maker with a Cotton Carnival, a series of parties and parades in May. A king and queen—a successful middle-aged man connected with the cotton industry and a young society girl—were selected to reign over the festivities. The carnival was held by and for white people, of course. To Nat D. it seemed the greatest irony that a celebration to honor cotton would ignore the very people, the blacks, without whom the crop could not be grown.

Black people were not entirely excluded, however. They were recruited to pull floats and to lead the horses and mules that pulled other floats. Black women were hired to sit on cotton bales on Main Street, bandannas tied around their heads, looking like the "aunties" and "mammies" of slavery times. And well-built young blacks, dressed in scarlet breeches and naked to the waist, acted as attendants to the white man who was king.

But that's where the black participation ended. Not one black musical organization marched in a single parade and not one black gospel group sang spirituals at the ceremonies. So the black community, led by Dr. and Mrs. Venson, decided to have its own celebration. The move was triggered, Mrs. Venson said, when they took their five-year-old nephew to see his first Cotton Carnival parade in 1935. "Did you like the parade?" they asked him after the floats and marchers had passed. "No," he said. Asked why not, he said, "All the Negroes were horses."[23]

The black celebration was first called the Beale Street Cotton Makers' Fiesta and later the Cottonmakers Jubilee. The whites loved it. Thousands of white people turned out for the grand parade, to watch the black bands march and the drum majorettes strut like no white aggregation they had ever seen. Whites took the best seats in the bleachers on Beale and lined the street as

23. Ed Weathers, "Carnival Knowledge," *City of Memphis Magazine*, II (April, 1977), 34.

well, mingling with the black crowd to watch the lengthy spectacle. At the Beale Street dance after the parade, the king was crowned—a king chosen in Beale Street tradition, by the amount of money he had raised for the celebration—and a new dance was introduced, like the jubilee dip, the dark rapture, or the jubilee wham. The dancing would go on all night with white spectators gawking at the show and white newsmen taking pictures and writing stories.

In 1936, Paul Whiteman's orchestra serenaded the whites at the Cotton Carnival dance in the auditorium, and Handy's orchestra came to town to play for the jubilee. When Handy, the only man in the room wearing tails, was introduced at the carnival ball, Whiteman handed over his baton for Handy to conduct his orchestra. The crowd applauded and the *Commercial Appeal* the next day said the white dancers had called Handy "dignified and polite."

In 1939 Handy returned to Memphis to play at the new Blues Bowl, an appearance that would become a tradition for him. The bowl, George Lee's idea to raise money for the black Elks Club Christmas charity, pitted the two top black high school football teams in the Mid-South against each other at Booker T. Washington stadium. Several hundred whites, seated in a separate reserved section, and several thousand blacks gathered for this first bowl to hear Handy's horn, to see the elaborate half-time festivities, and to listen to Booker T. principal Blair Hunt thank the city fathers for installing lights at the stadium. In the years that followed, Handy would come back many times for the bowl, to be met at the railroad station by a city hall delegation, serenaded by a group of aging musicians, photographed for the newspapers, ridden through downtown, and finally led into the spotlight to blow his cornet for the crowd.

Handy's appearances, the cotton fiesta, and the Blues Bowl were moments of gaiety for Beale Street during that somber era. The death rate among blacks was nearly twice as high as among whites, infant mortality rates were about two-to-one blacks to whites, and Negroes were much more susceptible to diseases such as tuberculosis and typhoid fever.[24] Unemployment remained high, and money and hope almost nonexistent.

To top off the troubles plaguing blacks during the depression was the flood. The Mississippi River posed a constant threat to those who chose to live in its rich floodlands, and in 1937, thousands of people, whites and blacks, were driven from their homes in the area around Memphis as the flood threatened to break the levees. Temporary housing was set up in the auditorium and at the fairgrounds for people displaced by the rising water. Many of them lost everything to the river except what they had on their backs. Some who had waited too long to flee were snatched from housetops and trees by squads of rescuers in boats.

The homeless sang to break the monotony of their days and alleviate the pain of their losses. Of the flood they sang:

> Down at the Fairgrounds on my knees
> Praying to the Lord to give me ease—
> Lord, Lord, I got them high water blues.

When the danger grew acute, blacks were conscripted and put to work reinforcing the levees. The Pittsburgh *Courier* reported on March 13, 1937:

> The rounding up of the men on Beale Street was done in the characteristic Memphis police fashion. Squad cars of officers and motorcycle patrolmen came down Beale Street, followed by trucks. They grabbed every man in sight and stood outside of the moving picture theaters, nabbing men as they came out with their wives and sweethearts. No excuses were accepted. No one was allowed to telephone home. No one was allowed to change his clothes and many were taken to the levee in their best suits and shoes. Many had no heavy work gloves or tools and were thus forced to work all night in the mud and cold rain in their bare hands and dress shoes. On the levee they were worked under armed guards.

The NAACP sent its assistant secretary, Roy Wilkins, to investigate the commandeering of the blacks. He talked with Police

24. Memphis *World*, March 22, 1932, p. 1.

Commissioner Cliff Davis, who said that "some deputy sheriff from out in the country" had "become excited," gone into Memphis for men, and gotten some police to help him. Davis said he didn't approve of the impressment and that he stopped it as soon as he heard of it. The *Courier* commented, "The truth of the matter is that the men were forced to work on the levee until the danger of a break had passed."

Even Boss Crump donned a pair of high-topped boots and went out to the levee to encourage the workers. When the blacks of the work gang saw him, they sang: "Oh, the river's up and cotton's down, / Mister Ed Crump, he runs this town." A weary workman asked one of the foremen:

"You think the levee will break?"

"Naw! It ain't gonna break."

"Why you so damn sure?"

"Mister Crump say it won't."[25]

---

25. Federal Writers' Project, *Tennessee: A Guide to the State*, 212–13.

Beale Street in 1976, after the fall.
Courtesy of Memphis *Press-Scimitar*

Sleepy John Estes, legendary country blues man, on the porch of his
home in Brownsville, Tennessee, in 1973.
Courtesy of the *Commercial Appeal*

# 7 · The Decline and Fall

Along with the discretion blacks had used for centuries to get along with whites had come a kind of impassiveness, an inability or unwillingness to be surprised by whatever whites decided to do. But no amount of imperviousness to surprise prepared Beale Street for what happened in 1940. E. H. Crump decided to close down the city's "high life." There had been raids before, and times when the "lid was on" until after an election or until crusaders were appeased. Bad national publicity had led to the shutdown of the policy houses in 1935. But this included gambling, whisky, women—all of it.

Of course, when it started, no one really believed that Crump would close down Beale and keep it closed. There had been too many similar attempts in years past, and the street had always revived, in spite of reformers. But this time it was different. Crump was determined.

Speculation ran high on his reasons. Some said it was because his youngest son, John, had been killed in a plane crash while making a Cotton Carnival goodwill tour in 1939. Others thought the boss had turned puritanical. Still others said that with the war coming on, and more and more young men in uniform showing up on Memphis streets, Crump wanted the town to be safe for the soldier boys. There were some who thought he was merely changing with the times. Bootlegging was finished anyway, with the 1939 Tennessee repeal of prohibition, eliminating many of his ward heelers. And the state Crime Commission had threatened to investigate voting practices of blacks; thus Crump was concentrating on white votes.[1]

Whatever his reasons, his methods were effective. He chose as his instrument Joe Boyle, former grocery store clerk who had held numerous courthouse jobs until he finally was elected city commissioner. Boyle was perhaps the most loyal of Crump's supporters, and he swung into action quickly when Crump ordered the clampdown. Beale's joints were cleaned up or closed up, the ladies of the evening were told to ply their trade in other cities, the bookies were ordered to fold up shop, and Beale entered into a new era. The rest of the city received the same attention, but Beale felt the change more because of its concentration of illegal activity and because much of its life revolved around the exercise of vice.[2]

Crump's new attitudes and tactics led to a break with, and a devastating blow against, Bob Church. For years the city had allowed real estate owners—Church included—to defer payment of taxes until sale of the property. By 1939 Church's back taxes had reached $89,000. During a tax collection campaign that year, the city held a tax auction and confiscated the Church property by bidding the amount of back taxes, penalties, and attorney fees. The Church family took the move as a personal attack[3], but similar action was taken across the city against both black and white, including United States Senator Kenneth McKellar and William Overton, uncle of Mayor Watkins Overton. Paul Coppock, at the time a reporter for the *Commercial Appeal*, recalled that Boyle spearheaded the tax collection so vigorously that he even took the overcoat off the back of a delinquent taxpayer he met in the courthouse hall.

Crump seemed determined to alienate blacks, perhaps to prove that he did not need black votes or black support. He re-

1. Tucker, *Lieutenant Lee*, 124–25.
2. Miller, *Mr. Crump*, 136, 276.
3. Tucker, *Lieutenant Lee*, 126.

named Church's Park, calling it Beale Avenue Park.[4] The black community complained that police violence increased against blacks. But the move that most angered Beale was the harassment of Dr. J. B. Martin.

Martin, owner of the South Memphis Drug Store, was one of Church's main lieutenants in the Republican party. In the national elections of 1940, the Republicans made an issue of the support of big-city bosses, such as Pendergast of Kansas City and Crump of Memphis, for the Democrats. Wendell Willkie, the GOP candidate for president, said he was proud not to have such support. Tennessee Republicans picked up on the theme. Martin directed the Shelby County campaign, during which speakers in black churches criticized Crump. Though warned by Crump aides to stop the meetings, Martin refused. Crump stationed police outside his drugstore—and the restaurant and pool hall of Elmer Atkinson, another Republican leader—with orders to search everyone who entered, supposedly for narcotics.[5]

Blair Hunt heard of the situation and went out to check on it. "The policemen were frisking people," he said. "Of course, they didn't bother me because I knew the police officer and he said, 'Professor, what are you doing out here?' I said I just wanted to see Dr. Martin and I went on in and they didn't bother me at all."

Hunt went to see Crump and asked him why the search was being conducted. Crump said:

"You're a preacher, aren't you?"

"Yes, sir."

"Well, do you believe in peddling dope?"

"No, indeed."

"Well, that's what's going on out there, and I mean to clean it up. That's a bad influence on Memphis."

4. Beale Street had officially been Beale Avenue since 1908 when the city made all the east-west streets avenues. Handy and almost everyone else ignored the change. In 1955, at the urging of comedian Danny Thomas, who had founded Saint Jude's Children's Research Hospital in Memphis, the City Commission changed the name back to Beale Street.

5. Tucker, *Lieutenant Lee,* 127.

"Mr. Crump, you're going to lose a lot of black votes."

"Well, I don't care if I lose all of them, if it takes that to clean up Memphis. I'm going to clean up Memphis."[6]

To those who complained about Martin's treatment, including ministers on the Inter-Racial Cooperation Committee, Boyle replied that they should leave control of lawlessness to the police. He claimed that Martin and his wife had gone to the circus and sat in seats reserved for whites, a move toward social equality. He also said black newspapermen had written inflammatory articles for months. "They must know they cannot write this character of stuff. They are not going to carry on and conduct themselves in Memphis as if they lived in Chicago, Pittsburgh and Philadelphia. We have never had it before and we will never have it. For after all this is a white man's country." He was sure most Negroes did not approve of "this fanatical, unappreciative group, seeking a social equality which will never come."[7]

Boyle continued his campaign of intimidation against blacks with a public threat in the *Press-Scimitar* on December 11, 1940, saying that he had his eye on certain black leaders who had been "fanning racial hatred" and that if anything should happen in Memphis, these men would be held responsible. "I say again this is a white man's country and always will be, and any Negro who doesn't agree to this had better move on." Boyle's threats did their work. No voice rose in the black community to take up the fight against Crump. Nat D. later explained the attitude that prevailed: "So, what must we do? Protest . . . yes . . . sue for redress of grievances . . . yes . . . grin and bear it . . . yes. That's the way we endured and multiplied in this country. Once we stop employing this technique of adapting ourselves to overpowering circumstances . . . like the Indian, we will become vanishing Americans. I don't believe most of us want to vanish."

After war came in 1941, Beale Street matched the patriotic fervor of the rest of the nation, though the need to grin and bear

6. Interview with Blair Hunt, February 6, 1973.
7. Memphis *Press-Scimitar*, December 5, 1940, p. 10.

it persisted. The Red Cross in Memphis told blacks they couldn't donate blood, but then it reconsidered and said it would accept their blood but keep it separate; the navy said there was no place in the WAVES for black women; the air corps severely limited the number of blacks it would accept. But blacks were welcomed as workers in defense plants, and their dollars were sought to finance the war. In 1942 Memphis blacks raised $302,000 in war bonds, surpassing the goal in each bond drive under the leadership of Lieutenant George Lee, chairman of the local Negro division of the War Finance Committee.[8]

Mayor Walter Chandler went to Beale to give send-offs to Negro boys called up in the draft, just as he did for the white boys. He told the draftees they were valued citizens of Memphis, whose contribution to the war effort was appreciated and whose return would be welcomed. "Beale Street audiences invariably applauded loudly and happily," Nat wrote. "Beale Street draftees left home with a new slant on Negro-white relationships, Beale Street stay-at-homes got a feeling that all was not so wrong with the world, that the bright stars still shone in the heavens."[9]

In the latter part of the war, however, the city administration's restrictive policies once again caused a conflict with the black community. A. Phillip Randolph, organizer of the Sleeping Car Porters Union and an outspoken advocate of civil rights, was scheduled to speak in Memphis in November of 1943. White officials, fearing Randolph's influence, called together black leaders, told them that the speech would bring violence, race riots, blood in the streets, and that they would be held responsible. The blacks agreed to cancel Randolph's appearance.[10] Crump took the occasion to tell the city that he did not want "imported" Negroes "to make unnecessary fire-brand speeches." The *Commercial Appeal* quoted him on November 14, 1943: "About one per cent of the Negroes will never be satisfied no matter what is done for them

8. Memphis *World*, January 8, 1943, p. 1.
9. *Ibid.*, August 16, 1946, p. 8.
10. Tucker, *Lieutenant Lee*, 140–41.

unless there is complete social equality. The few in this part of the country who want that had better give the matter serious thought as long as they live in this section."

In the spring of 1944, the Reverend G. A. Long, pastor of Beale Avenue Baptist Church and one of several blacks who had spoken out against the harassment of Martin, opened the doors of his church for Randolph to speak. An audience of seven hundred applauded as Randolph referred to Crump as "the Memphis political boss who out-Hitlers Hitler." Shelby County Sheriff Oliver Perry was infuriated. He raged to the *Press-Scimitar* on April 3: "Had I known that the negro Randolph from New York City and those he brought with him were to make blackguarding speeches defaming this community and speaking ill of my friends, Mr. Hale [E. W. Hale, County Commission chairman] and Mr. Crump, I would have pulled them all out of the pulpit in Preacher Long's Beale Street Church."

Long's answer was printed in the *Press-Scimitar* that same day: "I would have Mr. E. H. Crump to know I am an ambassador of Jesus Christ and take orders only from Christ. I did not ask Mr. Crump could I come to this town and I am not going to ask him if I may stay." Shortly after Long's defiant stand, city electrical and fire departments decided that the church needed thousands of dollars' worth of repairs and threatened to close the building if they were not made. The congregation got together the money to make the repairs and the church remained open.[11] But the debts were high and the congregation was small, probably in part because Long continued to make forthright statements against political bossism and racial injustice and not many blacks felt it was wise to have such an outspoken minister. In 1947, Long left Beale Avenue Baptist for Detroit. The feeling was that Crump had finally driven him out, but a report in the *World* on November 11 quoted Long as saying he left because of a conflict with the secretary of the National Baptist Publication Board in Nashville.

11. *Ibid.*, 143.

When the war ended in 1945, Beale Street celebrated with as much jubilation as the rest of the country, but Nat D. wondered if there was all that much for blacks to rejoice about. "Beale Street went wild on V-J Day. Why, no sober-minded person could truthfully tell. After all, Beale Street is a colored man's street . . . and the folk who believe in lording it over other folk are in power. . . . Negroes must watch everything in the post-war world if they are to survive."[12]

Nat D. was already beginning to wonder if Beale Street itself was to survive. True, the entertainment area picked up after the war; Robert Henry was booking the big bands and other top entertainers. In addition to the older spots, the new, white-owned Handy Theater was preparing to open on Park Avenue. Henry, as the manager, went to New York to get Handy's permission to name the theater for him. Handy readily agreed. "It's about time something was named after somebody besides Booker T. Washington," he told Henry.[13]

Notwithstanding the prosperity in some areas, the seeds of decay had begun to grow on Beale. Many of the buildings were deteriorating, and their owners were either unwilling or unable to repair them. Nat complained about the number of black businessmen being forced out of their locations, either through loss of their leases or through high rents. They were being replaced by whites, "their pockets stuffed with money from war work, entering business fields which have long been more or less the private property of Negroes." The newcomers were "sharp-eyed and shrewd white business folk who are on the ave. to make money, not necessarily to make friends as most of their white predecessors used to do."[14]

Appealing to the Negro Chamber of Commerce would do no good; as respectable pillars of society, most of its members never approved of Beale anyway and were not too concerned about the

12. Memphis *World*, August 17, 1945, p. 2.
13. Interview with Robert Henry, October 19, 1973.
14. Memphis *World*, July 16, 1946, p. 8.

street as long as they didn't lose money. "Like the white folk down town, many of our Negro upper crust view Beale Street very objectively indeed," Nat said. "They take their out-of-town visitors thru the street on slumming tours and laugh just as idiotically at the avenue's gaucherie manners. These folks have long since accepted the view that Chocolate Avenue is a place which is 'owned by imported Jews and Italians, policed by poor white trash and enjoyed by cotton-patch Negroes.' That's not the real Beale Streeter's point of view, of course, but it's what a lot of folk say and think."[15]

Beale, to the real Beale Streeter, remained a symbol of escape from white prejudice and arrogance. President Harry Truman's civil rights program was gaining momentum, but Boss Crump would have nothing to do with the wave of postwar liberalism. He battled racial mixing as never before. Even a child could not cross the color line. In May of 1946, the Boy Scout Circus was held before a packed crowd. When the announcement was made for all scouts to come down and take part in the ceremony, dozens of Negro Boy Scouts were among those who started for the spotlight. It was up to J. L. Beauchamp, the head of the Negro Scouts in Memphis, to stop the young black boys and tell them they were not included. "Negro Boy Scouts will have to learn the score," Beauchamp was quoted as saying in the World on May 10. "Just like all other Negroes we simply have a job of work ahead and should reconcile ourselves to doing it."

To Nat D. and others, such incidents made the civil rights movement appear hopeless. Yet, a few weeks later, on August 2, 1946, his column in the Memphis World expressed poignantly and eloquently the hope for a new day.

Too long and too deeply has consciousness of color pervaded our lives. It sinks into the souls of our saints, tainting their saintliness. It seeps into the minds of our children, making them old before their time. It rides into the consciousness of our young men, warping their dreams.

15. *Ibid.*

It shackles the minds of our scholars, making them intellectual eunuchs.

. . . . . . . . . . . .

Too long has it been dinned into my ears and seared on my consciousness that the Negro woman's bed is the playground of the world. . . . The Negro press, stage and screen glorify only the Negro woman who has white features. The world's press and movies portray the typical Negro woman as an Aunt Jemima, despite the counteracting refinement of a Madame Bethune or a Marian Anderson.

. . . . . . . . . . . .

I hope I live to see the day, black as I am, when white men will not be afraid to be fair . . . when they can welcome justice into their courts . . . allow truth a real hearing in their schools, churches and homes; and make the lust for gold and power secondary to the urge for service and human welfare.

. . . . . . . . . . . .

I hope to live to see the day when men may learn to turn their aggressive drives away from the organized slaughter of war and towards the organized effort to construct a world in which men won't fear for bread nor be forced to cower before tyrants.

. . . . . . . . . . . .

I hope I can live to see the day, black as I am, when colored folks, particularly those in the United States, will have a common ideal rather than a common misery.

The Crump administration's hard line on the color line sometimes worked to the disadvantage of whites as well as blacks. Protecting the citizens of Memphis from any glimpse of integration in the entertainment field, for example, was Censor Board Chairman Lloyd T. Binford, a rabid foe of any liberalism on the racial theme. Binford banned the musical, *Annie Get Your Gun*, starring Mary Martin, in 1947. He objected to a Negro's playing the role of a railroad conductor and to blacks and whites dancing together in some scenes. "We don't have any negro conductors in the South," he was quoted as saying in the *Press-Scimitar* on September 29. "Of course, it can't show here. It's social equality in action." Lena Horne's scenes were cut out of the movies *Words and Music, Till the Clouds Roll By*, and *Stormy Weather* for their Memphis showings. And a film with Eddie "Rochester" Anderson, the black comedian, was banned because the picture had too much racial mixture and because Binford said Rochester had too familiar a way about him.[16]

Contradictions were basic to the system of segregation. Nat wrote about an incident in 1947 when white people were crowded, sitting and standing, in the front of a city bus while black passengers were boarding and trying to get to the rear, where it was fairly empty. But they couldn't get through the solid wall of whites. The conductor yelled to the white passengers to let them through, but the whites didn't budge. The blacks had to decide whether to buck the barricade of whites or get off and wait for the next bus. Many of them chose the safer course. The incident illustrated one of the complications of survival for the black man —how to get along in a world where the rules were often ignored by those who actually made them. In writing about it, Nat said the practice of separation had been so widely and so long observed that it had become a habit, even with Negroes. A departure from custom left them uneasy and outdone.

In the first place, no self-respecting Negro can truthfully say that he likes the Jim-crow system. At the same time, no self-respecting Negro wants to barge into company where he is not wanted and where only humiliation and embarrassment are the likely results. And as long as the pattern of segregation persists, most Negroes find it to their best interests to adjust themselves to it. After the adjustment has been made, only a Negro who wants deliberately to disturb his own peace of mind tries to change it. It disturbs him when others seek to break the pattern.[17]

When the Jim Crow pattern was applied to the Freedom Train, however, Beale Streeters seethed with anger and frustration. Crump refused to allow the Freedom Train—carrying a collection of historical documents on a cross-country tour arranged by the Truman administration—to visit Memphis because there were no provisions for segregating blacks from whites. "A custom of 150 years can't be sidetracked in a day or a year and made

16. Tucker, *Lieutenant Lee*, 145–46.
17. Memphis *World*, March 12, 1946, p. 6.

workable," Crump was quoted as saying in the *Commercial Appeal* on November 24, 1947. "It would be a regrettable mistake—a costly mistake to have the whole crowd, whites and colored, men, women, and children, surging through at the same time—what a gamble—a desperate gamble, and it must be avoided. . . . There are many whites and colored who hate one another viciously and there is no patent medicine overnight cure for it."

Beale Streeters grumbled that blacks and whites had viewed the Freedom Train together in other cities and nothing vicious had happened. Nat D. sampled their opinions and allowed them to vent their anger in his column but concluded: "All in all, I've paid too big a price already for my ideas on things. I'm still in the same job I held 17 years ago. I still get the jitters about my future meals. Now I have a wife and possible other mouths to feed. And I'm sure they'll love to eat, too. . . . If I blow my top too far, you know and I know what will become of Mrs. Williams' oldest and darkest son. I have 'none further to say.' "[18]

But Nat D. had much yet to say. The following year, 1948, was to be a milestone for him and also for Crump, whose authoritarian power in state-wide politics would finally crumble.

Crump backed Governor Jim McCord for reelection over Gordon Browning and supported Judge John Mitchell, a relative unknown, for the United States Senate seat held by Tom Stewart. Edward J. Meeman, editor of the *Press-Scimitar* and a long-time Crump opponent, joined with businessman Edmund Orgill and attorney Lucius Burch in forming a coalition supporting Browning for governor and Estes Kefauver in the Senate race. Black businessmen allied themselves with the white liberals working for Kefauver and Browning. Nat seemed apprehensive about this activity. In July of 1948, he warned blacks who were "getting out on a political limb" that, as the old-time preacher told a young man in his congregation, "Young man, your arm's too short to box with God." Beale Street was not concerned about politics, he said.

18. *Ibid.*, November 21, 1947, p. 8.

"Beale is a realistic street. Beale faces the 'fact' that rights are harder to get than heads are to keep. . . . Beale Street is scared to vote its political convictions. So, most likely Beale Streeters, with the exception of the 'committed' boys, will stay away from the polls. . . . I am saying that the Negro in Memphis is not ready and is not in the position to do anything much about his status politically." Most Negroes were concerned about getting paid and spending their money either on booze or the church, he said. "And that's the way the white folk want it. Such Negroes are 'good Niggers.' And such Negroes are the ones who live the longest and safest in the land of cotton and corn. . . . Yet, what can Negroes down home here do about it? The answer is 'nothing' . . . unless someone is ready to get his head whipped. And the other consideration is 'why get your head caved in when you know your arm is too short to win in a pitched battle?' "[19]

Just a week after this column, in which he said he would not give Negroes advice on how to vote, Nat spoke out in support of Crump's candidate, Governor McCord, undoubtedly influenced by the endorsement of McCord by the Negro teachers' association. Nat commented that education in Tennessee had advanced more under McCord than in the history of the state.

Browning and Kefauver won. On August 10, after the elections, the *World* proclaimed "Boss Ed Crump's Power Broken" and praised the whites and blacks who had helped the city emerge from its "long night-mare of fear." But Nat pointed out that the majority of blacks did not depart from their usual position—right behind Crump. The largest wards of Negro voters went for McCord and Mitchell, not Kefauver and Browning. The vote showed that the blacks of Memphis voted with the white leadership, he said. "Most Negroes like and do what the 'Man' says do, just like most white folk like and do what the 'Man' says do."

Although Meeman, Orgill, Burch and their black allies demonstrated that Crump could be opposed without dire personal

19. *Ibid.*, July 20, 1948, p. 6.

consequences, the major factor in Kefauver's triumph probably was not so much a result of their coalition as it was Crump's error in running an unknown against an incumbent senator. Crump's state-wide influence was diluted but he retained the political reins in Shelby County until his death in 1954.

Even though the majority of blacks backed Crump in 1948, the support was no longer unanimous and the black vote now carried new weight. Black leaders, including *World* editor Lewis O. Swingler, pushed for black policemen, and the machine, attempting to hold on to the black vote, gave in.[20]

More in Memphis than just the city government was beginning to recognize the importance of its black population, which now was approaching 150,000. While black businesses had not grown sizably, black buying power had. The whites were beginning to take note. The Black and White Store and Kress became the first Main Street stores to provide lunch counters for black shoppers. The *Commercial Appeal* began referring to black women as "Mrs." and capitalizing Negro.[21] And, in late 1948, radio station WDIA decided to aim its programming at a black audience. Owners Bert Ferguson and John R. Pepper hired Nat D. and billed him as the Mid-South's first Negro disc jockey.

Nat wrote about them in his column on November 23, 1948, with both candor and optimism. "They are businessmen," he said. "They don't necessarily love Negroes. They make that clear. But they do love progress and they are willing to pay the price to make progress. One of the most neglected markets in the Mid-South is the Negro market. And that's true because so many white businessmen take the Negro for granted."

After the first year, WDIA hardly ever received a white complaint and, in fact, retained a good portion of its white audience. There were some complaints, however, from upper-class blacks who objected to Nat D.'s "clowning" and grumbled that they

20. Tucker, *Lieutenant Lee*, 147.
21. It was fifteen years later before the city's other major newspaper, the Memphis *Press-Scimitar*, followed suit.

would have been better represented by a more dignified personality.

Nat D. began the first black newscasts, started having short
segments on black history, and used the basic titles of respect in
referring to everyone. But probably the most important contribution by him and his show, Tan Town Jamboree, was his role in
the integration of black rhythm and blues into mainstream music.
As he recalled:

> We came up with the idea of giving them some blues. Only thing is,
> the only black record the station had was "Stompin' at the Savoy,"
> which became the theme song for my show—and it was by a white
> writer. We started scrounging around and finally got some records
> by blues artists—like Fats Waller, Ivory Joe Hunter—and then we
> had to clean them up. Some of those records were . . . well, suggestive.
> And the way I cleaned them up was, when it got to the suggestive part,
> I just started talking. First thing you know, it caught on. The listeners
> were ready for a different sound, it seemed.

Among those who became caught up in that different sound
was a thirteen year old living in a public housing development
in Memphis. Elvis Presley began collecting the records of such
bluesmen as Arthur Crudup and Big Bill Broonzy. Later, still in
Humes High School, he started going down on Beale and emu-
lating its musicians, not only in what they sang but the way they
sang it (and also in what they wore). He became acquainted not
only with Nat D. but with Robert Henry, who introduced him to
many of Beale Street's entertainers.

"I taken him to the Hotel Improvement Club with me, and he
would watch the colored singers, understand me, and then he got
to doing it the same way as them," Henry said. "He got that shaking, that wiggle, from Charlie Burse, Ukulele Ike we called him,
right there at the Gray Mule on Beale. Elvis, he wasn't doing
nothing but what the colored people had been doing for the last
hundred years. But people . . . people went wild over him."[22]

Nat D. spoke warmly of the young white entertainer who bad-

22. Interview with Robert Henry, October 19, 1973.

gered him into giving him a chance to perform along with black contestants on the amateur shows at the Palace Theater.

We had a lot of fun with him. Elvis Presley on Beale Street when he first started was a favorite man. When they saw him coming out, the audience always gave him as much recognition as they gave any musician—black. He had a way of singing the blues that was distinctive. He could sing 'em not necessarily like a Negro, but he didn't sing 'em altogether like a typical white musician. He had something in between and made the blues sort of different. . . Always he had that certain humanness about him that Negroes like to put in their songs. So when he had a show down there at the Palace, everybody got ready for something good. Yeah. They were crazy about Presley.

We had a boast that if you made it on Beale Street, you can make it anywhere. And Elvis Presley made it on Beale Street.

But after Elvis made it big with his blue suede blues, Nat D. raised some pointed questions in his December 22, 1956, column in the Pittsburgh *Courier* about Presley's hero status on Beale.

Maybe it's the Indigo Avenue's blase blues sophistication, native ignorance of the important, or just pur-dee meanness, but ordinarily nobody generally excites Beale Streeters enough to cause them to cue up to buy tickets or crash lines for autographs. . . . But Elvis Presley has 'em talking. And they ain't talking about his 'art.' Beale Street's more or less miffed at Elvis. And many of the brethren in black, brown and beige are plumb flustered by the man. You see, something happened the other night that the average Beale Streeter doesn't altogether dig nor appreciate.

It was like this: Memphis' famed radio station WDIA staged its annual goodwill revue for the benefit of needy Negro children. Naturally everybody for miles around was invited . . . along with scads of topflight Negro entertainers, like B. B. King, the Moonglows, the Magnificents, Ray Charles, the Five Blind Boys and various naries.

Well, more than 9,000 head of God's chillun showed up . . . along with Elvis Presley. Now, why Elvis came and how he got in the middle of such a concentrated kodachrome crowd, one may never know. But he was there. He tried to stay backstage. But somebody spotted him, and asked him to come out and take a bow. Well, he did. And that did it.

A thousand black, brown and beige teen-age girls in the audience blended their alto and soprano voices in one wild crescendo of sound that rent the rafters . . . and took off like scalded cats in the direction of Elvis.

It took some time and several white cops to quell the melee and protect Elvis. The teen-age charge left Beale Streeters wondering: "How come cullud girls would take on so over a Memphis white boy . . . when they hardly let out a squeak over B. B. King, a Memphis cullud boy?"

Both the boys have made names for themselves. And some folk feel that Elvis might just barely have borrowed something from B. B.

But further, Beale Streeters are wondering if these teen-age girls' demonstration over Presley doesn't reflect a basic integration in attitude and aspiration which has been festering in the minds of most of your folks' womenfolk all along.

That basic integration in attitude and inspiration was taking its toll on Beale as a whole. The steady gains in civil rights meant that Beale Streeters were no longer confined to Beale. Main Street department stores began to cater to blacks. New shopping centers opened, draining off still more of Beale's customers. White theaters no longer relegated blacks to the topmost balconies. Just around the corner were the sit-ins that won blacks the right to sit side by side with whites at lunch counters. And as the integration movement continued to build in momentum, Beale continued to disintegrate. The old street crumbled more and more, the old buildings deteriorated.

Beale was still clinging to life, still had some shoppers and sight-seers. But then came the sanitation troubles of the 1960s, the strike of sanitation workers and the assassination of Dr. Martin Luther King, Jr., in 1968, and the riots that wracked Memphis, riots that began on Beale and its surrounding area. The riots and looting rampages left shops with broken windows and ransacked counters. Stores closed, buildings emptied.

The Memphis Housing Authority, after years of talk about razing Beale and rebuilding it, began to act. Down came the Panama, the Midway Cafe, the Palace Theater, and other landmarks. Rubble and empty lots were about all that remained. A few young men idly shooting pool at Robert Henry's, until his death closed the doors in 1978; a few old men walking about, with no place else to go; a few straggling stores; a handful of old buildings; a die-hard collection of old-timers: they were the only life on a street full of memories.

Nathaniel Dowd Williams, hampered by a stroke, was retired now from all his jobs—but not as a Beale Streeter. He walked the street often, retracing his footprints of other years. "I hate to see it look like this," he said. "It looks like a coffin."

But there was yet another irony to add to the contradictions that figured so prominently in the history of the mile-long maelstrom. As Beale lay dying, the blues that had helped bring it fame sprang to life again. Elvis Presley's blue suede blues branched out into amplified hard rock, rock-and-soul, and progressive country rock; the Beatles acknowledged their debt to blues old-timers like Lightning Hopkins; the Rolling Stones took their name from a Muddy Waters song; and there was born a new interest in the roots of what Beale Streeter Willie Blackwell called the "true blues—the old-time, natural blues." Musicologists and researchers from around the world fanned out into the field to rediscover the pioneers, concentrating on the southern wellspring from which had flowed so much of the blues. In Memphis alone, living their blues in forgotten corners of history but singing and playing them little because of fingers gnarled by time and voices uncertain with age and disuse, were Furry Lewis, Memphis Minnie (Minnie Douglas McCoy), Gus Cannon, Bo Carter of the Mississippi Sheiks, Will Shade, Booker White, Piano Red Williams. Sleepy John Estes was found huddled in almost unbelievable poverty in Brownsville, Tennessee.

Joe Callicott, rocking gently on his porch at Nesbit, Mississippi, just outside Memphis, summed up the feelings of the old blues people, and perhaps spoke for the blues as an enduring art form, in his reply to a researcher who asked him where he had been so many years: "I ain't been nowhere. I ain't been lost. I been here all along."

PART II

# THE BLUES

• "I'm afraid I came to think that everything worthwhile was to be found in books. But the blues did not come from books. Suffering and hard luck were the midwives that birthed these songs. The blues were conceived in aching hearts."

      W. C. Handy, *Father of the Blues* (New York, 1941), 80.

• "Memphis blues was like a big, lazy, carefree fellow sauntering down a road pouring his heart out in song, and New Orleans music was like a man rushing to a street car, cursing with every leap."

      George W. Lee, in an interview in the Memphis *Press-Scimitar*, April 25, 1967. Lee said New Orleans "took our music and speeded it up, gave it some razzle-dazzle, but what they got was a style, and what we had was the music."

• "Blues is a song that lingers with certain people in trouble, and nothing do them no better than to get to singing the blues."

      Alex Sims, in an interview at his home in Memphis, November 11, 1973.

• "It's what you feel, you know; any type of song, you got to feel that song before you can play it. You got to feel that song before you can sing it. I'll tell you like it is. White people do not have blues because they ain't never been in no trouble or nothing like that. Now we's born with the blues. See. That's why we could do it. A white man never will play no blues."

      Walter "Shakey" Horton, harmonica player, in an interview at his home in Chicago, September 14, 1973.

• "You get anger, you get frustration, you get melancholy [in the blues]. There's a stringent quality to them, there's a strong quality to them. It's not sentimentality. It's not boo-hooing. It's a been-down-so-long-down-don't-worry-me kind of thing. It's its own. That's the reason the word came into the language. It's its own kind of sorrow, its own kind of grief, its own kind of way of looking at life. I think the blues transmute the griefs. I think they change them. I think they answer them. . . . I don't know of any other people with a segment of music so important in their lives as the blues. I don't know of any immigrant group. I don't know of any Polish parallel, I don't know of any Jewish parallel. I think it's very significant that a very simple kind of rural expsession catches the attention of the whole country and catches the attention of the world."

Sterling Brown, author, poet, critic and teacher, in an interview at his home in Washington, D.C., June 6, 1974.

• "At the pulsating core of their emotional center, the blues are the spiritual and ritual energy of the church thrust into eyes of life's raw realities. Even though they appear primarily to concern themselves with the secular experience, the relationships between males and females, between boss and worker, between nature and Man, they are, in fact, extensions of the deepest, most pragmatic spiritual and moral realities. Even though they primarily deal with the world as flesh, they are essentially religious. Because they finally celebrate life and the ability of man to control and shape his destiny. The blues don't jive. They reach way down into the maw of the individual and collective experience."

Larry Neal, "Any Day Now: Black Art and Black Liberation," in Woodie King and Earl Anthony (eds.), *Black Poets and Prophets* (New York, 1972), 152.

• "I think the church could be called the father of the blues and the honky-tonks the mother. I think the blues are a kind of lament of oppression. At the same time, they're a kind of rhythmic outlet, emotional, happy; they seem to be a combination of sadness and gladness. And the same way with the old jubilee songs. I call them—if not brother and sister—I call them at least first cousins."

Reverend Blair Hunt, in an interview at Mississippi Boulevard Christian Church in Memphis, February 6, 1973.

• "Behind the blues, there is really a bit of hidden gaiety. There's a spirit of willingness to go on living despite all the sorrow and weariness the singer feels."

Nat D. Williams, in an interview in the *Press-Scimitar*, January 12, 1970.

Furry Lewis, patriarch of the Memphis country blues, at his home in Memphis in 1972.
Courtesy of William Leaptrott

# 8 · Furry

Something about the very title of the show—the Cotton Carnival Blues Festival—pricked the conscience and tugged at the sensibilities. Although black hands in white cotton inspired many a blues song, blues people never felt a kinship to the annual week-long carnival produced and enjoyed mainly by white socialites. But the two old blues men cavorting on the stage of the auditorium in downtown Memphis were enjoying it immensely: Furry Lewis with his electric guitar and Snowball Nichols, the one-man band—drums, kazoo, guitar, accordion—up from Greenville, Mississippi. They obviously had passed the bottle frequently before their introduction, but their blues licks and "mislicks" just as obviously pleased the mostly young, mostly white audience.

Suddenly, with flourish and flurry, the Cotton Carnival king and queen and entourage marched into the arena and down the aisle. The appearance wasn't part of the program and drew only polite applause, along with scattered grumbles.

Furry was equal to the occasion. He swept off his battered hat, bowed solemnly, announced the presence of their royal highnesses and broke into the carnival's theme song:

> Oh, I wish I was in the land of cotton,
> Old times there ain't n'er forgotten,
> Look away, look away, look away, Dixie land.

Whether thick-tongued tribute or mocking irony, nobody knew—perhaps not even Furry himself. What everybody knew was that Furry was always ready to perform any time, for any-body. His stiffened fingers lacked the dexterity they once had, his voice cracked with the weight of his years, but he remained very much the blues singer, the entertainer—even the buffoon if he thought buffoonery would please his audience.

• • •

A knock on the screen door of the faded green, rickety wooden duplex brought the chorused response from within. "Come in, come on it, it's open, the door's open."

A double bed, a couch, one chair, a dog bed, a veneered dresser, and an amplifier stuffed the dimly lighted living room-bedroom. Walter "Furry" Lewis lay on the bed, a mongrel dog curled up at his side. Tacked on the walls were a number of blues posters, a calendar, a hand-printed note saying "Lord help me keep my nose out of other peoples business," and pictures of Dr. Martin Luther King, Jr., and John F. and Robert Kennedy. Other photographs and clippings traced his recent blues excursions. Nothing indicated that this modest half-house on a narrow street with no sidewalks had become a favorite tourist attraction for blues buffs from all over the world.

Furry always greeted the famous and obscure with equal courtesy, inviting them to sit a spell and share his beer or whisky if he had any or, if he had none, broadly hinting that the visitor provide. ("I was wishin' you all had a little bottle," he told us on our first visit. "When you called me, I started to tell you to bring me a small one with you. But I didn't tell you, though." On the next trip, we carried along a small bottle that Furry promptly broke open and offered to an elderly woman he introduced as his "schoolmate, Miss Margaret Mintz." "Get yourself a glass," he told Miss Mintz, and the two sat and sipped straight whisky from water glasses throughout the interview.)

"Excuse me for not getting up," he said as we walked in. "I don't get around so good since my operation." He'd had cataracts removed, and his thick-lensed, horn-rimmed glasses almost hid his eyes from view. "I can't half see. When I get ready to go somewhere to play now, there be somebody to take care of me. I can see some, but I can't discern certain things."

He waited patiently as the tape recorder was set up, then responded cautiously to questions.

Born in Greenwood, Mississippi. That was the sixth of March in eighteen-and-ninety-three. My mother is named Victoria Lewis and my father is named Walter "Furry" Lewis, like I am. They farmed. I was six years old when I came to Memphis to stay and I been here ever since. My mother moved here and my father died. She done, you know, day work and cook, you know, like that, and taken in washing and ironing.

I went to school, Carnes Avenue School. I didn't get no higher than the fifth grade. And I quit then and work, help my mother, riding a bicycle and carrying drugs and working in a drugstore, like that. Let me see, I was about seventeen, eighteen years old.

As he talked, the replies to questions gradually became a bit longer, the phrases lengthening into sentences and the sentences into paragraphs. "Well, I guess I was 'bout twelve, thirteen years old, something like that, when I first started playing guitar. I didn't have none so I got a cigar box, I cut a hole in the top, put a board and nail it on there. And I taken four nails, put wire on 'em from a screen door for strings. I couldn't play it, but I rapped the sides, hootin' and hollerin'. I thought I was doin' somethin', you know."

He strolled the streets with his guitar for nickels and dimes, played parties for his neighbors and jived with jug bands for bigger to-dos. Most prized, and most repeated, were the memories of playing with W. C. Handy, even though Handy preferred trained musicians who could read music and follow his elaborate orchestrations.

"I never was a regular with Handy," Furry confessed. "I never did have just a regular job with Handy, but I played more than some of the regulars did 'cause they's off all the time and every other night I filled in for one of 'em."

Then came his treasured story, told as though it was his true claim to fame. "My first good guitar, I got it from Handy. The one I went around playin' with, it wasn't so much, but I was gettin' good with it and he just went and got me one that was worthwhile. Only one what I know he did it for. Just myself. I kept it 'bout some thirty odd years."

· · ·

Handy went on to New York and Furry went on the road with medicine shows, more as a comedian than as a musician.

I'm just a good comedian, you know. I be a whole show by myself sometimes, just do anything to get a laugh.

I was with Dr. Benson's doctor show. Selling Jack Rabbit medicine, pills and such as that, corn medicine, too. We had a whole jug band with us. We travel in T-model cars, had a big old flatbed truck we go 'round in, that was our stage. We used to crack jokes and tell funny tales and do this and that up on the stage. Sometimes have on pants with a patch on it, everything funny. That's something like a clown, you understand. Sometimes we wear frocks—that's a coat, long in the back. Wear those kind of hats, derby and all like that. We was all messed up. We work blackface comedian, you know. Just take lamp black, some grease, put it all over your face, like in those vaudeville shows.

I used to sing a song about black, you see, 'cause I have the black on my face. I used to sing a song about black everywhere I went.

Without guitar or accompaniment, Furry sang his song.

> Some people don't like their color.
> Well, I sure do like mine.
> I know I'm black and ugly.
> But I gits along just fine.
> I was going down the street the other day
> Two high browns I did meet,
> Say, "Lord, ain't old Furry black,
> But he sure looks good to me."
> Well, I'm black, I'm black, I'm B-L-A-C-K, black,
> I'm black, but I'm sweet, oh, God.
> I don't wear no diamonds,

Don't wear no pearls,
I don't have no hard time
Coming through this world,
You can tease, squeeze, just as much as you please.
I know I'm black, but I ain't unease,
I'm black, black, B-L-A-C-K, black,
I'm black, but I'm sweet, oh, God.

He leaned back, smiling as his listeners applauded. "I made that up," he said. "That's the song I made up. I never did record nothing like that. Wouldn't do no good nohow."

. . .

In the 1920s Furry came off the road and took a steady job, cleaning the streets of Memphis. Earlier, he had had a succession of jobs, some just pick-up work like delivering groceries and cutting grass, others more substantial like being cook's helper on the excursion boats or running the "whisky train" (hauling cases of whisky from the riverboats to a roadhouse on Beale).

When I started working for the city, it was payin' fifteen cent an hour, then it went up to twenty, then it went up to thirty-five. When I first started there, the city didn't have trucks. I drove a mule and car for the city, I was a street cleaner, I hauled garbage, I worked on the city dump, and I worked washing streets. I was a night watch up there for nine years, up there where they fix the city trucks and police cars. I worked there forty-four years. Just retired me here in 1966.

Furry played as hard as he worked. He lived around the corner from Beale and, always carrying his guitar, became one of the street's most familiar fixtures, playing in honky-tonks, in Beale Street Park, for Amateur Nights at the Beale Street Palace Theater. But Beale Street wasn't his boundary. He was called upon to play at Memphis' fashionable homes, at picnics, barbecues, and political rallies, and for serenades by young swains. However, the rewards came more in pleasure than in profit. Whites paid little and blacks paid less, usually only his supper and sipping whisky, with a few dollars on the side. He didn't just play at parties; he also loved to attend them.

It were one thing I can say about every party I ever went to in my life—just had a nice time, everything went along smooth. There was never no violence, there were no fightin', there were no argument, there were no nothin' but everybody sat down and played funny cards—won't be playin' for money, just play cards for fun. Funny cards, you know. I'd have my partner and you'd have your partner. If we won a game, we take this bottle and pass it 'round your old nose and you all have to smell it. If you all beat us, then you all would drink and pass the bottle around and we'd smell it. That was called "drink or smell."

In them days, we all just got so drunk, if anything had happened we wouldn't have noticed. Just had a ball every time I went to a party. And I was glad to go to one.

Furry recalled those glory days of Beale with as much relish as anyone. Still, he stood alone among Memphis blues people in applauding the urban renewal restructure of the old street.

It's best to put new things up, 'cause you know there's a long lane got no end and there's a bad wind on every change. You just got to change things. It's best to renew anything that's been old. That's my idea. Some of them buildings been there for a hundred and some years, I expect, and they's falling down, and people still livin' in 'em. I think after they get through with it, it's gonna be a beautiful place. I think it's gonna be a better place, anyhow, 'cause it would run off a whole lot of rats and things.

At precisely that moment, a rat scurried across the bare floor of the kitchen adjoining Furry's bedroom-living room.

· · ·

Many of the people who watched and applauded Furry through the years never knew he had but one leg. He lost one in 1916, during his hoboing days, when he hopped a freight at Du Quoin, Illinois.

I done been up there playin' and had money to come back, but I just wanted to save the money. I could have paid my way; I had the money. I just tried to catch the train, and I missed it and my foot went under the wheel. It was four or five of us together, and one of 'em just got up on top and walked the boxcars up to the engine and told them about it and they stopped.

I was at the Carbondale I.C. Railroad Hospital about a month. Was nearly a year before I could wear an artificial leg. I had crutches. I kept on as a musicianer, though.

He kept on dancing, too. His shuffle and strut and pigeon wing formed as much a part of his act as his singing and clowning. "I used to do pretty good," he said. "I can dance now."

· · ·

Little Laura Dukes burst through the door of Piano Red's house, grabbed Furry around the neck, and whirled him around the room as Red banged out some barrelhouse blues. Furry stayed with her, step for step, rock for roll.

"I can still shake a leg," he said, grinning.

Little Laura hugged him again. "Happy birthday, Furry. How old you now, anyway?"

"Old enough to sleep by myself," he retorted. "I ain't resigning yet."

"How's your health?"

"Better'n the man's at the Board of Health."

It was Furry's birthday, and jazz-blues buff Harry Godwin had arranged a party. Piano Red (John Williams) had some home brew to go with the barbecue and beans. (Red's beer wasn't really ready, he said, because it was only two days old and needed to be six—or, anyway, four.)

Red, six-foot-two and 250 pounds, pounded the piano while Little Laura, four-foot-seven and 85 pounds, rattled the roof of the green clapboard house with "Shake, Rattle and Roll." Furry recalled singing it with Gus Cannon in the days of the Beale Street jug bands, years before it and other old blues songs were converted into rock and roll hits in the 1950s.

But those jug band buddies—James Maynor, Jim Jackson,

Frank Stokes, Son Brimmer—were gone. Even the fellow blues men of today were conspicuous by their absence. Most of those present were from newspapers and television stations.

With the television lights blazing, Furry sang "Let Me Call You Sweetheart" and "Furry's Blues" and said, yes, he sometimes got to thinking about how it would have been if the fame of his recent years had come sooner. "But the Good Lord has been good to me, I guess, mighty good," he said. Godwin gave Furry tributes and letters, framed for hanging, and an honorary commission as a Tennessee Colonel, making him one of the few blacks so honored in Tennessee. Furry grinned and said softly, "I reckon it's about as nice a thing as has happened to me."

• • •

Furry talked in a matter-of-fact way, without bitterness, about the lack of nice things. Long ago he sang the song that provided the title of a hit Broadway play, "Been Down So Long It Seems Like Up To Me."

I been hearin' that ever since I been in the world, 'cause that's the truth. I been that way all my life. Look, you know, a rich fellow, he come up to me one time and said, "Furry, how do you feel, broke?" I say, "I feel fine broke because I hain't never had nothin'. I hain't had nothin' in my life, been broke all the time. I got to feel all right like I am." Just like you say, you never miss a thing you never had. I'm down now. I been down so long, it seems like up to me. I don't know what up is.

Even as the posters on his wall touted his appearances at blues festivals, in Madison Square Garden, on college campuses, the financial gains from these shows were nowhere to be seen. The most expensive items in his house—in fact, the only expensive items—were his electric guitar and amplifier. Nothing else indicated this was the home of someone who had become a blues cult idol.

Outward appearances notwithstanding, there was a time when,

if you wanted to hear Furry, you probably had to get his guitar out of hock first. If you asked him to play for a function, he'd say yes; if you paid him five dollars or five hundred, he'd thank you. But with more money coming in, he had become more conscious of his drawing power and less agreeable to performing for nickels and dimes. Money and the things money can buy, however, still weren't as important to him as his music. Furry liked to talk about where and how he played, not what he was paid.

I go somewhere and people ask me if I am going to practice. I tell them, "No, I don't need to practice 'cause I knew what I was going to do before I left home." Just like you got a guitar and I got one and I don't care what you play, I go right on behind you and it sounds good, too. I just know how to do it. Go on and play; I'll be witcha.

Elvis Presley, I tell you, he's good. He's fine. He made plenty money, more'n I ever will make. But he just couldn't play the blues and sing the blues like I can, I'll tell you that right now.

Besides playing and singing the blues, Furry liked to boast that he could make them. "I could just sit up here, make a song about most anything and make it rhyme out right," he said. He set up a singsong rhythm, a cappella:

> Some people say the worry blues ain't bad,
> And I said they must not have been the blues
> that old Furry had.

"You see?" he said, and then continued.

> They says again, some people say the worry blues
> ain't tough,
> And I says if they don't kill you, they handles
> you mighty rough.

Harry Godwin recalled the time he went to interview Furry for a radio series.

The Hong Kong flu epidemic was right at its height here in Memphis. Furry was taken bad with the flu and I had just gotten over it. Furry was lying in bed, but he sat up and said, "I told you I'd do this today and I will." And he sat up and started strumming on the guitar. I asked him if he could make up a song. "Oh, yeah," he said. And he started out saying:

> I'm so sick I don't know what I'm gonna do,
> I got the Hong Kong flu;
> I called my best friend Mr. Harry
> And he had it, too.

Godwin sent the tape along with others to Paramount in Chicago, and the song, called "The Harry-Furry Blues," ended up on a Biograph album that included other songs by Furry and some by Fred McDowell of Como, Mississippi. The album was titled *When I Lay My Burden Down*.

. . .

The day was as hot as only an August day can be on a dusty country road in Mississippi. It was more than one hundred degrees inside the frame church house near Como, a small town on the fringe of the Delta. There were easily 500 people jammed together in the church, 495 black and 5 white—Harry Godwin; Steve LeVere, a Memphis promoter; Stanley Booth, a free-lance writer; and two New York musicians who had driven all night to pay their last respects to blues man Fred McDowell.

The weeping and wailing—one woman became so hysterical she had to be carried bodily from the church—made it even hotter. Cardboard fans stirred the air without cooling it. Each of three preachers delivered a long, hard eulogy. Then they called on the congregation to testify, inviting the white people first.

When Furry Lewis and Booker White were called on, they talked about how Fred was just a fine man, a fine friend, and a fine guitar player, and about where they had played together. Someone asked Furry if he would play his guitar. There had been no choir or organ as part of the service; only Furry was there to bring music to the funeral of a man who had made music all of his life. Alone, he played and sang "When I Lay My Burden Down."

•  •  •

"They don't have music like they do at funerals in New Orleans," Furry said, a little indignant at the suggestion.

No, they don't do that. They just go there for last respect for him. No, they don't have no music or nothin' like that. They don't have nothin' like that. We all just goes to see him for his last time. I'm quite sure that some of the musicians come see me when I pass. I don't think that no one—me or other musicians—are 'sposed to take a church song and make the blues out of it. I tell you what I call it. I call it playin' with God. You can go on and have all your fun and foolishness and make up your own blues songs and everything else. You ain't got no business singin' "Old Rugged Cross" and all like that in no blues fashion and no jazz fashion and no such mess as that. "Old Rugged Cross" ought to be sung just like they sing it in church and, then, all church songs ought to be let alone from the jazz and the blues. I really don't think nobody ought to take God's songs and just go on and take 'em 'round like they do the blues or jazz and get out buck dancin' and jumpin' and all that mess. I don't think so. No. And I think I'll get a little "amen" on that from somebody. I think we have one here to help. [His schoolmate, Miss Margaret Mintz, gave him an "amen."] I just don't believe in mixing up. National wide and everybody hear all that kind of mess. That's the reason the world ain't no better now, ain't no better now and never will be.

Now, I'm not no better'n nobody else, but a few little years or a few little days I have to be here, I really wants to be all right. And I been tryin' to be that way all my life. You can't get to heaven like I'm doin' now, though. I'm kinda doin' a little wrong, singing the blues, but some of these days I'm goin' to retire from it probably and won't do this job. Probably go to church myself.

•  •  •

As affable as Furry seemed to white people, and as free of social protest as his songs usually were, he was capable of an occasional barb. Like the song he wrote about a certain city court judge, known as the "hanging judge" because of the high rate of conviction and often harsh punishment in his court.

> "Good morning, Judge, what may be my fine?"
> He said, "Fifty dollars and eleven twenty-nine."
> I said, "Arrest me for murder and I ain't never
>      hung a man,
> And arrest me for forgery and I can't even
>      sign my name."

Such sarcasm, with an underlying note of seriousness, was rare in his singing, but with all his clowning on stage—tossing his guitar around, playing it on his lap, cutting a stiff-legged pigeon wing—Furry took his craft seriously. He had been known to take a drink before going on stage—in fact, he had seldom been known not to—but he was never too drunk to perform and often continued for forty-five minutes to an hour. Usually the audience was young, tolerant of his clinkers, and appreciative of his corn pone jokes. But not always.

Don't care where you go, somebody ain't gonna like it. I was playin' at the Gaslight in New York. There was a white fellow there. He got up there and he was jes' doin' a whole lot of talk and he said I was up there actin' a fool. And I just explained to him, says, "Yes, I'm actin' a fool. But you're a bigger fool than me. I'm up on this stage actin' a fool and gettin' money and you're the fool who paid to come see me." Now, I didn't act no fool. That's my livin' with my guitar, gettin' out singin' and carryin' on my fun. That's my livin'.

· · ·

The River City Blues Festival had boogied with Piano Red Williams and jived with Little Laura Dukes backed up by Charlie Banks and his band. Now it was time for Furry. He was led onstage by a young white boy, who held a steadying hand under Furry's arm and carried his guitar. Furry moved at a shuffle, his glasses reflecting the bright lights, his eyes behind them seemingly near blind. His halting steps came to steady applause that continued as he sat down in the single, straight-backed chair at center stage and took his guitar on his lap.

"Thank you, thank you. Thank you all," he said. "Now I think
I play for you 'Furry's Blues.'"

> My Monday's woman live on Beale and Main,
> My Tuesday's woman bring me for to change,
> My Wednesday's woman bring me daily news,
> My Thursday's woman buy my socks and shoes,
> My Friday's woman puts it on the shelf,
> My Saturday's woman gimme the devil if she
>     ever catch me out,
> My Sunday's woman cooks my Sunday eats,
> I got me a woman for every day in the week.

Wild applause. Furry delivered more thank you's and a smile
that showed open space where front teeth once were. "Let Me
Call You Sweetheart" followed, the guitar quavering in imitation
of the Hawaiian style popular when Furry learned the piece sixty
years ago and the voice quavering because it had been sixty years
since he learned it. But the young audience, as high on the music
as on the cigarettes that sent smoke billowing toward the ceiling
of the auditorium, whooped and cheered as though every note
was perfect.

"This is a piece wrote by Mr. W. C. Handy," Furry announced.
"He give me the first good guitar I ever owned." Handy's "Saint
Louis Blues" came home, away from the fancy orchestration and
Spanish beat and back to its blues roots.

With "Waiting For The Train," the old Jimmie Rodgers song
on which Furry even tried an abortive yodel, and "I'm Goin' To
Brownsville," he got up and tottered off, the boy rushing out to
help him but letting him return alone for the four bows the audience demanded. Furry gloried in it, but most of his usual mischief
was missing. Only once had he swung the guitar up, spun it
around and caught it on his lap, never missing a lick; there was
none of the usual comic soft-shoe. As he waved slowly to the
audience on his final bow, there was the aura of a farewell performance by a man who wondered if he would pass this way
again.

But it was far from farewell. Furry "went ahead on" as never before. He even won a role in a Burt Reynolds movie, playing an old-time blues musician, of course, and Reynolds and costar Art Carney arranged an appearance for him on Johnny Carson's television show. Never altering his manner nor his style one whit for national television, he sang "Furry's Blues" and told the joke about not needing a wife when the man next door's got one. (Some of his Memphis friends were afraid he'd tell the one about why he had broken off a long-standing relationship with a woman friend: "My key," he would say impishly, "don't fit her keyhole no more.")

The Carson show helped generate new interest in Furry's kind of blues, bringing him more concerts with higher fees than ever before, along with semi-celebrity status and recognition by late-night television fans in his travels across the country. Still he moved at his own pace, joking and laughing and being himself—whatever you might think you wanted him to be. And he said: "I just thank the Good Lord for lettin' me be here this long. I just always tried to do the best I could, whatever I'm doin'. Never did try to hurt nobody or nothin'. Just gettin' along, that's all."

Booker T. Washington White, bottlenecking with his steel slide on his nickel-plated guitar, at his home in Memphis in 1972.
Courtesy of William Leaptrott

# 9 · Booker

Life had been harder on Booker White than his reminiscences reflected. He had sung the hard-row-to-hoe, hungry man's blues and how-long-before-I-can-change-my-clothes prison blues, but his mood was far from indigo. He preferred to remember rollicking through life as if it were a stage show, playing the girls as adroitly as he bottlenecked the strings on his nickel-plated steel guitar, singing his song to an applauding world, and trigger-toeing out of the tight spots.

Booker (his spelling, though it's *Bukka* on his records) looked and sounded the part of a barrelhouse blues man—bull-necked and barrel-chested, with a rumbling voice roaming from field holler to Southern Comfort growl. Unlike many of his blues contemporaries who were content to let their songs speak for them, Booker was loquacious. He slurred the words and mauled the grammar. But he got his message across with an expressiveness all his own, nowhere more evident than in his descriptions of the women he had known.

There were the Saint Louis women when the sun was just coming up on the blues career of the thirteen-year-old guitar picker from Mississippi.

They'd come around and they'd kiss me and pick me up. And I could just feel myself stretching in my skin, just growing on up. And you know there was a lady there 'bout thirty years old. And she had some kind of cologne on her that almost give me the asthma, so sweet. And she said, "When you grow up, you gonna be my boyfriend." And, sure enough, when I got fifteen years old, me and her commenced to dating. I was a man then, you know, fifteen years old, and I carried money to the bank. I didn't have to steal nothing, you know.

. . . . . . . . . . .

The prettiest girl was down there in Mississippi. Woooee! She was so pretty, when she walked the weeds would spread for her. It looked like the weeds and things just get back to let her have a state view without scratching her.

. . . . . . . . . . .

My heart used to stop three and four minutes when I'd see them women get out there and do that shimmy-she-wobble. One night a great big lady there, weigh about 170, she was shaking that whole house. My nose started bleeding and I started to weaken down. I couldn't budge, I couldn't move, I couldn't bat my eyes—my eyes got locked. Man, I just couldn't stand it. My cousin had to take me away from the place. I believe I was going to fall dead, 'cause I don't remember breathing.

. . . . . . . . . . .

The ugliest woman I ever seen, I got so jealous of her I wouldn't let her even dance with nobody. But now Maude was the ugliest woman that God ever made—had a face just like a monkey. But she was built up through the waist, she had legs just like a twisted possum and, God, she was made back here [he patted his hips] just like you take and fix it just like you want it. I don't care how ugly a woman is, if she carry herself, keep that hair fixed right and that lipstick ain't too thick on her lip and put that right dress on and fix herself up nice, the best-looking man that could walk the street, he going to fall for that woman. I done experienced it.

. . . . . . . . . . .

I wasn't doing no work. What the men didn't like to see, I walking with my silk shirt on, sharp as a tack, and while they was plowing, it would be about fifteen or twenty of them women and me in some grove right off the side of the road. Just me, one man, and my guitar. And the men, they'd come to the pump and get some water and just roll their eyes at me. And I'd say, "Hey, buddy, how you doing?" Some of them say, "Go to hell," you know.

. . . . . . . . . . .

I married this girl Susie, I was old enough for her daddy—she'd say, yessir, nossir, to me. She was low and chunky and big-legged and neat in the waist like a wasp and two dimples in her jaws, one in the forehead, and one in the chin. And every time she'd smile, look like fleas and gnats just run all over me. She was just what I wanted, and I wouldn't have took a city for her. Susie looked so good to me, I couldn't sleep at night. I talked to her when I was awoke, and when I'd go to sleep I'd be talking to her in my sleep. If I was gone from her, when the sun go to going down I'd feel like somebody what had the double pneumonia.

. . . . . . . . . . . .

My girl friend, Pearline, she'd come to see me in Parchman [Mississippi State Penitentiary, where Booker served time for killing a man]. And the clothes she wore, they would shine just like the Prodigal Son. . . . One of the prettiest women that ever was was in the women's camp down there. And I said to the Sergeant, "If I get out, I'm going to get this girl out." He said, "Booker, you know what that damn woman done did? She done cut two men's heads plumb off their shoulders. The last one, she cut it off with a ax. And the first one, she cut it off with a razor. She jealous and she don't allow her man to even tell another woman good morning." I said, "Well, y'all keep praying for her when she dies."

. . . . . . . . . . . .

I'd be in my hotel room [in Chicago]. I'd get my table and put it right at the door, with a fifth of whisky on it. I'd sit there, be playing my guitar and singing, to draw the women when they come through the aisle. That's just like you trying to catch a crawdad with the bait swinging off your hook. They stops. "Would you like to have some company?" they say. When one came I like, I'd shut the door and we'd just sit and drink. I'd give her ten dollars to go get whatever kind of brand she like, five dollars to go get a big plate lunch. They say: "Oh, Mr. White, you so nice. It just don't look like you're from the South. Look like you raised in the North." I'd say: "It ain't where you from. It's just what's in you. I just got good cleanness in my heart."

Booker still had his eye out as he traveled the college concert circuit during the 1960s. "Some of them girls, they look like God done throwed some of them angels out of heaven, they look so pretty. I just look at them. I say, 'If I had another heaven somewhere, under this heaven, I'd carry y'all up there.' "

. . .

Much of his love for women, song, and dance came from his

father, John White, whose railroad job and moonlighting as a musician kept him on the road most of the time. Born in 1909, Booker grew up on his grandfather's farm near Houston, Mississippi.

My daddy was a big performer. He played guitar, mandolin, violin, saxophone, piano; and, man, could he dance—outta sight. I always said my daddy wasn't no full Negro. You could hardly tell him too much from white. All the girls, they wasn't falling for his color, though; they was falling for his music. He could read music, you know. He read any kind of music you could put on paper. I started off like that, but it was too much complicated for me. I say to him, "I believe I can just reach up and get mine. I can go faster in my way." I couldn't fool with no paper, you know.

His father gave him a guitar, and by age nine he was playing at country frolics and suppers for fifteen cents, two apples, and a box of sardines a night, as well as learning about the black bottom and trigger-toe.

I just went to the devil. And my grandfather, he was a bishop. I did a heap better with them guitar strings than I did with that mule, so help me God. My grandfather had me hauling fodder with the mules. Them mules was so slow, I'm just steady whupping them with a bullwhip, and they got slower. I say, "When I get you to the barn, old buddy, you won't be bothering Booker no more." Them mules ain't seen me from that day to this. That just wasn't my talent to fool with nothing like that.

He drove the mules to the barn's back gate, left them there harnessed, and, barefooted, hit the road to Houston. He worked at a store and sawmill long enough to get himself shoes and a knee-pants suit and then hitchhiked a hundred miles across the state to the Mississippi Delta, to an uncle in Glendora. "That was the greatest place, I believe, on God's land at that time, 'cause the people around there, they had plenty of money. They had nice automobiles, and the girls was going to most certainly worse'n hell. The girls would go to dances, and the parents would let them go. Sometimes the parents would be there with them."

In the Delta he was introduced to the cotton patch, which he didn't like any better than the mules, and he began to yearn to go upcountry. His departure came sooner than he had planned, perhaps partly by accident. "I was, I reckon, thirteen or fourteen, and me and some other boys were playing with that freight train that day, all of us jumping on the train. When the train got a little faster than we thought it was, well, they jumped off. I was scared to get off, and I went ahead on to Saint Louis."

Saint Louis was bigger than he had bargained for, and as he wandered alone and afraid and crying, an old man sitting on the riverside spotted him.

So he called me over and asked me where I was from and everything, and he said, "Aw, stop crying and stay here with me. I ain't got no kid. I'll bring you up to be a great man one day. I'll call your parents and let 'em know where you're at and so just be quiet." So that satisfied me so I stayed there.

Old man Ben, his name was Ben Wright, he was decorated, man. You know, old man millionaire. He had a big nightclub which kind of favored a big hotel. It had a band, understand, and the band would let me play in the break hour, you see. And I just started playing the piano and I played my guitar. I was like a game rooster, and I'd jump up for any big kind of congregation and do my thing. I wasn't ashamed or nothing.

Besides an opportunity to do his own thing, he could watch others doing theirs. Among the blues men he remembers playing there were Peetie Wheatstraw, St. Louis Jimmy (Jimmy Oden), and the great Lonnie Johnson. "All those old players just give me such a good encourage to go along to do my thing with them, you see. And so that put my boots on, so I just didn't have nothing to do but just walk shallow water and sing the blues."

Eventually he and other teenagers formed their own band and took it on the road in the Saint Louis area, "playing the blues sky high," he said. But it wasn't until he was drawn back to the Mississippi Delta that he made his first recording in 1930. Ralph Lumbo, a record-store owner in Itta Bena and occasional scout for record companies, talked him into trying out.

I went on up there and Ralph give me a big glass half-full of bonded whisky. I don't believe I ever had tasted a bonded whisky. It taste just like syrup to me, it was so good. And I drank the last of it and he caught me licking the glass, just holding it up getting the last drop. And I could feel it commencing building me up. I played "Downtown Women Sic 'Em Dogs on You" and he just had a fit. He said, "Can you stand another half a glass?" I said, "You can fill it up; it ain't gonna hurt." Well, I had sense enough to didn't drink it, I just sipped a little on it till I got through, then I killed it. Ooooo, I was the happiest soul going down that highway. You be hearing my foots hitting them rocks like somebody had a sledge hammer hitting on the rock. Man, I was feeling good.

Lumbo took him to Memphis for a Victor recording session at the auditorium. A preacher was there to record and a keg of apple brandy was there for refreshment and the two got together.

Apple brandy is sweet and it's good, you know; and if you don't watch yourself, you'll drink a gallon before you will a glassful. And that's what Reverend did. Every time I see him, he had the faucet wide open. And he got drunk. Ralph, he ask me, "Booker, do you know how to preach? Hell, I'll give you the job." I said, "Naw, I don't know how to preach and I'm not going to mess with God like that." We had to let that preacher take a nap and git hisself back together 'fore we could do any recording.

"Panama Limited" and "The Frisco Train" were among the sides Booker cut that day. Lumbo paid him seventy dollars, Booker said, "and that just give me a good gift to want to really get out and make some money."

Unfortunately, the hard times of the 1930s left their imprint on the recording industry. Some companies folded, and those which stayed in business cut back drastically on their field trips to the South to record black blues. The money Booker made from his music in those years came from playing at roadhouses, mainly in Mississippi but occasionally as far north as Cleveland and Saint Louis.

It wasn't until 1937 that he recorded again, this time in Chicago where talent hunter Lester Melrose added him to his stable of major blues musicians, including Big Bill Broonzy, Tampa Red (Hudson Whitaker), St. Louis Jimmy, Washboard Sam (Robert Young), and Memphis Minnie. He recorded two sides for Vocalion, "Shake 'Em On Down" and "Pine Bluff, Arkansas," and doubtless could have contributed more to the resurgence of the blues, but again he went back to Mississippi.

I couldn't get the Delta out of my mind. There was more money in the Delta than was in Chicago to me. I know it was, 'cause I could make more. And I knowed more people down in the Delta, see. I didn't have to do no work 'lessen I want to work. I was just around there with them old musicians and we'd have a ball. Pick cotton some days, some days I didn't do anything. We'd just sit around at the house and have our white whisky and frying fishes and just have a big time. Go to a frolic at night, we were going to ball all night long. Well, I like it that way.

It didn't stay that way long. Booker was caught up in a shooting scrape near Charleston, Mississippi, as he waited one afternoon to catch a ride on a log truck to go to a dance. He insisted he was threatened by a gang of men resentful of the fact that he was playing his guitar and courting the women while they were working in the fields. At any rate, one man lay dead after the fracas and the judge sentenced Booker to Parchman. Booker boasted that his music made prison life easier for him. "The way they'd do us good musicians, we'd go from one camp to another, playing. God knows, hear me say, I couldn't be treated no better." Still, some of his bluesiest songs came from his prison days, such as "How Long Before I Can Change My Clothes."

> It would be so cold till you stand and look
> At your dirty clothes and wonder how long,
> I wonder how long before I can change my clothes.

Parole came after he had served two years, and he changed his prison clothes for silk shirts and blue serge, he said, and headed back to Chicago, where Melrose put him up in a hotel, gave him a meal ticket and started recording him again. On

March 7 and 8 of 1940, using Big Bill Broonzy's Gibson guitar and accompanied by Washboard Sam, he recorded twelve sides for Okeh and Vocalion, including "Parchman Farm Blues," "Sleepy Man Blues," "A Special Stream Line," "Bukka's Jitterbug Swing," "Good Gin Blues," and "A Fixin' to Die Blues," which Bob Dylan was later to popularize with his own version in the 1960s.

Booker impressed Melrose's musicians enough that they took him into their circle.

Memphis Minnie, Washboard Sam, Tampa Red, Big Bill, they were my favorite 'cause they really would knock the cover off a house. They play in the nightclubs, would play house parties through the day. Otherwise they were rehearsing; people would be there as many as they would be at the nightclub sometimes. You have all the company you looking for, something free. Which I was on the Freedom Train, too. I could play some, you know, but it's so many there that I mostly couldn't do nothing except pass the bottle.

I played with them a lot of nights at the club, just one song or two songs, make me seventy-five, eighty dollars, just like that. When I go to the stage, they just set a shoebox or hat on the edge. Sometimes I make more money than the guys that was in the band.

They said, "You got at least eighty-five or a hundred dollars. I didn't make but sixty dollars."

I said, "I ain't counted it. I don't think I got that much."

"Yes, you is!"

The 1940 sessions were Booker's last recordings until the blues revival more than twenty years later. There were a number of factors: the government's restriction of shellac shortly after America entered World War II; the cutback in race releases; the ban that J. D. Petrillo, president of the American Federation of Musicians, imposed on all recording because of his concern about the effect on live music; the changing interest of the audience; and, perhaps most important, Booker's inclination to keep one foot in the road. He roamed through the forties, mostly in the South.

Just wherever I thought I could make a hit, that's where I would go. I just forgot about work. When I was working, I wasn't getting nowhere. Work wasn't on my mind. I wasn't looking for no job at all. I was playing at juke houses. Out from the city, they call it the roadhouse. I would play in them and I made good money. And everybody, white and colored, they went for it.

So in the forties I played my music everywhere, west or east. And then it got to where I wasn't doing nothing but playing the girls. Which I had always made my own money, I never did want to live off no lady, but it was kinda time for me to take some rest, you know.

I run up on a lady, she was a beautician and she had plenty of money. I didn't work myself so hard, just set myself in her front room there and play the piano or either my guitar. Many weekends Della have put three hundred-dollar bills in my hand. See, that will make a fool out of you if you don't watch yourself. What you gonna do when she get tired of spending money on you? Then she gonna leave you just like you just come in the world. Well, it run down. The hundreds, fifties, stop coming in my hand. And I was glad it was. I went on back out and started getting around and make me some more money.

His wandering took him to Beale Street, where he met up with such well-known Memphis blues men as Jack Kelly, Frank Stokes, Gus Cannon, Piano Red Williams, Furry Lewis, Walter Horton, Dewey Corley.

Shoot, I used to sleep on Beale. We used to play in that park on Beale. Every Saturday night, if you want to find anybody, you go to Beale Street at that park. This where they at. Just like we do when we's in the small towns, we had our hat down, let them throw the money in it. The polices used to come stand there, listen at us play. I knowed the police many times to turn around, chunk us a half or quarter.

If there ever was a good time, so help me God, there was good times on Beale Street. People from everywhere was coming to find out about that place; people you see there you ain't ever seen before in your life. You know, Beale Street was a joint street, it was a drag street, it was a drawing street.

But the good times are gone for good. They done tore up near about everything. I hate to go down through there now. I hear a lot of talk what they going to do. The most I see them doing is putting car lots, you know, parking lots. I don't see no building going up nowhere no more. I going to just tell you the truth: I just don't believe it's going to be no more Beale now.

He enjoyed Beale enough to decide to settle in Memphis and

to get a steady job for the first time. "I quit playing, I got tired of playing, and got a job at a place where they made truck tanks. I wanted to work so I can get me up a lot of social security, you know."

During this period, Booker's cousin, B. B. King, moved to Memphis from Indianola, Mississippi. While he was struggling to make it as one of Beale Street's itinerant blues singers, he lived for a time with Booker, who charged him three dollars a week for bed and board, "and he was eating the very best food 'cause I likes to eat." When B. B. went on to become a singing deejay at radio station WDIA, Booker would join him occasionally on the air.

In 1963, two young blues buffs, John Fahey and Ed Denson, persuaded Booker to go to California to record for their fledgling recording company on the Takoma label. "John and them was just beginning to get in this racket. They just started. They used to sleep in the car shed, sleep on the side of a big old hill. I pulled them up and they pulled me up. We helped one another," Booker recalled.

After that, he traveled around the country and the world, becoming one of the most popular of the country blues men on the college circuit in the late 1960s and early 1970s. "All the playing I ever did, I did better than I ever did in my life. I scrapped up pretty nicely."

As far as money goes, Booker probably fared better than many of the country blues musicians, especially during the rediscovery era. His appearances at concerts and blues festivals had brought him a respectable income for the first time in his life, but it hadn't changed his life style. He still lived in a rented room in a modest apartment in Memphis' central city, just a few blocks down the street from Furry.

Although times were better and the pay, too, insecurity remained a constant companion. Booker got a small royalty check about every six months from the Melrose estate, but he said there was never enough money to relax. "You got to be doing something all the while 'cause six months to six months mighty long for you to don't eat nothing. You got to be scuffling all the time. If I sit here and don't try to get out and do no job or nothing, the way I likes to have fun and get around, I'd be in bad shape. But I be fortunate enough to always have something coming in all the time 'cause I'm going all the time."

For his latter-day audiences, Booker used the same approach he used in playing the juke joints, roadhouses, and street corners.

Everything I do, I tries to do it all right. I do's what I tell a man I will do. And so that give me a good comeback. That's the way you got to do your job. Just do it right.

I played my guitar, and I was an easy guy to get along with, and people like that. I was good mixing. Every time you was good mixing, you don't have no hard time. I'm the same thing every day.

But I do say this, you got to pick your peoples now to associate with 'cause you just can't associate with everybody. That's the main question, just pick your people, 'cause everybody grinning you in the face is not no friend to you.

Booker T. Washington White died in Memphis on February 26, 1977.

Piano Red Williams, playing and singing the workingman's blues, at his home in Memphis in 1973.
Courtesy of William Leaptrott

# 10 · Piano Red

On the porch of the rented frame bungalow in a neighborhood that had long since switched from working-class white to working-class black, John Williams sat puffing a cigar and taking the air on a hot afternoon in late summer. Even in the shade, he wore dark glasses; his eyes, like those of most albinos, were sensitive to light. And like most albinos his pale, biscuit-colored skin was flecked with freckles and he was called Red—Piano Red.

As he got up slowly to shake hands with his visitors, his clothes—open-necked sports shirt, navy trousers, and black-and-white spectator shoes—strained at the task of covering the bulk of his body. As though some potter molded him out of speckled beige clay, he was shaped with no sharp edges. One giant, rounded mass flowed smoothly into another, huge neck into enormous shoulders into gargantuan chest into thick torso into tree-trunk legs. Even his head was outsized, a shiny bald dome set with massive features and a forehead of rippled furrows of flesh.

He led the way inside where a blond upright piano shared the living room with gold-toned composition furniture upholstered in red velvet. He turned on the large revolving fan and settled himself on the piano bench.

Then, through a long afternoon, he talked about his life with the unselfconscious charm of a natural yarn spinner. He chuckled over his own tall tales, looked only slightly abashed about his brawls, and earnestly related his basic belief in his Maker and his fellow man.

Born in 1905 in Germantown, a small farming community outside Memphis, he wandered—rousting on the river, hoboing on
the rails, playing piano in the honky-tonks—for more than twenty
years before settling down in Memphis in the late 1930s to take
a job doing heavy-moving work for a storage and transfer company. Even at nearly seventy years old, his strength was his pride.

'Course I have pretty good power now. I carried one end of that piano
there up here when I moved. Them young fellows, I ain't afraid to face
'em, not today. No, ma'am. I can work a thirty-year-old man to death
almost, right now. I could work from now—from right here standing
now—work 'til this time tomorrow.

And I do like work, sure. I like those big trailers, that truck line
work, moving vans. I'd like that work right now.

I was always a large-size fellow. When I was somewhere about
seventeen, I taken a job rousting on the steamboat. I just had nerve.
All the fellows was able to tote those three-hundred and four-hundred-
pound sacks of meal. One man would lift a five-hundred-pound bale
of cotton. I would work right with those fellows. I was stout as a
mule.

How it would be, you would stop at some landing, you'd have to
pick up five hundred bags of cottonseeds. And you'd have one or two
families to move. Then you would have to worry with some mules.
But three or four men get a poor mule, he wasn't more than a little
puppy. A mule! They'd get him, they'd carry him on there, sometime
he be yellering.

The baddest thing you could handle was a crate of chickens 'cause
they be flopping and going this side and that side in that crate. Chickens and hogs, they was the baddest fellows. Those big sows, they
don't care nothin' about a gang of men. Get one long as this table and
you've got something on your hands.

Then, after you get them on, well, you ride about two hours or
three. You got a rest period, then, that far.

At night, that's all where the fun was. You know, they usually
carried passengers, too, colored and white. You'd be up there with the
passengers, trying to court, first one thing and another, 'til Captain
run you back down with the crew.

You know what a corkscrew is, don't you? That's something like
an auger, got a piece across it and a sharp end, see. You could take
that and go down in the hold 'til you find you a sixteen-gallon liquor

keg. And get you some liquor and be high as a Georgia pine. I remember some old fellow that stole liquor, stole it from the keg 'til the keg was light as his hat.

Now don't you think you won't lose your pass if that old captain catch you down there. 'Course I fool around there and go in the cheese and eat up the "stage planks"—that's a old, long cake. Two together and have icing on one side, call them "daddy wide legs."

Oh, it was lots of fun in it. Well, you don't make but a very little money. Say your pay 'spose to be a hundred and seventy-five dollars. Now you never know what that meant 'cause when you get to payoff time, you just be lined up and he gonna shove you some money. And you just take what he give you and don't say nothing.

And they didn't put no roses on your shoulders. Give you slices of meat, you wouldn't have no knives and forks. Just reach in there all together. Had some old light bread that wasn't sliced; you had got to break it and give this one a piece and him some. Day-old bread. And that's the way it was. No, you didn't make all that much. But you didn't have to go wondering where can I make some money to pay my little house rent. You just get off the boat on the street, somebody grabbed you, "You want to work some?" That's the way it was then and a whole lot better than it is now. Your house rent then was eighteen dollars a month—that was a six-room house.

It was pretty good fun. But sometimes you catch the devil and some of them old men was stout. They catch a little boy on there and they'd on and kill him. They didn't care. I remember my last trip, in this high water of twenty-seven. This little kid was sixteen years old, trying to work his way to Memphis for he and his mother. You know them cutting machines what they use in the printing shop? This old man picked up one of them on that little kid, just put all the weight on the kid and almost kilt him. That was low down. And I ran to that child and I put it on that old man just like he done the little boy, and they taken him off that boat, put him in Rosedale (Mississippi) Hospital. Yeah, I put it on him.

You see, you could just put your heels together thisaway [Red stood up and moved to the center of the room and clamped his heels together with a snap]. Hold your knees thataways [he bent his knees in a slight crouch and curved his forearms as though getting ready to lift a tremendous weight]. And you *got* some men. [He sat back down, obviously satisfied with the memory.]

He was trying to kill that little boy. He didn't care. Well, I ran to him, to his rescue. And I had something for that old fellow. And I just put it on the old fellow and wouldn't turn it aloose, I wouldn't turn it aloose. 'Cause I was just hard, as hard as my leg was. They broke me in rough. That was an easy job, but it was low-down type of people. You wouldn't find very many people have a heart, you know.

Sometimes I just hoboed around. You see, when I called myself leaving away from home, I was somewhere about fourteen. And from then on, I just learnt how to go and go and go and go and go. And I ran around all over Mississippi, Arkansas, Missouri, and Alabama and Georgia. I had a pretty nice time and I had some little rough times. 'Course I didn't never harm nobody, and everywhere I ever been, I can go back. Didn't do no harm like people go in, steal and things. And I would go in a little town and I would ask the law, I'd go right up to him and say, "How you, Mr. Officer?"

He turn around and look rough at me. He say, "Well, how you, fellow?"

I say, "Mr. Officer, would you mind letting me have a quarter or a dime or something to get me a little food. I'm a little hungry." I say, "I'd work if I had something."

"Can you cut grass?" he'd say. He'd carry me somewhere, it looked like a plantation it was so big. But I go on, cut it, and I made it everywhere. I could always talk to the law.

Over there in El Dorado in Arkansas, I come through and the boys got to gambling up on the railway in the highway. It wasn't thirty cents in the game, two pennies shooting, but they got to fighting and somebody called the marshal. And so the man come over there and he lined all of us up. "Where you from, young man?" he asked the first one. "I'm from Smackover." That's a little place that ain't far from El Dorado. "Where you from?" he say to the next one. "I'm from Smackover." He asked me, "Where you from, old fellow?" I said, "Kenton, Missouri." And he got some more Smackover and he say, "I'm gone to smack every one of you over there in that jail. That's what I gone do with you." And told me to get lost. Yeah, lost. And I was plumb glad. I'd rather be bit by a snaggletooth mule than go to court.

I played all around, around Cairo, Illinois, and all around Helena and Greenville, Mississippi, and Saint Louis. I played all around Mobile and New Orleans, Chattanooga, Knoxville, and Nashville, too.

Way I got my start, there was a little place called the White House where they would go for the weekend get-together when I was a little fellow. My sister Blanche would say, "Well, I'll carry you where they playing, then you'll learn how to play, Red." So I would go and I would stand on the corner of the piano and watch and watch them and watch them. And I get home, I'd find an old log and then I begin to play a little tune. Later on, where I stayed, the lady had a piano, you put a nickel in, and I'd watch that. I watched the keys and I would catch on like that. She'd run me off every chance she got. And so I just kept on and kept on; I learnt one little song and then you learn yourself. I hoboed around about twenty-two years trying to learn.

I did play some on the riverboats. How it was, I could mock the captain when he talk, call the men names like you would pigs and roosters, call 'em Ringtail, Bear, and Mule. And I mocked him and he heard. He seen it was me, he got up and say, "I'll throw that scoundrel off in that river!"

And I outran him and went up those steps to the white waiting room. All the little children playing the piano. I played, "It Ain't Gonna Rain No More." And, oh, they got crazy about me; them kids had a fit over me. When they come up there after me, that's what kept them away from me, them kids raised so much sand over me. And then the old captain told me to stay up there and entertain them kids, and that's how I got my start.

I played a little bit at little house parties. That was all through Memphis, you know, ten cents at the door and fifteen cents a couple, serve spaghetti and crackers, and give a dollar and a half to the best dancer, all like that. You had to go up to the courthouse and pay a dollar and a half for a permit to keep from getting raided. 'Cause they had a plenty of that moonshine whisky there. But it was good, and if you had some and kept it from now to Christmas, it really would be fine. And if you had some in a charred keg, you'd remember it.

That's what everybody dranked, that moonshine. It wasn't no bonded whisky then, without you go down to New Orleans, just that old Uncle Tom whisky. All them joints on Beale sell it for twenty-five cents a half-a-pint, that Pee Wee's joint and the Club House and the Red Front and Midway and the Gray Mule. I played at all of them.

I went up there to Saint Louis in Missouri, and I come back playing the blues like them fellows there was. That was new. And all of them wanted to come see who's that playing down at the Gray Mule. Like one somebody run a joint, he say, "I know you, Red; you know me. Come on up here and play for me." One want to swipe you from the other one. If you be a good blues player and could sing good, they always be one want to steal you from the other one.

In the old days on Beale, you could say it was never nighttime. They just stayed open from dawn to dawn. Everything was lively. You go to playing at five o'clock, play until four-thirty in the morning. Sometimes would be some old fellow come by, and you give him a drink, he'd go take a lick or two for you. Then sometimes, it be three or four, this one don't like the way the other one play; he think he can beat him, he come play. And here come another one play. And another one play. You get a chance to rest all night almost.

They dance. They have a little contest, the best dancer. At that time women shoes costed one dollar and thirty-nine cents. And the next morning, they be in there "catching the tiger" and doing the "scratch" and be just as barefooted as a goose. Had nothing but the tops; done danced the soles plumb out.

Catching the tiger—you remember the "Tiger Rag"—that was to that. That was foxy, something like a six-eight swing. That was really nice. The scratch, it was a funny kind of peculiar. I sees them do it now. Something like what Rufus Thomas called the "dog."

I'll tell you what—it was bad in a way—I was playing at the Gray Mule. And I had on some old corduroys that weren't too good. And so, it was an old millionaire man here, his name was Homer K. Jones. And his chauffeur, he done got drunk in there, just laid out drunk. These guys sitting there, they liked me, said they going to fix me up. And they start taking clothes off that chauffeur, and every time they take a piece off of him, they put it on me. They didn't act nasty; they just borrowed his clothes. He had some shoes, they were awful beautiful shoes, brass in there; he had some of them velvet-looking corduroys on. Just fit me. We were the same size. I didn't need that cap, but all that other business, they put it on me. And them rags of mine, they put that junk on him, got my old piece of shoes on him, and trousers and everything, and turnt him a-loose like that. So I know he was a nice-looking chauffeur when he got back to old man Homer K. with them rags on.

The Gray Mule, it had a lively bunch. It was kind of crowded, but it was a nice little joint. Had good food in there. They served plenty black-eyed peas and cornbread and baked sweet potatoes. And they would have candied yams and baked ribs, have peach cobbler, apple cobbler, or blackberry cobbler. Sell you that dessert for ten cents a little bowl. Or bread pudding or rice pudding. Neck bones and Irish potatoes and beef stew.

There was all different kind of places on Beale. Them places I played, they was mostly just joints. To tell the truth, some of them

was just real scalawag joints, like old man [Nello] Grundy's and the
Red Front. Folks go there, wear overalls, work in the coal yard, and
go to the joint just like they quit work.

But then there was places like the Monarch. It was the classiest;
it was the town talk, the Monarch. Well, they're real dressed up,
gambling men with diamond rings on and suits of clothes. And them
pimps would go there—but, Lord, they wasn't nothin' like these
ragged fellows 'round here now sayin' they're pimps. Them men,
you'd thought it was a preacher or lawyer, way they dressed then.
Some of 'em would dress twice a day. When they come out in the
mornin', they wear that 'til noon, and see 'em again, they's different.
They had tailor-made suits, nice gray and blue serge, and brown
broadcloth, Manhattan shirts, and Stacy Adams shoes, and Knox hats
and stetsons. Yes, Lord, they were nice dressers. Wear two-and-a-
half-dollar gold pieces in his cuff links, five-dollar gold piece for a
stickpin. They drive them fancy cars—Studebaker, Hudson Super Six.

You want the truth, some of the places you go, you tell them you
were from Memphis, you'd be treated like a boy dog. Sure is, really
the truth. I remember when you could name three towns and you
could forget it. You could say you were from Memphis, New Orleans,
Birmingham, you were out the back door. I can't explain why. They
just thought the people there were so slick.

'Cause Beale was rough. But it still was better than it is now.
'Cause a fellow stayed in his place, else them bouncers would carry
him out of there and give him a good brushing up. But now, these
little fellows, they don't think a old man forty-five years old got no
business with no money. They gone take yours and beat you up.
That's all I think about them—they nothing. But I remember that
time you could walk all night everywhere you wanted to go, nobody
to bother you.

Well, there was fighting, that's right. Specially when they was
gambling. And one would stick one with a knife, and you'd find him
over there in the corner, gone away from here. They'd drag him over
there, and they just shoot right on, they'd shoot craps right on. They'd
go right straight on.

The Royal Gardens, that was a famous little nightclub at Hernando
and Beale, upstairs over the drugstore. That was high powered. That
was a little high-powered place. Fellows throat cutting and throw
them out the window, three stories down onto Beale and Hernando.

I remember two got to fighting at the wagon yard at Second and
Beale. That was where the country people left their horses and wagons

when they come into town on a Saturday. These two was gambling, and one kept on hollerin' 'bout what he would shoot. The other one say, "Man, you too old; you fifty-five. You too light." And the first one just give him a back-hand lick, slapped him in the mouth. He say, "This is Mr. Bear"—that what he called himself—"This is Mr. Bear, jumped in the mouth."

So Mr. Bear, he went on. The other old fellow, he went on for two or three weeks. Then he caught Mr. Bear up there, just gambling in that dust, and he gave him a good going over. Then he says, "This Mr. Wolf." That's what he told him. After he paid him back, he say, "This is Mr. Wolf."

Yes, sir, I seen some pretty tough things. Where the water plug is, right at Second and Beale, I seen a man lying down there dying, and he said his last thing, he said, "A buddy is the worst thing in the world to have." He was gambling, and every time he would get lucky and win, his partner would come up and want some money. And he said, "Why don't you let me try to work while I'm lucky," and he just got up and popped him. Other man took his knife and made like he was going to hit him in his face. When he throw his hands up—*bim!* with that knife. That's the way he killed him. Yes, I saw quite a few things here, sure have.

Now here what would go on. Some place where would have been so many people butchered up, they would change the name. They had a beautiful little place here. They used to call it the Blue Heaven. Before that was the Cotton Club, and before that they called it Sunset Hall. When it got to where some people wouldn't go there, the name is changed, you know.

Now about the baddest and low-downest little place was on Beale Street was the Hole in the Ground. That was a honey down there, sure was. You go down some steps, that's where they gambled, but you come upstairs to drink and dance. That's why they called it a Hole in the Ground.

I always was afraid of that Hole in the Ground. There's some bad ladies was there, they was bad, they was just mean. They're old grown women but I was a young fellow. One of them called me. "Come here, Red," she say. Say, "You like me?" I say, "Yeah, I like everybody." Half-scared. And she just taken her teeth and got a good mouthful of my forehead and she just worked, she just bit, just left a bad place where she just taken her teeth and just worked it up in there. I was trying to get away from there. But when I did, I made up for lost time. I got on the good foot and done myself some running from that Hole in the Ground.

I got a friend girl, name Alma. She was going to school, but she was just a outlaw. They caught her with a long pocketknife, she cut one of those old teachers on the hand, and they put her out from there. And so I left her for another lady. And Alma, she got hold an old pistol—they called it a 32-20—and she come over to old man Grundy's, where I played. And she got over in the corner. And it was dark over in the corner and she was dark and the gun was dark, so I didn't know what to do. She say, "You ain't gone do no good here." So I just had to get loose. And lose my job. I went back and told old man Grundy about it. He was nice as he could be, and he told me I ought to have told him about it then. But I couldn't have time to tell him, she standin' in the corner, corner dark and she was real dark. No-o-o, I couldn't stand that, she standin' in that corner, I don't know what's going to happen directly. Alma, she run me away. She live in Peoria, Illinois, now. And I hope to the Lord that she always stay there.

I will tell you this about playing in them joints, playing the blues. Some say the blues is devil music, but I say playing the blues ain't bad. It ain't nearly 'bout like a big lie and a peace breaker. The truth is you can play the blues all day, and if you don't pat your foot or sing, you won't feel it. 'Cause I play the blues and it don't get under my skin. I ain't studying it, ain't thinking about it. I just do it to help me along, that's all. I played a many a nights a whole lots of places, played with them fellows, have a time, play all night, and be talking to the Maker. He knows what's in us. He knows what's in all of us.

Besides which, some of those church people can make a pure monkey out of you in drinking. One time I ran around with preachers and that's when I learned something. One old preacher wanted me to go around with him. I lied and told him, said, "That lady that I had, she ran off with all my clothes. I'm not fit to go with you." I would lie to 'em to get away from 'em and it wouldn't do any good. And I say, "And I make fifteen dollars a day. I can't lose that."

He say, "Here." Hand me a twenty-dollar bill. Now, he tell me about all the hideouts. That's right. Don't you think old Rev never can dance. You wrong. Old Rev can dance. They go to a nice private little place, they got a portable record player, and the ladies all come, fine sisters, all sitting around the wall, just sittin' there. That's right. I learned a whole lot about that.

I tell you the way I am. I never be interested in trying to harm people. I never did have time for that. I wouldn't do nothing but try to live. I like to be nice to somebody, treat everybody right.

But I can tell you what you don't know about. Them real dark people, they don't like me. I don't know why not. I wonder myself. I don't know what ails them. Some people are just like that. They just evil. They won't stay away from you, and there are some evil people. They have some kind of grudge against you or jealous. I had eight or ten battles.

I had some eighty-dollar glasses that the superintendent of the moving company had made for me 'cause I had a hard job but I kept it goin' every day. And this other old musician who use to live with me, he and his friend lady, he done away with my devilish glasses 'cause the people thought I was a white man when I wear them. He done away with those glasses. They were tough people all right.

But I had it out with them here. That lady owed me eleven dollars and cursing me out before she would pay me and told me she would call the police. I just told her, "I don't like no violence. We don't suppose to fight." She told me what she would do to me. And I said, "I will have to ask you to leave, please." And she started it again, and I just treated her like she was a man. I sure did. I sent her head over heels. She weighed about one hundred and seventy, and I carried her out head over heels. And I said, "You go get all the law you can get. I'll be right here when you get back."

I don't know why people act that way. I had one say to me, he say, "I'm dark and you bright and wonder what happened?" I say, "Well, one was born in the daytime and the other at night, that's what." But I don't let them people bother me. No, I enjoy myself every day. It's like Christmas every day. I'm proud of me.

I try to do what it say in the Book. I read my big Bible yonder. I don't have no grade in school. Not no one. I don't. I learnt how to read by trying to spell the name of boxcars; well, I just started. And I read in the book, it says, "Love one and another at all times." That's right. That's the reason I learnt to be friendly. I am. I be nice to white and colored.

I have youngsters come out here, them old boys about nineteen or twenty. I treat them nice, tell them what's good, try to show them the way. One of them, a little white kid, he brought me a pint of Heavenly Hills for my birthday. You know, that will kill a brick nearly. But he brought it and it was very courteous and the bottle was pretty.

A fellow told me, he said, "Red, what you let them boys in for?"

I said, "Look here, you understand me now. I been their age. They ain't never been mine." Ain't that right? You don't scorn people. You treat everybody right. When you get down to it, if people think about trying to love one another, brother, everything would be good. If it was like that, they wouldn't need no jailhouse, would they?

Now you got to have feelings. See, that's your religion. You go get that Bible and look under there under the Lord's Prayer and start to reading and that will learn you today. It say, "If you don't forgive man his trespasses, your Heavenly Father will not forgive you." You can't go along on there, got a devil picked up in your heart, say, "I hates him, I hates her." You can't do that. 'Cause if you don't forgive, He won't forgive. And that's final. I believes that. So that's the reason I don't tote no junk like that in me.

If I leave away, if I pass away today, I'll pass away a happy old fellow. I ain't got no black heart.

Lillie May Glover, "Big Mama Blues," at her apartment in Memphis in 1973.
Courtesy of William Leaptrott

# 11 · Big Mama

The woman called Big Mama Blues eased her two-hundred-plus pounds onto her daybed. Lillie May Glover, also called Ma Rainey Two, was ready to talk about her blues and her hoodoos—mojo charms and healing potions, spells and spirit roots, the socks she planted, conjure, chicanery, and bluff.

"Honey, you want me to tell you about that hoodoo? That ain't nothing but junk, just junk," she said, chuckling, slapping her palm on her knee. "I tell you, it's just a racket. Jim Hayden —he was the fellow what stole me away, carried me off on a carnival show to be a blues singer when I was thirteen—he started me on it. He told me that we could make a lot of money telling fortunes, playing like I could read the people's minds and things. He got me a great big marble once, and I set that marble on a glass of water. And I would look at the marble and play like I could see things in it."

"Could you see anything?"

"Not anything, not *anything*." She laughed uproariously, slapping her knee again. "But the people would go for it. Their mind was weak to that. All you got to do is whisper in their ear, and they believe anything you say."

Big Mama's public housing walk-up was but a stone's throw from Beale Street, where mojo artists, herb doctors, peddlers of love potions, dealers in dream books, conjure men, and con men always thrived. Mama—after years of blues singing on the minstrel, carnival, and vaudeville circuits—settled in Memphis in the late twenties and found her hoodoos as much in demand as her blues. She became one of Beale's "hidden hoodooists," unadvertised, unlicensed, and unpopular with the law. Though once she had a hustler at the bus station, waylaying travelers and showing them the way to her door—and keeping a wary eye out for the police—it was mostly through word of mouth that her clients continued to seek her out for solutions to their problems.

One woman wanted to get rid of her man because he beat her and took her money.

"Bring me one of his socks," Big Mama told her. The woman brought the sock, and Big Mama "dressed" it, that is, doused it with cologne and muttered some "magic" words over it. "Now you take this sock and take it down to the creek and throw it in," she commanded. "And just like the water take away that sock, the spell is gonna take away that man." The woman fell into the creek, and her irate sister visited Big Mama later.

"You almost got her drownded," she complained.

"Well, you see she *didn't* get drownded, don't you?" Big Mama said huffily.

"Well, she like to got drownded."

"Just overbalanced. Wasn't nothing gonna happen to her."

In time, Big Mama said, the woman actually did get rid of her man some way or another. "They broke up. It was just one of those things, but she thought for sure I done it."

One client wanted Big Mama to bring her man back. "Poor old lady was on a walking stick," Big Mama said. "Her old man done gone. I said to myself, 'What do she want with a man? She's on a stick, poor old thing.' But I told her to go and bring me some of his socks, I would plant them to make him come back. She went and got a sack full of socks—I mean a tall sack—and she had them stuffed in there. And, honey, all of them was mixed-matched. And I laid out and cried. I hollered, I laughed so hard. God knows, I ought to be ashamed of myself. But she'd washed them socks, and I say, 'Honey, they got to be *dirty*. You gonna have to wait until you get you some dirty ones.'" The woman returned several times, giving Big Mama money as a retainer, but finally told her, "Don't look like he gonna lay down for me to get his socks."

Another client was the old woman with arthritic legs who paid no attention to the fact that Big Mama had similar aches and pains of her own.

I told her I'd give her some medicine for twenty-five dollars, but her case would cost one hundred and fifty dollars outside of the medicine. I got the medicine—some vinegar, some wintergreen, some alcohol, it's a wonder it didn't take the skin off. I told her to grease her legs and rub it on her knees and that would cure her. And she did get cured. She just knowed that I done it, but I guess it was just God's will.

One day I was coming in from the clinic, a-hobbling and trying to get up the steps, my old legs was hurting me so bad. This girl I had rooming with me, she says, "Mama, kinda lighten up, this damn fool's in here waiting on you to give you some money."

I come on in there, and it was this same old woman, but she didn't pay any mind to me limping around. She paid me the money, and when she left, my girl friend say: "She been here two hours talking about how you cured her. There you crawling up the steps. I wanna know this, ain't they got sense enough to know if you can cure them, why in hell don't you do something for yourself?" Which that's the truth. But people, they don't be looking at that, you know.

Like other hoodooists, she made frequent use of the most widely known talisman or charm, the mojo hand, which supposedly can bring back wayward lovers, cast ill fortune on adversaries, or bring good fortune. Many mojos contained such ingredients as Samson's snakeroot, devil's shoestring, or a sandbur called Seed of Earth, all wrapped and sewn in red flannel. Big Mama's wasn't quite so exotic. She relied on flour, sugar, and cologne, with a lump of coal to add weight. "You don't have to have no red flannel, just any kind of red rag will do," she said.

As she recounted the tales of her hoodooing, Big Mama kept insisting that mojo wouldn't work for her or anybody else, but she might not have been quite as skeptical as she professed. "It's some people can tell you things," she avowed. She visited one of them at the insistence of a friend who had volunteered to pay her fee.

"At that time I thought that the doctors I was going to were wrong, that my sickness wasn't real," Big Mama said. "The woman tell me, 'You kind of half-way think that your sickness is not what the doctors tell you. Your sickness is real. But I tell you one thing, you gonna have plenty luck when you leaves here.'" Big Mama paused dramatically. "And sure enough, I have had luck."

What Mama called luck had to do with the regular poker games at her apartment and her success with the cards. Other kinds of luck seemed in short supply. Burdened with heart trouble, diabetes, and rheumatism, she was virtually a prisoner confined to the three rooms of her apartment. But she traveled in time, relishing the recollections of those days when a stagestruck thirteen year old defied her family and ran off with a carnival. "I am the sheep of the family," she said, with only a tinge of regret for "shaming" her family by singing the blues and then compounding the disgrace by trafficking in hoodoos.

All my people church people, understand. My father was a pastor. See, the blues was borned in me, but my people never sung the blues in their life. That's the worst thing in the world to them, the blues was. But they couldn't get those blues out of me.

I was brought up in a sanctified church, but I wanted to be a blues singer. My people paid out more money on me than they did the rest of the children. They tried to make a music teacher out of me. I learnt how to play my scales, do re mi. That's all I learnt in three years. I don't care what you done, what you tried to make me be, I just had to sing the blues.

We were living in Nashville, Tennessee, and they had a carnival show that came there. You could sing the blues for a prize. My people didn't allow me out, understand, but I slipped up there with another girl and slipped up on the stage and I sang the blues. Someone went home and got my people. They like to killed me.

But the prize she had won in the singing contest—and perhaps the whipping she got at home—led her to run off with Jim

Hayden and the carnival. Hayden, whose ability as a trumpet player and comedian was exceeded only by his skill as a con artist, found a natural pupil in young Lillie May Hardison. The two split off from the carnival and joined a medicine show, traveling in rattletrap cars and a flatbed truck from one small southern town to another. The troupe would park in an empty lot, let down the platform, and start the music and the jokes to draw a crowd. All the performers hawked the medicine—cure-all salves and tonics ("which it wasn't good for nothing," Big Mama said) —but Hayden and his protégée added a few concoctions of their own. They mixed potash and iodine, for example, as a tonic for rheumatism ("It ain't gonna hurt you," she assured us. "Potash and iodine is good for your blood."), and they combined glycerine and calamine lotion as a makeup to lighten the complexion.

"We almost got run out of Mississippi for selling that stuff, that crap, that medicine, and telling fortunes. The sheriff told us that if we didn't get out of town, why, he was going to throw us in jail, on account of all that phony stuff we put down. We left there, all right enough, but we kept on; it didn't stop us. We took our old piece of car and went on to the next town."

In their wanderings from one traveling show to another Big Mama at first worked mainly in the chorus. Finally she persuaded Hayden to give her a chance as a comedian. She was convinced this made her an early women's liberationist; the "dirty dozens" and off-color humor that characterized the comedy of the traveling shows were largely a male domain.

I made me some red plaid overalls and bought me a white shirt at a Salvation Army. I taken those white tennis shoes and put some of the plaid in them, and I put the tennies on the wrong foot. Then I got in front of the looking glass and locked the door and talked to myself to say what I was going to say, just so I could get it down pat. And I didn't mind looking in the looking glass in them days. I was small then. I used to didn't be as fat as I am now. I used to didn't weigh but 135.

One night Jim taken a chance on me and let me open the olio. The olio, that's when the comedian come on behind the chorus and start to doing the jokes. So I come on out in blackface, everybody wondering whether I was a boy or girl or what. And I danced a while, then I told them, "Hold it, hold it, don't go no further till you hear from Mama." And I commenced a-talking, doing my jokes, and I just brought the house down.

From then on it was as comedian and blues singer that she performed in medicine and minstrel shows, carnivals, and vaudeville. Her traveling began in 1919 and continued through the golden age of the classic women blues singers, her path crossing at one time or another with Bessie Smith, Ida Cox, Ethel Waters, Sara Martin, and Ma Rainey. She recalled appearing on the same show with Ma for two weeks at the old Frolic Theater in Birmingham.

The original Ma Rainey was fat, just like I am. And she wasn't quite as tall as I am. And she wore a wig all the time. Now, she was hard. Her people, she couldn't get along with her people. She drank, and you know, quite naturally when you drink, you don't do so well with your people. And she was one of these types, she knew that she was the manager over you and she was just absolutely the boss.

But she had a voice from here to yonder. You would hear her, I guess, three or four blocks. That's the reason they started calling me Baby Ma Rainey, because I had a voice just like her. I have worked with the Rabbit Foot Minstrels in a big tent when the mike got out of fix, and I sang without a mike. The boss said he had never had nobody do that. I had a voice.

Besides the Rabbit Foot Minstrels, she also traveled with the Bronze Mannequins, the Vampin' Baby Show, the Georgia Minstrels, Harlem in Havana, and others. She was with Nina Benson's Medicine Show when she first visited Memphis and Beale Street in 1928; and from then on, even though she was "backwards and forwards" on the road, Memphis was her home base. After her marriage to Willie Glover, a cook in a Memphis restaurant, her on-stage appearances were at night spots around Memphis and occasionally at the Midnight Rambles, the risqué revue staged weekly for white audiences at the Palace Theater. She also performed frequently in the Palace's amateur shows, and at one time or another sang in many of the clubs in the Beale area—Citizens Club, Manhattan Club, Coca-Cola Club, Hotel Improvement Club. And when she wasn't working on Beale, she'd be playing on Beale, roaming from joint to joint, drinking corn whisky out of short, flat bottles called "slabs" at twenty-five cents a bottle.

"It was always a piano in the back of the joints, and drums," she said. "The boys would play and I'd sing, and we'd just call ourselves balling. Especially on Thursdays, which is cooks' ball day, when the cooks got paid. The boys would be on the stem for the cooks on Thursday because they knowed the cooks was going to get off and spend their money."

Among others Big Mama recalled singing and drinking with on Beale in various eras were Memphis Slim (Peter Chatman, blues pianist, now living in Paris) and none other than Bessie Smith. "I had met Bessie on the road, and when she came to Memphis to play the Palace, she'd stop to see me," she said. Bessie's favorite hangout was the Chicago House, a back-alley cafe where she could get her favorite food, pigs' feet. "It wasn't nothing but a dump, but we'd go around and have a jam session, see if we could out-sing the other. Lots of times we'd sneak off in the daytime and go to those clubs and drink. Bessie was drinking pretty heavy then," Big Mama said.

Tough, explosive, often belligerent, Bessie was known for her brawls with men or women, and she found a kindred spirit in Big Mama. In the rough days on Beale, when staying out of a fight was often a problem, Mama went looking for trouble. Banned from some of the joints because she had raised so much hell, she'd stand outside—often with a pistol in her purse—while her companions went in. "We'd go just to start a fight. We'd look them up." Once the fight began, she would post herself by the door to polish off any combatant who got that far, usually with a good lick with the pistol butt. "One time there was a garbage can by the door. Somebody would come out and I'd slap him across the head with the garbage can lid."

She regarded her reputation as "a pretty tough boy" in much

the same manner she considered her background in hoodoo: she was a little ashamed and a little proud. "It was the mean low-downness in me. I don't know why I did it," she said.

In those days, Beale was the place to be for action, and where the action was, Mama was: shooting craps on the corner on Sundays, with a lookout posted for the police; missing a meal to put her last dime on the numbers, the policy game that all Beale was devoted to like a religion; playing pokeno (a form of Bingo) in the back room of Pee Wee's saloon; getting juiced on corn whisky bought from a barrel in the back of a honky-tonk; playing the dozens, both for fun and for fights; cavorting until 3 A.M. on Sunday because "they say if you didn't have a ball on Saturday night, it wasn't worth living."

By the late 1940s, Beale was still the place to be, but both Beale and Big Mama had become tamer. Some of the clubs had closed, and those still open were relying more and more on jukeboxes instead of piano players and blues singers. For most musicians, Big Mama included, times were harder than in the hard times of the 1930s.

Among the hungry blues people walking the street was Riley King, just up from Indianola, Mississippi. Big Mama took a liking to him and claimed credit for talking him out of quitting the blues. She told of meeting him at Hamburger Heaven after a gig that brought each performer fifteen cents. "I'm telling you, Mom, I'm ready to give it up. We ain't doing no good," King said wearily. "No, you can't quit," she told him. "I think I'm quitting the racket, 'cause I been at it so long, but you keep on, 'cause you're going places."

One of her proudest moments came years later after B. B. King had indeed gone places. He took her with him to Jackson, Tennessee, for a concert and called her to the stage to thank her for her early role in his career.

By the 1950s Beale Street had slowed down so much that Mama found herself playing more and more for white audiences

—at variety shows, at parties, in major hotels such as the Peabody, and on riverboat excursions.

It was at a white night spot—the Cotton Club in West Memphis, Arkansas—that Mama spent seven years performing, the longest booking of her life. Being at the Cotton Club was something like old times for her; the brawling in this hangout for roughneck whites was as prevalent as it had been in the dives on Beale. "Them women would have a hair pulling and a pocketbook fight. If their man got in a fight with another, they'd start to jumping on the man with a pocketbook, take off their shoes, and hit him. I had me a ball. I used to get on the bandstand and referee."

Often she carried her own troupe—a "shake dancer," a band, and Robert Couch, a dancer-comedian known as Bones, who had played with her on Amateur Nights. At times she sang with other bands, even a white hillbilly group. She sang their country and rock-and-roll songs (appropriately enough, in view of her other career, "I Got My Mojo Working" was her most popular number), but she sang her songs, too—what she called "the plain old everyday blues." In so doing, she took her place alongside better-known black singers who popularized their music among whites and thus helped to create the so-called blue-eyed blues.

Wherever she sang them, the blues were always special to her.

You got to sing the blues with your soul. It looks like you hurt in the deep-down part of your heart. You really hurt when you sing the blues. Blues can make you cry. I was singing at a little old club and I'd just sit down and sing, just sing, I'd sing the blues. I remember times I sanged the blues, I just cried, just deliberate cried. And I told the people I didn't know what was wrong with me, but it just got me. And my boss man used to tell me, "Go on and get it out of you, old lady, just help yourself."

There was never enough money to live on from either of Mama's careers, and so almost always she had an outside job. She worked as a cook, as a cleanup woman for a trucking line, as a stacker for a fence company, and at a lumber company where "my boss said I was the best man he had there."

Money or no money, though, show business came first. "I'm gonna tell you about show business," she said. "I have worked shows, come in before day, and gone up there and clean up at that trucking line. I have quit many a job to go and make fifteen cents a night."

She had never lost the longing for the spotlight. Even with her many ailments, at times she slipped off to some small night-club out of her past. Invariably the crowd demanded that she sing, and invariably she obliged. She even took occasional book-ings, along with other old-timers, for promoter and blues buff Harry Godwin.

Everybody say my voice still strong, and when I get a band, I can swing. My words get tied up a little bit on account of my teeth, and I can't stand those (she pointed to her upper plate she had placed in a glass of water). I do get hoarse. I are easy to get hoarse quickly. But my voice is not trembly like some of the old singers. My voice ought to be wore out by now as much as I have hollered—screamed and hollered all night long.

I'm sixty-some years old, and it look like I can't get over show business. I tell you, I used to cry after the first time the doctor told me I'd never be well no more and I couldn't work. I was just hurt itself. Now, sometimes things come over that TV, dances and things I used to do, and I lay here and just boohoo. I was a good dancer. Can't hardly walk now.

I sing the blues for myself. Sometimes they do me some good. It helps you to sing the blues when you're feeling blue.

The blues continued to come, but so did her laughter. The great raucous roars rocked her round stomach and her daybed as she regaled her visitors: small boys who came by to take out her garbage and earn rewards of homemade cookies and cakes, shake dancers and bandsmen who worked with her, occasional clients seeking Madam Ma Rainey's mojo, and poker-playing buddies (all male) trying to recoup earlier losses and, quite often, de-parting still poorer.

She was satisfied that she didn't go to the devil, after all, despite the warnings from her family that the blues were the devil's music and she would come to no good end. "I've been out in the world and I've scuffled for myself and I've never been in no trouble—nothing but fighting," she said. "I have fought, you know, but serious trouble I've never had. My family, they tried to make something outta me. They wanted me to be somebody. Which I made somebody, but not the type of person they wanted me to be."

Hammie Nixon, worldwide traveling companion of Sleepy John Estes, playing his kazoo at a blues festival in Memphis in 1980.
Courtesy of Memphis *Press-Scimitar*

# 12 · Sleepy John and Hammie

They came in the back door of the place called High Cotton soon after it opened for business at noon on Sunday: the old man, gaunt and stooped and in dark glasses, led gently by a rotund companion wearing a beret and a blue happicoat with a dragon stitched on the back. He put down the guitar case he was carrying and seated the old man at a table. "This here is Sleepy John Estes, and I'm Hammie Nixon," he said to the waiter. "I and John gonna sing you some blues."

Lunch was part of their pay. Hammie tucked a napkin under the collar of John's faded work shirt to protect his wrinkled tie and worn suit. He reached over occasionally to guide John's fork to the potatoes or to dab away the ketchup on his chin.

Their audience trickled in, mostly young whites. Several came by the table to meet Sleepy John for the first time. He left most of the talking to Hammie, who told about their blues tours in Czechoslovakia, England, and France, where he got the beret, and to Japan, where the promoters had given him the happicoat. John preferred his battered hat and his old suit. "We gonna have a pretty good congregation, John," Hammie said softly. By the time they were ready to begin the show, there were about fifty present.

John carefully tuned the electric guitar Hammie had bought him for the foreign tours, and they swung easily into the songs that had brought Sleepy John Estes some fame if not fortune— "Someday Baby Blues," "I Ain't Gonna Be Worried No More,"

"Diving Duck Blues," "Corinna, Corinna." They did the latter in a call-and-response style, John's high-pitched but soft wail mixing perfectly with Hammie's more guttural harmonizing. Hammie alternated between kazoo and harmonica, then brought out an empty gallon jug that he whirled and twirled and blew into. A young white man from the audience joined them with a jug of his own, and Hammie gave him some pointers. With some coaxing, Hammie did one of his "blue blues" numbers ("I'd love to dig your potatoes, / I'd like to get tangled up in your yellow yams"). They closed the performance the same way they'd been doing for years, against the objections of those who said they shouldn't mix sacred songs with devil music, their voices blending fervently on "Holy Spirit, Don't Leave Me in the Hands of the Wicked World."

John had another beer and Hammie another diet drink as they packed to go. It had been a good day; they'd had a satisfying meal, put on a good show for an appreciative audience, and picked up a few dollars. Hammie led John to their old car and drove them back home to Brownsville and the living blues.

• • •

We visited them on a chilled gray afternoon in January. It was thawing after a recent snow, and the car barely made it through the mudholes along the short, crooked road leading to the dirty-white clapboard shack with tin roof. We were a quarter-mile off Highway 70, the straight shoot to Memphis that was to West Tennessee blues musicians what Highway 61 was to those in the Mississippi Delta.

Ankle-deep mud filled the yard and pathway leading to the tiny porch where John Estes preferred to sit and play his blues, and talk about them, for his visitors. But the day was too cold, and his wife ushered us inside. She told us not to worry about the mud we tracked in; the bare wooden floor was already streaked with it, almost slippery.

Three young children were half-sitting, half-lying on the floor, chins cupped in their hands, watching television. The television set itself rested flat against the floor. In the middle of the room, contrasting starkly with the rest of the furnishings, stood a shiny new avocado-green electric cook stove. Mrs. Estes was heating a pot of water on the stove.

She showed us to the other room where John waited, sitting on one of two ancient iron beds next to an open gas heater. It seemed stifling, but he had a tattered coat on over a wrinkled plaid shirt buttoned to the neck. He wore his large black sunglasses with rubber on the ear-pieces to make them stay up. The socks sagging over the tops of his mud-smeared brogans were mismatched, one blue and one red.

"Y'all make yourselves to home," he mumbled through his chew of tobacco. "Just set anywheres." He gestured toward the other bed and an old sofa with springs sticking out and foam rubber showing. Dirty clothes were piled high on both the bed and the sofa, as well as on two decrepit upholstered chairs and in two large pasteboard boxes. Cardboard from other boxes patched the walls and the gap at the bottom of the door. One of the cardboard sections on the wall pictured a smiling middle-class family telling us to BUY NOW AND SAVE.

Hammie Nixon stomped in, jovial but—without his beret, bundled up in two sweaters and a heavy coat instead of the happicoat—not so dashing a figure as in his appearance at High Cotton. He immediately solved the problem of how to work the tape recorder in a room with no electrical outlets; he ran the cord under the door and plugged it into the single socket in the living room, thus cutting off the television. "Y'all run along now," he told the children. "I and John gonna be interviewed."

Thinking hard, talking softly in monosyllables, pausing occasionally to soothe his whimpering two-year-old grandson he held in his lap, John Adam Estes told about being born into the natural blues as one of sixteen children of a sharecropping family on a farm near Ripley, Tennessee, in 1903. His introduction to the blues music born of such a life didn't come until after the family moved to Brownsville, when he was eleven.

A fellow was going with my sister, and them days a boy walk about four or five miles, you know, to see a girl. He come through by our house every evening, and I got to following behind him. There was this little old place called Low Gum Tree, and my sister said, "Brother, don't go no further than Gum Tree, hear? Turn around." Well, I go back in them hills anyway, come out playing a song every evening. I didn't have no guitar, but I acted like I had a guitar, don't you know.

Then I got me a broom handle, took the wire off of it, and made me a guitar out of an old cigar box. Started playing on that one finger there, I'd catch the sound from that one finger. And finally I playing. My daddy told mother, said, "That boy's going to make music. You live to see it." So I get out there and get to scrapping that cotton, and he bought me a real guitar.

And so I taken that guitar, started playing. I could play as long as it stayed tuned. I'd take it over to a friend's house and he'd tune it for me. That lasted me about a week. I kept on, finally learned how to tune one finger at a time. That's where I started from.

Soon after that, young Estes slung his guitar over his shoulder and hit the road, though at first—and for several years—he stayed close to Brownsville. He'd join other musicians playing for "cotton pickings"—parties blending work and pleasure late in the harvest season. When cold weather came, the field hands often would pull rather than pick the cotton remaining to be harvested, yanking boll and all from the stalk. "A wagon bring it up to the house, and that night they have a cotton picking inside the house to get the cotton from the bolls," he said. "We'd set up and pop popcorn, bake a cake, and have lemonade or something, all you want to eat and drink free, and then they pick cotton for a while." Sometimes his music making brought him, in addition to free food, as much as a dollar a night.

Later he performed on various medicine shows and in the twenties traveled a regular circuit with other blues men around

Brownsville, Ripley, and Jackson—a golden triangle with a blues vein as rich perhaps as that of the Mississippi Delta. The coterie included Willie Newbern, Brownsville guitarist. ("That's the one that started me out," said Estes. "He played all around everywhere, never would do nothing but play the guitar.") Also included was the original Sonny Boy Williamson, Jackson harmonica man. ("I started him out. He traveled some with me on weekends. He was the best there was.") And there were Yank (James) Rachel, Brownsville mandolin player; Jab Jones, piano; Brownsville Son Bonds, a guitarist; and Noah Lewis, another harmonica player, from Ripley.

During his rounds in the 1920s, Estes discovered young Hammie Nixon. "I was eleven years old, and up come John, had a little old picnic to play for at Union, where I was born and raised up at about ten miles from here," Hammie said. "And so he had heard me playing that harmonica, which I had learned it from Noah Lewis, and John said, 'Come on, help me,' said 'We'll just rack the money.' I think they was paying him about six dollars. That was big money. He asked my mother, said 'How about letting him go to town with me? I bring him back tomorrow.' 'Course, John was always a big liar, you know. And he kept me about six months, all in Memphis, Arkansas, Missouri."

John smiled. "He was just a kid. He'd get homesick and I'd say, 'You play good tonight, now, I take you home tomorrow.'"

"So we ease on back in about six months," Hammie continued, "and then he begged me to go with him somewhere else. We took out again, went to hoboing."

Even though Estes was the leader, Nixon the follower, John recalled that it was Hammie who taught him how to hop a freight.

He'd take my guitar and his jug, which he played the jug, too, and he'd take all that stuff and swing onto the train with one arm. I couldn't even catch it with not anything. I be holding onto that train with mouth, teeth, knee, and everything. And sometimes when I finally catch ahold and climb on, we get throwed right off. Them special agents, railroad police, they all over the place. We at Bowling Green, Kentucky, and every time we try to catch the train, we got drove off. So I said, "Hammie, I'm going to make a song about this." And I made a song, "Railroad Police Blues." But me and Hammie, we liked to leave our tracks on the railroad.

At one point, John worked for the railroad, singing for a lining gang, in the call-and-response technique so prevalent not only in the blues but in church songs. "Captain, Captain, what time of day you got? Bam!" Hammie sang, illustrating. "He holler, 'Hurry but I'm taking my time.' Bam! Everybody hit at the same time." John sang:

> John Henry had a woman.
> The dress she wore was red.
> She went down the tracks, she never look back
> But I wonder why John Henry fell dead."

"Bam!" said Hammie, laughing.

If they weren't on the railroad, they were on the dusty country roads leading to some frolic, church picnic, or house party, the good timer with the guitar and the young companion with jug and harp. "We go up and down the road playing music," Hammie said. "Sometimes mostly it was for whites. White folks be after us when the sun go down. We sneak off and go play for some colored folks, white folks come get us. I and John played everywhere you can think of and then some—churches, barrelhouses, picnics, parties, just anywhere we'd get paid or fed." John grunted. "And a lot of places where we didn't get nothing," he said. Then, almost wistfully, he added: "But me and Hammie, we liked them days. Out there traveling with my guitar on my back, that was the best time of my life."

The best time of all perhaps came just before the hard times signaled by the Wall Street crash of October, 1929. Starting in mid-September, Estes made his first recordings for Victor in Memphis. They included "Broken Hearted, Ragged and Dirty Too," "The Girl I Love, She Got Long Curly Hair," and "Diving

Duck Blues," which is similar to "Rye Whisky" and which he said he heard Blind Lemon Jefferson sing on Front Street in Memphis. James Rachel on mandolin and Jab Jones on piano joined Estes in those first recording sessions. He cut several more records the following May—"Milk Cow Blues," "Poor John Blues," "My Black Gal Blues" among them—but the deepening depression blocked the field trips of the recording companies, and Estes and Hammie went back to scuffling on street and roadside. They spent much of their time on Beale or in the Memphis "hobo jungle," a commune-like collection of drifters like themselves. Hammie still speaks in awe about their days on Beale.

"Now it sounds like a story but I'm telling you the truth, Beale Street wasn't nothing but good timers and guys walking the street and telling fortunes and conning you and cheating you," he said. "They was just slick people going up and down that Beale Street. You never seen anything like it."

He chuckled about a blues contest on Beale, in which the great Big Bill Broonzy finished second but grabbed first prize—a bottle of whisky—and ran off with it. About that time Hammie picked Big Bill's pocket. "I never pulled a trick like that before, but Big Bill had a pocketful of money, and I fooled around and went to work with these two fingers and got that pocketbook, got the money out and stuck the pocketbook back in his pocket. So he didn't know which way the money went. I decided that I ain't gonna do that no more."

When the young, adventurous Nixon split up with Sleepy John to hobo alone to Chicago, he made the mistake of boasting that he was up from Memphis. He learned that there was less respect than distrust for, and sometimes fear of, Beale Streeters.

You know, when I first went to Chicago, I couldn't hardly get a room. I thought maybe it would help me to say I was from Memphis, but come to find out, everywhere I go, they'd say, "You from *Memphis*? Oh, I done already rent that room out." And finally someone told me, said, "What you say you from Memphis for? Don't tell nobody you from Memphis, man, you never do no good here."

You know, many people who live in Memphis don't hardly know what Beale Street is. But anybody away from there, they think everybody out of Memphis comes off of Beale Street.

He figured that was about like thinking anybody in Chicago of that era was connected with the Capone gang, for whom he occasionally made music with his jug, harmonica, washboard, and washtub. Hammie told of playing for Al Capone himself.

That's the goddog's truth. They strictly dope people—you know, Eye-talian gangsters. I never did hustle that dope, but they liked our music. And the head knockers, see, they had barns set up all over, where they'd send the mens out from, on calls. And we'd go there to play for them. And Al Capone, he used to be at the barn there, you see. Come up in one of those big cars with chauffeurs and everything, you know. And he'd come in there and drop some money on you, maybe twenty dollars at a time. As he was coming back, he liable to throw another twenty at you. Oh, he was crazy about that music, now. You got to cut up and act a fool, though. I always acted a fool. See, I'd take them jugs and turn them over and flip them thisaway and thataway and throw them away from me.

Nixon teamed with another Tennessee traveling companion, Brownsville Son Bonds—on their blues-gospel numbers he became Brother Son Bonds—at three recording sessions for Decca in 1934. But the partnership was short lived; Nixon returned to Tennessee and persuaded Estes to hop a freight with him to Chicago. "We jumped back in there moving. He was looking for me and I was looking for him," Hammie said. "So I and John been together ever since. And—well, we did pretty good."

They played mostly at house rent parties and in Chicago's Maxwell Street market area, which became a gathering place for many of the blues musicians, particularly those from the deep South. It was there that Sleepy John attracted the attention of recording scout Mayo Williams, who rented a new guitar for him and told him and Hammie to report to his recording studio on Lakeshore Drive the next day. Hammie laughed as he told how John promptly ruined the guitar and almost wrecked his recording career that night.

We done got ahold of some moonshine, you know, and that stuff went to working in John's head there. We going along on the street, John with that new guitar and me with that jug, only it wasn't a empty jug, you understand, and some ladies hollered down from the third floor, say "Hey, y'all come up and play us a tune." So we hauls up on that third floor, and it turns out that it's a *preaching*. We commenced playing for them, and they said, "Oh, now, we don't go for these blues," and so we went to playing that song about "I'm going to live so God can use me anywhere and anytime." We had them preachers jumping up there and shouting. And then one of the girls, she didn't talk like John thought she was going to talk, and so he got mad and jumped up to make the go out the door and stepped over the steps. And he fell all the way down from the third floor down to the bottom, and he fell plumb through that guitar. Plumb *through* it. And John is out cold, and—well, here I am handicapped. I'm like a ship without a trail. He ain't making no kind of move. And I went to rubbing his neck, and I picked him up and swung him a few times, and then I bought him another half-pint, and he finally came around, but his neck was sore. So I and John finally got straightened out and went on up to the record shop there the next morning.

Two sessions during which they cut six sides for Chess in July of 1935 brought them an invitation to record in New York for Decca, and they hit the road, hitchhiking and freight hopping all the way. "Hey, Hammie, you remember that one lady, when I asked her for a drink of water, she was going to charge me a dime?" Estes said. "And the toll bridge, it took us a dime to cross that toll bridge, and us with not a nickel to both our names. Hammie said, 'Come on, boy, hit that guitar.' I hit the guitar, and they let us walk on across the bridge."

In New York, Charlie Pickett's guitar and Lee Brown's kazoo joined them on August 2 and 3, 1935, as they recorded some of the songs born of hard times and hard living. They included "Hobo Jungle Blues," "Floating Bridge," which grew out of a high-water drama in which Hammie saved Sleepy John from drowning after their car went off a bridge, "Poor Man's Friend (T-Model Blues)," "Government Money," and "I Ain't Gonna Be Worried No More."

They returned to New York in 1937 for another session, and again in 1938. Estes was at his peak as a country blues man in these years, and by 1941 he was even beginning to branch out. In September of that year, he jived with Son Bonds and Raymond Thomas on "When the Saints Go Marching In" for Bluebird in Chicago. But then came the union war on jukeboxes and the cutback in recording and, for Sleepy John and Hammie as well as many another blues man, a decade of nomadic obscurity.

Their hoboing ended in 1949 when John married, settled down in Memphis, and started a family. Hammie took a job as a chauffeur and sometime cook, dropping in frequently to check on his old friend, whose vision by now was fast fading. He had lost the sight in one eye as the result of an errant baseball years before; he blamed bad working hours and bad whisky for the loss of the other.

"In 1951, they carried me to John Gaston Hospital (City Hospital in Memphis)," John said. "A doctor got to working on my eyes, and it worked. Done pretty good for a while. And so then he put me on the bed, and he told one boy to hold my hand and the other my feet. I come up off that thing. I got loose and ran with my gown on, came on home."

Soon after, he moved his family—with Hammie following—back to Brownsville. There they remained, not so much singing their blues as living them. The interest in old-time blues men in the 1960s, their trip to Europe as part of the 1964 American Folk Festival, and their subsequent overseas tours, helped—but not much. A few past-due royalty checks for Sleepy John, thanks to the efforts of a lawyer friend in Brownsville, also helped—but not much.

Hammie swore he never received a penny in royalties. "Some people," he said, "got black hearts."

• • •

When we returned a month later for another interview, the sun was out and the wind was still, and they had set the stage—the tiny front porch—for a show. They started it with some "cross firing," a cousin of the minstrel show patter, the way they did in their days on the road.

Then came song after song, delivered as though they were giving a command performance before a huge audience, Sleepy John in the spotlight first, followed by Hammie, gulping down a diet drink and then blowing the bottle into musical life, mocking the hounds on his harp, making music with tissue paper and comb, and even yodeling as he sang the train songs of Jimmie Rodgers. This time they let their music do their talking. It was as though they were saying, "Listen, if you want our story, hear what we sing, not what we say."

Leaving, we asked them who they considered to be the best at their kind of blues. "Sonny Boy Williamson, I guess," Sleepy John said. "The original Sonny Boy. He learned it from me." Hammie didn't hesitate. "I and John," he said.

The living blues for Sleepy John ended with his death on June 5, 1977, the same day he was to leave for another tour in Europe.

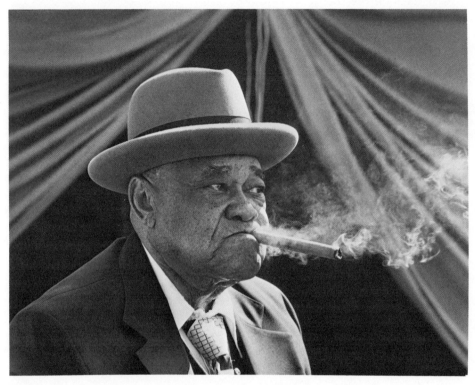

Roosevelt Sykes, "the Honeydripper," in New Orleans in 1980.
Courtesy of Lee Crum

# 13 · The Honeydripper

It was November in New Orleans, and the sultry heat of early fall had eased into balminess. The windows were up in the living room of Roosevelt Sykes's house on Louisa Street, and he wore a short-sleeved white shirt open at the neck and light-blue, summer-weight pants. His heavy stomach pushed against the buttons of the shirt and spilled over the belt of the trousers.

He ignored the overstuffed sofa and chairs slip-covered in a flower-and-bird print to sit astride a straight-backed chair, his stomach bumping the rungs. In one hand he held a stumpy black cigar that he brandished, munched on occasionally, but never lit.

"My name is Roosevelt Sykes, professionally known as the Honeydripper, born in Helena, Arkansas, January 31, 1906," he started the interview. Only the flecks of gray at his temples gave any indication that he was that old. His light-tan, freckled skin was unwrinkled, his receding hairline hadn't receded any farther in the last thirty years, and his barrel-shaped body—its roundness suggesting the kind of toy that bounces back when it is tipped over—was unbowed by age.

He talked about living with relatives in Saint Louis, where he was sent to go to school after his parents died, and the summers he spent with his preacher-schoolteacher grandfather, working on the farm outside Helena. He was about fifteen, he said, "when I got a little mannish and runned away. Well, the main thing was, I said there *must* be something better than me gettin' up early in the morning. If I could get up after ten or eleven o'clock in the day, then I wouldn't mind go and chop the cotton, plow, whatsomever to be done. But I got to get up *early*. I say, 'I'm leaving here. There must be something better somewhere. I can't do no worser.' Well, I lit out and been out ever since."

Then came years when he rode the rails and wandered the roads, based at first in Saint Louis, then later in Chicago. "I wasn't going no place hardly to stay too long," he said. "Nobody crying about nowhere I just left, and wasn't nobody expecting me where I was going. I had nothing to worry about, nobody looking for me, and I ain't looking for nobody. I's happy as a lark."

And in all the years, from the time he started playing at joints in Helena for "a dollar and a red pop," music was his master, and his way of life.

People used to call guitars "starvation boxes." When a guy couldn't play good enough to make no money but he refused to work, he wouldn't put that guitar down, then they'd say, "You put that guitar down and do something, get you a job." He'd say no. They'd say, "That's starvation. Just going to starve you to death, that guitar." Well, that's the same way with me with the piano. When I did get started, I wouldn't do nothing else, just play the piano. Sometime I had something, sometime I didn't, but I just stick with the piano. If I didn't play, I didn't eat.

To help out with the eating, he bootlegged whisky, ran fried fish and barbecue joints, and operated a cab, but always as a sideline. Music was always the main line. In a career that spanned more than fifty years and touched upon the lives of most of the major blues musicians of this century, he worked the levee camps and sawmill towns of southern Mississippi with Little Brother Montgomery, Lee Green, and Sunnyland Slim (Albert Luandrew); he played at Katy Red's honky-tonk in East Saint Louis when Peetie Wheatstraw, Henry Brown, and Alice Moore were regulars there; he traveled with St. Louis Jimmy Oden and wrote several songs with him; he was one of the dominant figures of the Chicago scene when Tampa Red, Lonnie Johnson, Big Bill Broonzy, and Sonny Boy Williamson held forth. He recorded early—beginning in 1929—and prolifically; from 1934 until the beginning of World War II, he had a new record issued every few weeks. Muddy Waters grew up with his record of the "Forty-four Blues," Memphis Slim emulated his style for years, and thousands of whites who didn't know his name knew his music, like "The Honeydripper" and "Nighttime's the Right Time."

One of the biggest names in the blues revival, he had made the blues concert circuit in Europe for the past fifteen years and, with Little Brother, practically had a lock on the piano spot for major festivals. He traveled out of New Orleans three or four times a month, playing colleges, theaters, festivals, nightclubs.

"Look like I'm going more now than I ever did," he said. "I don't stay here. I'm always going someplace, Chicago, New York, France. I traveled so much, you know, I been everywhere. I seen so many cities and towns and countries 'til I get to sleep at night, sometimes I wake up, forget what town I went to bed in."

In all those years, he played many types of music, but in his own mind, he remained a blues man. And on that balmy day, sitting spraddle-legged on his straight chair, his gold tooth flashing as he smiled, he talked about the blues.

Blues is a peculiar thing. You mostly have to be done born with it. You can't teach it. It's a feeling. It's the same as trying to teach somebody how to feel.

Jazz you can learn from reading music—they got notes for you to read and go by. Now the guy that wrote a song, he got a feeling, he can feel, he could be a blues man. He wrote it. But the guys who play it, they don't know how he felt when he wrote, but still they can play it like he got it. They got the shell. They didn't get the solid insides.

Some people, they's supposed to have been playing the blues, but they wasn't really playing the blues. They were finished musicians, but they didn't really want to get deep because they says, well, blues too low. Well, one thing about it, they can't understand it. Anything you can't understand, you just say, "I can't handle it, can't do it like I wants." Some of them could play, like Duke [Ellington], he can play it. But nobody can teach you. You ask me to teach you to play the blues, I says, "I can't do it, you got to get it yourself." It just have to come out of you.

Blues is just mostly from the heart. Jazz, you can learn it. If you want, you can read it. You can play jazz from your eyes. Put the music up there, keep your eye up there, and you can still go, playing from your eyes. But blues, you play from your heart. If a big wind come and the band playing and the wind blow the music off the stand, you ain't gonna hear no more jazz 'til they done picked their music up. The wind stop the band. But when you playing the blues and it's coming from your heart, can't nothing stop it. And play *your* way.

It's good to know music. But it's best to learn to play by your ear, by your heart first. And then you won't let the music take you over. You'll begin to want to do nothing but what you can read. You say, "Oh, it's the easy way." You can just slap it up there. See now, to compose something, I got to sit down and figure it out, how I gonna do it. Then I make it, it become a song, and then people can do the song. But I sat right there and done it on nothing.

Blues is like a doctor. Doctor studies medicine—'course he ain't sick, but he studies to help them people. A blues player ain't got no blues, but he plays for the worried people. He has the talent to give to the worried people. See, they enjoy it. Like the doctor works from the outside of the body to the inside of the body. But the blues works on the insides of the inside. See?

Everybody has the blues that I know. You couldn't say that a person plays the blues 'cause he got worried, because there's a thousands a people worried to death, house done burned down, lost their family, and can't sing a tune. If that's the case that worried people play the blues, you'd be surprised at how many people sing the blues. That's not the case. Blues is a talent you're born with from God, Jesus Christ.

See, you have to be born with that talent. It's a gift given by God. The Heavenly Father, He give me the gift. I don't take no credit. I give the credit to God. I didn't even take a lesson in my life.

Like anything else, the more you do it, look like you're successful with it, why then you get after it more, get more into it. Same with a mechanic. Be surprised at the kicks he get out of a old jalopy when he get through with it. It's crickety when it roll up there. When he get through with it, it sound so pretty that he just gets a thrill, just what *he* done. So that's a gift to him, see.

Blues is like salt. It has to go in everything. You make a cake, it's sweet, but you got to put a little salt in it. Ice cream got salt in it. If you go to a place and order a steak, it can be a every-so-fine steak, cost you five dollars, but look what they got settin' side of it for nothing—salt and black pepper. Now that steak, as much as it cost, it's no good if it don't have a little salt on it. Blues is to music what salt is to food. Blues most have to be in all music. Classic and the opera got five percent blues. And jazz got fifty percent blues.

Blues is in all nations. All races has got the blues, Chinese people, Germans, everybody got something that is blues to him in his vocabulary. We say yes—that means okay. Frenchman say oui—that means okay. That's French for yes. "You going downtown today?" He say oui. That means he going. If you going, you say, yeah. You going right on. Same going, you know.

So that's the way it is with the blues. All races has got 'em, but they ain't like blues; they're different, but within them, they got something. I went to a place in Weims, which is Vienna, Austria. It was a festival we played there, and this guy was playing a strange kind of music on guitar. Some of them peoples was crying, them Germans, sitting there crying. Wiped me out. He didn't sound like nothing to me while he was doing it, but it was knocking them peoples out. So I say, "Oh, that guy's got it. He's got the blues."

Blues is different in different places. It's something can't be explained. It comes with the sound. It's different style. Like people talks different, well, their blues is different, too. You can tell what style it is when you hear it, but you don't know why.

By me being a-traveling and associating with different musicians and folks give me music in all parts of the country, I play a little like the Memphians, little like the Chicagoians, play a little like the Vicksburg, Mississippians, play a little bit like the Texians, a little western stuff, do a little jazz of the New Orleans style. See, I had a variety, which I do have now, you know.

This town here, New Orleans, this is actually a jazz town. So is Memphis, so is Chicago. Memphis always was a jazz town. But a lot of blues players come in there. Just like Chicago. They say Chicago blues. Sure, they had blues—blues players all left the South and went there. But every one of them blues players, including me, they all from the South. Chicago ain't got no blues.

When I first go in Chicago, you could play the blues from Twenty-ninth Street up to Thirty-fifth. When you get to Forty-seventh Street, no more. Nothing but jazz. But later years, blues would ease on in. Muddy Waters come up with good blues, and then they wants us to play. People thought that was the very thing.

I went in a place—all those people, they're high up and they say they didn't like the blues. Well, then I went down there where Muddy Waters play, it's about three o'clock in the morning, the joint was packed. I went to looking around. Top peoples there, them lawyers, them big shots. I say, "Oh, you don't like the blues. You done hid back down here where Muddy Waters at."

If you'd ask one of 'em, he acts like he ain't even ever heard of the blues. Sometimes I go to somebody's house and I knock on the door. Blues just a-going on the victrola. I knock on the door, the music stop, and they slap a jazz on there, go to playing jive and then open the door. I say, "I heard them blues."

When I come in this town here, New Orleans, they didn't want no blues. But I know that when I come. So when I walk in a place and they ask me to play a few, first thing I went to playing jazz. And the man said, "Okay, I'll give you a job." After I was there about a couple of nights, then I come to stomping on the blues.

In Memphis, the blues did get popular, but jazz was the thing. They judge you by your music ability. You couldn't play jazz, they didn't much recognize you too much, even though you were a good blues player. If you couldn't play no jazz, you're in pretty bad shape.

People get the idea that Memphis a blues town because Handy made the "Memphis Blues" and the "Saint Louis Blues." Actually I wouldn't call 'em blues. It was a little blues in them, but they're not the regular blues.

See, blues didn't come from the city. They come from the country; then the city got 'em and dressed 'em up. They was playing jazz in the city. They wasn't playing no jazz in the country, out in those little bitty towns. Nothing but blues. And they first started with them guitars, harmonicas, and they transferred them to the piano, horns, so forth.

You see, guitars were really looked down on. People never did recognize 'em that much. But those guitars had their way, though. See, they'd walk down the street, everything's quiet, they would strum on that guitar. They music sound good and somebody'd yell, "Come over here." He go sit on their porch, they'd go to crowding around, and he's a big shot. He would walk around and sit in the parks, crowd come up, people give a quarter, he'd pitch it in a box. He wound up, he got seven or eight dollars, he'd go to another spot. I's just setting there playing in some joint, two dollars or two and a half a night, fifteen dollars a week. In the good times, out in the parks, he'd make more in two hours than I would in a week.

When I started to making records in 1929, I was playing at a little barrelhouse joint over in East Saint Louis for a dollar a night, room and board. 'Course I didn't have nothing to bother about 'cause everything was cheap. You could get a twenty-four-pound sack of flour for a quarter. So I could take six dollars and raise a lot of sand.

There was a fellow in Saint Louis, he had a music store, sold all kinds of blues records and jazz, had the loudspeaker coming out to the street. I'd just go by there and sit outside and listen. So one day I walked in there—they had a piano—and I asked, "Lady, do you mind me playing a piece?" She said, "I don't care." So I sat there and I commenced to playing a few blues. I played the "Forty-Fours," and some more numbers. Her husband come in—he's called Jesse Johnson—he listened and he said, "Hey, play that other piece of music you just played." I played that and he say, "Play another one, different style of that." So I played another one. "Well," he said, "it's nice. You got any more?"

I said, "Oh, yeah, I've got a lot more songs." He said: "No, you got a lot more words. Your music's going to be all the same, I can see that. You sang the same thing. Well, play me something."

So he went on back there, selling records, and I kept banging out there. He said, "Step back here." And I went back there. Now this is on about Friday evening. He said, "How would you like to go to New York and make a record? Like these records here."

I said, "No, I can't play good enough for no records."

"Oh, yes," he said, "you sounds all right. Now if you want to go, I can take you. I'm going to take a couple of more fellows over there tomorrow."

I said, "Well, I'll try."

He said: "I'll pay you good."

I said, "Well!"

He said: "You be here in the morning at eight o'clock, we'll catch the American, run down to New York and record."

I never know how much money I's gonna get, nothing. So I's over there, and they took me on the train. It was fine. I's been riding them freight trains. Well, I went back in the back end, in the big observation car, little rugs on the floor, and the train's flying. I said, "Lookahere, man, I'm in a fine train and going to New York." Well,

I would have paid *him* a thousand dollars for that, that was a great thing.

I got there, very first thing, I recorded "Forty-four Blues," "The Way I Feel." I made four tunes. He said, "Okay, come in the office and get your money." The big fellow of the Columbia Record Company—the label was the Okeh, but Columbia was the big boss—he come in there to pay me off. He said, "Sit down." He's counting out, and he had these hundred-dollar bills in a bale. I never seen money wrapped up. I said, "A bandit!" I got fifteen hundred dollars, and so he shoved that over to me and he said, "Sign this right here, that's yours." Well, I started to sweating. I like to fell out. I couldn't hardly write my name. Fifteen hundred dollars and I been working for a dollar and a dollar and a half a night all my life, and in just a few minutes, a guy give me fifteen hundred dollars. You know, money going to kill you, too much of it dropped on you at one time.

And I picked it up and, boy, I was sweating, and I says, "I got *all* the money, ain't no more money." I think the Piggly Wiggly was some big store then. I said, "They ain't got nothing, Piggly Wiggly, if they had the money I had." And some fellows take me by the drugstore, and I'd stop and say, "Them drugstore people ain't got nothing, if they had the money . . ." I put some here and some there. I kept changing it. I'd put it in my inside coat pocket and take it out if it stayed too long, and I put some in my back pocket and I'd take it out of there. I's just steady working with that money. I couldn't let it be still.

But let me tell you about this contract, this contract with Columbia. I read on there Roosevelt Sykes agree to record and we going to pay him quarterly royalties; every three months you get a royalty check. And I see that—all the months down there, the quarterly months in the contract. Then lot of fine reading down at the bottom. After I see you get paid quarterly, I didn't pay no attention to the rest; then I just signed.

When I got home, three months passed, I didn't get no check. Six months passed, I didn't get no check or nothing. So I went down and talked to this fellow, Jesse Johnson. I said, "I didn't get no check."

And he said, "Well, you ain't supposed to get any. Didn't you get fifteen hundred dollars and get paid?"

I said, "Well, man, I got to get royalties."

"No," he say, "read your contract."

So I read the contract, down there where it says royalties, say, "Royalties to be paid one hundred percent to Jesse Johnson." Now that was the case 'til the contract run out in a couple of years. But thereafter made me had to read, you know. But I figured everybody was fair. I didn't think nobody would pull nothing like that 'cause I meant well myself. I thought everybody was good like me.

After I got the fifteen hundred dollars, I moved across the river back to big Saint Louis, and got me a little house over there and commenced selling whisky myself, had bootlegging, selling fried fish, and everything like that. I'd get me a couple of gallons of whisky and set them in the middle of the floor and have all my friends to come sit around there and drink it, for free. "Tonight's for free." And I'd go down to the fish market. You could get I don't know how many fish heads for a nickel or dime. I'd get a big bag of fish heads and come back and fry 'em up, say, "Everybody eat." I know how to live, you know. It's a lot of meat on them fish heads lot of times. I ain't buying no fish when I can get me a little fishhook, get me a bait, and catch me a few of 'em. Why should I go there and pay him no dollar and a half for that fish and I can take one worm and pull out a three or four pound fish? [He laughed.] I really was kind of on the cheap end on that.

I made a pretty good living in that place. Way back there I got along well with the police. They come in, say, "Who run this place?" I say, "I do." They say, "Well, I tell you what to do. Keep down cuttings and shootings. And have your fun. And every night we come by here at eleven o'clock, you give us two dollars apiece." I say, "Good." They say, "Go on and have your fun. Just don't have no cuttings and shootings." That's all. No license or nothing. Four dollars. And I'd make that back on a couple of drinks.

I had a bunch of little places at different times in Saint Louis, maybe for about a year. Then I'd move somewhere. I'd just leave my house and everything. I had an old lady, she's keeping it, and if she didn't, I wouldn't care. I never stayed no place that long. Don't care if I made a million dollars, I just couldn't stay there. I always had to go.

What I was doing was hoboing on freight trains, ride the freight trains, yeah. I could have a pocket full of money, wouldn't pay no fare. I just think it didn't make sense, all them free things running up and down the road. Oh, no, I didn't pay no fare. When I first started to paying fare, I hated to put my hand in my pocket and pay. "It's just a shame," I'd say, "I go right by the places on the passenger train that I been. I know all along here. Now why should I pay all my money coming through here?"

I just wasn't staying nowhere put. I'd leave Saint Louis, from there I'd go to Chicago. And I'd play around Chicago a while, and then I'd come back to Saint Louis. Go to Memphis, play around there a week or a month or two.

I played all over Memphis—out there in Boxtown, on Kansas Street, at Trigg and Florida for Tobacco George—I can't remember all of them. I played at Joe LaFonza's at Fourth and Beale.[1] Memphis Slim got his start in there. I taught him what he knowed at that time. 'Course he's ventured off on his own now.

Them places, they had a restaurant in the front, but you go on through to the back, that's the big part, that's where the action is, card tables and dice tables, and the bandstand was back there. And that's where all the musicians played. See, musicians in those days never played to the people who'd buy drinks. They played to the gamblers. That was the feature attraction, was the gambling.

Some good musicians, they just play music just for the kicks, but they really was gamblers. Just like Sunnyland Slim. He's a gambler; he was dice and cards and all that. Memphis Slim, too. All them guys, they just would only play if they get broke. Then they'd say, "I'm going to play the blues," start playing because somebody'd give 'em a stake to get back in the game. So really they wasn't very much the music end of it, but they could play the blues. Then, too, they could get the women—lot of girls'd fall for blues players, you know. Anybody who could play, when he'd get there, if he ain't got no girl and done got broke and ain't got no roll, he go to playing the blues; somebody come up, some girl'll give him five dollars, and he go and get back in the game.

Then in the early forties, I played at the Palace Theater in Memphis. I had me a band in there. I come on right behind Chick Webb. The Palace was awful popular. They'd bring all the leading names in.

That was when I was on the road with my big band, from about nineteen forty-two. I always had my own band. I couldn't play with nobody's band because I's original, see. Somebody want me to play like he wanted, he'd set a pace, and I'd say, "I can't do that." I ain't able to play that right like he want it.

Lot of times when I had my big bands, I'd get different fellows, good musicians, schoolteachers, musicians finished up in music, they could read. I'd say, "Now ya'll play this in a nine-ten piece of time."

1. Joe Raffanti owned the Midway Cafe at Fourth and Beale for many years. He was mentioned by a number of blues musicians but never as Raffanti, always as LaFonza.

They'd say, "Wait, don't play thisaway; you putting too many bars here and you're taking too many from here."

I say, "I'm glad you told me." I say, "Now, you is the better musician than I am. You can come more near playing what I'm playing than I can what you playing. Now you get with me 'cause I ain't good enough to get with you." I say, "You done been along here where I am; you done passed by here. Well, I ain't been up there yet; you come with me." I say, "Two wrongs makes a good right, so long as we hit along together."

That was my own style, see. I'd be in the right bars and what have you, 'cording to Hoyle, but I put a little something else in the middle I wasn't supposed to, that was getting way out field. And it would be a hit, see.

So that's why I always had my own band because I wasn't good enough to play with nobody else. So everybody was good enough to play with me.

I took up harmony, by me having a band. I had to tell the fellows what I wanted them to do. That's all I did. But I didn't play what I told them, see, 'cause I never could play anything over again just alike. I can't do it just alike every time 'cause I got a different feeling than what I had when I went over it before. I wouldn't play it like the music was wrote. I always add a little of me in it. So I still do that now.

I had my big band from nineteen forty-two till nineteen fifty-four or fifty-five. Them fellows, you know you got to be a mama and a daddy. They come up, say "Hey, man, put me in the book for five," "Hey, man, I'm in a tight spot, I wants ten, man." You got to be a mother and a father. You got to watch 'em, keep 'em from getting drunk. Which a lot of musicians would have been very good as of today, but they drank themselves out. People brag on them and then they take them out; when one bunch turn 'em a-loose, somebody else got 'em, and they wouldn't get no sleep. Just like Sonny Boy Williamson just dranked all the time. Had a fifth of whisky, a hundred proof, setting by his bed when he died, about half of it done gone. I guess it worked his heart too fast. That hundred proof, you know it'll make your blood go fast.

You got to watch 'em. I had a lot of that. I had a headache on me. I done that about sixteen to twenty years.

When I was on the road with the band, blues, that's what I was booked out there for. I was specializing in the blues, my records was hot out, and they booked me on account of my records. But I played some of everything once I get out there. I played jazz, I learned to play "Stardust," anything.

When I go out here at these festivals, I play different things. I always try playing whatsomever's doing. I have young people to play for, the middle, even the old, so I have to play all different styles. The young people wants the blues now, the young people wants the rock, so I have to play both of them. I got to learn to play the beat of rock. Rock is mostly a beat, and the music in it is patterned after a Baptist preacher. You notice how it's sung mostly as preaching and hollering and like a preacher would preach. [He sang.] "Yeah, da, do, da, di, yeah, do, da, da, do." That's rock. Do a little screaming there sometime.

Like the rock is today, you hear one rock band, go down the street further, he's playing something similar to the rock band you just left here. That's the way it was with the "Forty-four Blues." "Forty-four Blues" was a trend, was a style. Near about everything people play, they have a little "Forty-four" in it, years ago. But I grabbed them and copyrighted them, put words to it. Then Little Brother [Montgomery] made one called "Vicksburg Blues," but it was nothing but the "Forty-four Blues." They's lots of songs like that. People been singing them out across the fields. Somebody hear him and go on and write it and get a copyright from the Library of Congress. They got it, but the guy that made it is over around there plowing. It's really his song, but he don't even know it.

I really enjoyed those days, coming up in them days. If I had to live my life over again, I think I'd like to keep the same tracks all over again. I don't regret nothing, I'm telling you, playing music. I'm glad I didn't learn all that as I go along. Right now I learns a whole lot more daily as I plays. Well, God knows what you going to need later. See, if I'd been piled all that up in my younger days, I'd been done wore out on it now. Probably I'd been dead. He give me a little bit at a time. Like when I get eighty-five. He be laying a little more on me. And some of the money I didn't get, it'll come pouring in on me, see.

Roosevelt rocked back in the chair, almost lifting it off the floor, and laughed. We turned off the tape recorder, but before we left he obliged us with a mini concert. "Now this here is Helena honky-tonk," he said as he seated himself at the piano and swung into the barrelhouse blues. He played several variations on jazz and blues to illustrate the Memphis, New Orleans, Saint Louis, and Chicago styles. "And this here," he said, grinning broadly, "is *me*," whipping into his theme song. The Honeydripper never sounded better.

Sam Chatmon, the last of the Mississippi Sheiks, in front of his home at Hollandale, Mississippi, in 1976.
© Thomas Lea, 1976

# 14 · The Mississippi Sheik

At first, they were known merely as the Chatmon boys—nine full brothers and more half-brothers than anyone can remember.[1] From 1900 on, no party around Bolton, Mississippi, was complete without their music. Then, in the late 1920s, some of them started making records, and soon the Chatmons were known from Atlanta to San Antonio, from New Orleans to Chicago, as the Mississippi Sheiks. Now, there was only one—sprightly, tough, cocksure, opinionated, indomitable old Sam Chatmon, himself in his middle seventies. When his time came to go, he said, "God's gonna have to draft me, 'cause I ain't gonna volunteer."

On this dank, cold November day, he had ridden the bus up to Memphis from Hollandale, Mississippi, where he held down a regular job as a night watchman. A long, heavy overcoat hung loosely around his spare frame, his white hair curling around the collar. With his bush of white beard, high cheekbones, bright black eyes, and slightly swarthy skin, he looked like a Biblical patriarch in a snap-brimmed cap.

He accepted a ride to the Memphis Auditorium, where he was to play that night at the River City Blues Festival, and, with reluctance, let a younger man carry both his guitar and his beaten-up old suitcase. At the auditorium, he checked in with Steve LeVere, the promoter of the show, who was shepherding his collection of venerable blues men through a harried rehearsal with

1. The family name is spelled Chatmon or Chatman, depending on the family member or the record company involved. Sam used the Chatmon spelling, whereas his great-nephew, Peter (Memphis Slim), spelled his name Chatman.

the help of a handful of bearded youngsters in T-shirts and blue jeans.

Out of the hubbub, in one of the auditorium's spartan dressing rooms, Chatmon hung up his overcoat, settled down in a ladder-backed wooden chair, and took his ease. He was where he was supposed to be, he was already wearing his stage clothes—khaki work pants, khaki shirt, heavy brogans, and a sport jacket of English tweed—and now he was ready to do one of his favorite things, talk.

"There was nine whole brothers of us and ain't none of us took time to count the halves," he said of the family he was born into on January 10, 1899, on a plantation at Bolton. "There's Charley Patton, he's my half-brother; my daddy raised him. Joe Marshall's a half-brother. And Papa had seven children by a outside lady, Memphis Slim's grandmother."

My father played in slavery time and he had to tote his fiddle in a sack. He just picked it up; wasn't nobody taught him. That's the way with all of us; we picked it up. It was just a gift, I guess.

Didn't but one of us read music, that was my brother Lonnie. A man there in Bolton—he was a good violinist—he taught him notes. Lonnie knowed how to play, but he just wanted to learn by the notes. See, that's the way we learned all our pieces. He'd learn 'em and we'd play 'em behind him.

I started to picking when I's about four. I had been hearing my brothers pick. They asked me in California, "How did you learn how to pick?" I told 'em I learned by lying. They said, "Well, how is that? How come you learnt by lying?" I said I'd put chairs and boxes and climb up until I get Bo's or Lonnie's guitar down off the nail and get down there and pick and wind up on it 'til I'd break a string. Then I'd climb back up there and hang it up. When they come in, says, "Oh, my string broke off my guitar," I say, "I ain't had it. I ain't *had* it."

The brothers were Lonnie, Edgar, Bo, Willie, Lamar, Laurie, Harry, Charley, and Sam. Among them they played violin, guitar, bass viol, clarinet, banjo, drums, and piano, with most of them able to play more than one instrument. Among the keys to the band's success were its melodic, slightly swinging style that made for easy dancing and its wide stock of tunes—country dance numbers, folk songs, blues, and even occasional hillbilly selections. The folk-country background that carried over into all their music widened their appeal for whites.

In olden times, back when I was a real young boy, everybody square danced. They played "Turkey in the Straw" and "Old Hen Cackle" and "Can't Get the Saddle on the Old Gray Mule." I can play all them things yet. I ain't forgot 'em.

If we played for colored folks, we ordinarily'd get two dollars apiece, but we couldn't have but about four of us playing, at the highest. And if you wanted to eat anything, you had to buy it. Man, I have played for a dollar and fifty cents and sometimes have to take it in meat. Fellow didn't have a dollar to give me and I said, "Well, you got to give me something." He said, "Well, how'd you like to have a shoulder or ham?" I said, "Yeah, hand it here." I wouldn't leave it. Noooo.

But if we was playing at white folks' house, they'd give you five dollars a man, and they'd fix you plates and pass 'em on to you. You'd eat real choice. They'd have servants there waiting on you. They's through with you, go on home, you'd get your five dollars apiece.

Parties at white folks' house would go to about twelve or eleven-thirty, like that, and they'd be ready to go. Shucks, at the colored folks' house, they'd be there 'til sunrise sometime, next morning, and then they'd dance right on out the door on the grounds, keep on dancing, get some more men to stay and pick for them, keep dancing.

We'd play out at the wells, that was a place out there from Raymond [near Bolton] that had the healing waters, name of Cooper's Wells. And Brown's Wells. And then we'd take a tour out on the road, come on to Memphis here and play all the way back.

Among the musicians the Chatmons encountered on their wanderings from Memphis to New Orleans was a trumpet player named Louis Armstrong.

He used to come to Jackson, and he knowed us was playing, he'd stop there and blow a piece or two with us. And Lonnie used to go down there and play the fiddle for him. Any time he run short of a man, he'd ask one of us to come and play for him. I played with him in New Orleans, when he had his band called the Hot Five. Played with him a many time.

I always did figure he was going to be the best trumpet player there was around. He sang, too—well, I wouldn't call hisself singing, I'd call hisself clowning. He'd do all that kind of way—hrunff-hrunff— and the big handkerchief. Folks would want him to do that, you see, and he'd just be acting crazy. Just act crazy. I said, "Lord-a-mercy, that man ain't ashamed of nothing."

Jackson, only fifteen miles from Bolton, boasted the blues not only of Sam and his brothers but such top blues men as Tommy Johnson, Ishmon Bracey, Charlie McCoy, and Walter Jacobs as well.

I liked Jackson better than I did either Memphis or New Orleans. Blues was more popular. Any time you go to Jackson, they's be telling us, "Put me down there where they chunkin' tin cans." They mean just play 'em just as low as you can get to 'em, then. Where they goin' to chunk tin cans, that's in the alley. You don't find no tin cans on the street. "Put 'em in the alley," that's what they holler for.

We'd play them gambling joints. We'd play in this room and they'd have gambling in the other room. Sometime the law would come, and all them was in there in the gambling room, they had to pay a fine. You'd spy more pistols laying on the floor when the law come in. You could just look anywhere and find a pistol or big, long knife laying down on the floor, some of them stuck up under the heaters. You see, the houseman tell the law to come by to keep him from having a lot of trouble. Guys what got the pistols on 'em, if the law come and take their pistols, they wouldn't have nothing to act with.

Sometime we would have played until way late at night, be walking home with our instruments; the law meet us on the street, say, "Where you been?"

"Well, I been to such-and-such a place," I say.

"You walking mighty lop-legged there," he say.

I told him, "You'd walk lop-legged, too, if you had done played long as I done played. I'm sleepy."

He say, "Can you walk this line?"

I told him, "Yeah, I can walk any kind of line."

He look, say, "Oh, that's them Chatmon boys. Let 'em go on; they don't drink." He let us go on. I had just one brother who drank pretty heavy. All the rest of us, we wouldn't. We drank when we'd get through playing, after we get home. Whisky makes some people want to fight, and whisky makes some people want to be friendly. Now every time I have ever took a drink, it makes me sleepy.

But them what would drink, the law'd catch 'em every one at night coming home from parties full of whisky and put 'em in jail. They done made six dollars and be out about fifteen dollars in fines the next day.

In the late 1920s, the Chatmons started their recording career. In the next decade they made nearly a hundred sides for several companies and under various names—the Mississippi Blacksnakes, the Mississippi Mud Steppers, the Jackson Blue Boys—in Atlanta, San Antonio, Chicago, New Orleans, Memphis, Jackson, New York. It was in Shreveport, Louisiana, in 1930 that they recorded for Okeh their two most successful songs, "Sitting on Top of the World" and "Stop and Listen." Bo Chatmon, who also recorded under the name of Bo Carter, made more than a hundred sides on his own, many of them the double entendre "blue" blues. The last session for the brothers was in 1936. Bo continued to record for a few more years before he too was dropped by the record companies.

With the recording days over, Sam farmed, played Saturday night sociables, and just barely scraped by for years.

Then a man come from San Diego, California, come looking for Bo, just any of the Chatmons. All of 'em was dead but me. He asked me, "If I take some tapes back and get you some jobs to come to California, would you be in earnest to come out there and play for 'em?" I told him yeah. So I made him three songs; he carried them back. Everywhere he played 'em, they hired me. I got my ticket and twenty dollars he sent me to eat on from home out there. And I been on the go ever since; sixty-two, that's when I started.

I got ten places that want me to come to California and play now. I turned down two—it's between California and the state of Washington. Oregon. Ain't Oregon out in there? Well, I turned down two nights playing out in Oregon.

Although most of the performers were black, Sam found his

audience at the festivals and concerts made up mainly of young whites.

I'll tell you what I believe it is. The biggest majority of the white folks ain't never heard the blues before. Everywhere I play, they ain't never been used to nothing but rock and roll. That's all they said they'd ever heard. So when I go there and I play, they all scream.

I been all over the country. I ain't been to Europe. They tried to get me to go. I figure I'm going after while. They offered me eight hundred dollars a week and I wouldn't go. I told 'em they give Memphis Slim two thousand five hundred dollars, they can give it to me, too. If they want me bad enough, they'll give it to me.

I don't like to fly, but I'm gone fly to get there. But if it happened to go down, I'm going to take out enough airplane insurance so all my folks—all of y'all—could get rich if you wants. I'm going to break the insurance company up. ["Why was it you said you didn't fly?" he was asked.

" 'Cause I ain't got no feathers on my arms. I done looked all over my arms."]

My boy told me once, say, "Oh, Dad, go ahead over there with Memphis Slim. Boy, eight hundred dollars would be good for a week. You ain't going to die 'til your time come." I told him, "Yeah, but I'd look like a fool. I'd be way up over all that water and somebody else's time come and I had to follow him down for him to die. I'd look just like a fool following him down to die."

I went out there in Berkeley, California. It was so many folks there 'til it looked just like ants crawling. Just couldn't even turn for 'em. Thirty-eight thousand people—that's what the place holds, that's how many seats—but there was more than that there. The thing start off right down at the ground and go all the way round, just keep a-going round and round, getting higher and higher, higher and higher and higher, and every one of them seats was taken up. Five dollars apiece.

I played for a festival up there in Washington, D.C.; I ain't ever seen them many people. I believe it was two million there. Was out there in a street where it ain't nothing but some trees. Everything was free. And the garbage truck was hauling off beer cans; just as regular as he can go and come back, they'd have another load of beer cans. [This was the Festival of American Folk Life in 1974, held on the Mall area between the Washington Monument and the Lincoln Memorial. Sam, who took a bus to Washington, was the hit of the show, and when the crowd clamored to get him back on stage, he grumbled good-naturedly, "They got a good mule and they want to work him to death."] I likes playing for a great big crowd like that. Bigger the crowd, better I can play.

I played at the Wolf Trap [Wolf Trap Park Performing Center near Washington, D.C.] and the man told me, "Say, Sam, I sure want you back next year, but we ain't allowed to use the same talent every year. But, now, next year after this, we'll have you back." I told him, "Okay. If you don't, I have plenty places to play." I done already signed for one festival, and one more told me they want me to come out there to California.

But I likes to go like to Saint Louis where I can go and come back. I be going back home tonight after the show; I won't stay, catch the bus back. See, summertime, it's okay. Wintertime, now, all of my pipes and everything is exposed to the weather. They can freeze and bust, and now my wife, she don't stay well so good, and she got to get out there and worry with that herself. If I be at home, I worry with it.

I don't have no manager. Huh-uh, I don't need nairn. If I want to play, you see, if I want to take the job for twenty dollars and the manager, he won't want that, he want forty dollars so he can get part, and I done missed that twenty dollars. I don't have no manager. The cheapest more or less I gets at these festivals and things is four hundred dollars a hour. Play one hour and get four hundred dollars and sometimes five hundred.

Used to be that I have trouble with the church people over playing the blues. They have turned me out of church. But I don't have none lately, since I been doing pretty good. I go back home, they see me, say, "Where you going?" I told 'em I'm going to the bank. "What you done done this week?" I don't say nothing; I just hand 'em my checks. Like last week, I had three checks that was around fourteen hundred dollars, what I done made in the last three weeks. They say, "I wish I could pick that thing. I'd be holding it, too." They beginning to want to pick it some now.

But used to be, people feel that if you don't play a church song and you play blues, they think that's a disgrace, it's a sin before God. I been had religion ever since nineteen and twelve, and they have turned me out of church more than one time because I sang the blues. I go right on back there and tell 'em, "God give me the talent. If I take my talent and bury it somewhere, He'd take all the rest away from me."

Now, they have to take you back in the church, if you want to come back. You go to the preacher or either your deacon and tell him you going to do better. You don't tell him now that you going to quit. Just tell him you want to do better and you want to go back to church. He'll bring you before the congregation, and they votes you back in. You be a standing member again, get up and go.

I took my guitar and go to church, the same church turn me out, and play for 'em, and they raised as high as sixty and seventy dollars that night. They offered to pay. I told 'em, I said, "No, I's helping the church." Still, that's devil music. But long as I'm singing and they're making money, it's different.

They tell you to don't mix church songs and the blues, don't live straddling the fence. But now, every note that you make playing the blues, you make it on an instrument playing church songs. Same mouth you use to cuss with, you say Lord, have mercy with that same mouth. Tongue is so you can mix anything and say anything you want to, and that's the way I believe about playing guitar.

The preacher one time, he's telling me about my guitar, "That's a sinful thing you got there." I told him, I said, "Well, I wouldn't say that, Reverend. This guitar right here is just as holy as that Bible you got there. I can put this guitar in a case and stand it up in the corner and it'll never say a word as long as I let it set there. Now if I go to playing this guitar, you'd give me some money." He said, "I'd tell you to play 'til your fingers drop off!" I took my bottle-neck out and commenced playing "Nearer, Oh, My God To Thee." He run his hand in his pocket and give me fifty cents. Say, "Son, you go ahead and play that everywhere you go, hear?" I told him, "Yes, sir."

If I want to play a church song, I play it. If I want to play blues, I play it. I write church songs. I got about eight or ten. I likes 'em better than the blues. I tell you, I loves the church songs. When I'm sanging a blues, when I get through singing, I'm through with it. But I can sang a church song, and I'll set there and go to crying. But no blues make me do that. No.

I sing that thing I recorded, "I Want to Live with My Jesus When This Life End." Say, "I'm gettin' old and my eyes turning gray, I know by that my days can't be so far away, and I want to rest with my Jesus when this life end." Shucks, when I go to sing that, I have to cry.

You know the blues partly come out of New Orleans and jazz, too.

And they brought the blues down from church songs. That's where the blues originated from, church songs. And I'll tell you why the blues come about. It's a expression that a person have—he want to tell you something, and he can't tell you in his words, he'll sing it to you. See, back in—well, I'll just bring it right out in plain where anybody can see it—in olden days, if a white man do a colored man wrong, he couldn't tell him he was wrong. He'd go off on a mule or something and sing back to that man, the blues like, singing it to him. That's the way a plenty of them songs come up.

Take my daddy. When he's playing the fiddle in slavery time, he wouldn't want to play, but he *had* to play. So he'd go along and make up things and holler it out in the fields where the old boss man could hear, just singing away. Now that's what he meant—he's tired of playing nearly every night and then working in daytime. [Asked for an example, he sang:]

> Hey, Liza, Little Liza Jane,
> Oh, Liza, Little Liza Jane.
> Can't get the saddle on the old gray mule,
> Can't get the saddle on the old gray mule,
> Whoa, whoa, mule, can't get the saddle on the
>     old gray mule.

He's saying the white man done worked him so 'til he can't even put a saddle on the old gray mule. That's what he talking about.

> Chicken in the bread pan
> Picking at the dough.
> When he git through picking,
> He scratch for more.

That's what they'd be singing to the white folks what wasn't giving 'em enough to eat. Yeah, in slavery time. All them things come out of slavery time. All that happened in them days.

Ain't no white man yet that can sing the blues like the colored guy. [Asked why, he said:] Well, I'll tell you one thing. I think white people speaks they words more correct than would a colored person. If they going to put out or sing a song, they going to say "came." A colored guy say "come." He don't care if it's after or before, he going to say "come" or "go," whatever's rhyme. Now you take a white man, he's going to put that "came" there.

And then the next thing, a colored guy's going to say "mothuh" and just cut it right short. A white man will say "motherrrr." That's the way they was taught to speak English and they speaken it right. But no, you see, colored folks don't use it. That's why white folks can't sing the blues like a colored person.

This guy with a home here, he went overseas and made such a good mark—Elvis Presley. Presley sung one piece that I like and that's that "Jailhouse Rock." That was right at the blues. If he just had a shoved a little bit, he'd a went in.

I's hoping I'd meet upon these guitar pickers like you got up there now. I'm going to stir up a little bit. I can show 'em something. Man, yeah, I can teach 'em something.

He went on stage and sang "Saint Louis Blues" and "Corinna," and several more, including the rowdy "Diggin' Your Potatoes," a throwback to brother Bo's blue blues. He picked his guitar lovingly, in the Sheik style, with a sweetness, subtlety, and sophistication not seen in many country blues men. After each number, the crowd of young people in jeans and denims stomped and shouted and yelled for more. The last of the Mississippi Sheiks was indeed showing them something and teaching them something.

Big Joe Williams, the wandering "Po' Joe" who befriended and coached young Bob Dylan, at the Ann Arbor, Michigan, Jazz and Blues Festival in 1969.
Courtesy of Delmark Records

# 15 · Big Joe

The blues bred a strain of fiddle-footed ramblers. The blues fed them, clothed them, and opened almost any black man's door to them. In return, they followed the blues—or were pursued by them—all their lives. Their restless feet roamed the dusty backroads of the South and the back alleyways of the big towns. No steady job or weekly paycheck for them—they played for six bits and a pork sandwich when times were hard, for hundred-dollar tips when the high rollers hit it big, and for whatever the traffic would bear in between. Their songs told their stories of long, lonesome roads, of well-walked highways, and always of the need to move on.

Big Joe Williams was of that restless breed, one of the last of the rambling blues men of the likes of Leadbelly (Huddie Ledbetter), Robert Johnson, and Charley Patton. For more than sixty years he had gone wherever his mind took him and his guitar could make his way, to country suppers and Chicago house-rent parties, to crossroad honky-tonks and Beale Street dives.

For the moment he was back where he started, in Crawford, a small country town near the edge of the Piney Woods in east Mississippi. Like most small Mississippi towns, Crawford had a hierarchy of street surfaces—asphalt on the few streets downtown and in the white section, gravel for the black part of town, graded dirt toward the outskirts. At Joe's beetle-domed trailer on the edge of Crawford, gravel was unknown and muddy ruts were hubcap deep.

Joe sat just inside the metal trailer with the door open for the breeze and the screen closed against the flies. A squat, stocky man, he had a face to suit his body—broad. On both sides of his forehead his hair had receded, leaving only a thick patch in the center. A large wen bulged through the bare scalp at the right side. The trailer was parked only a few miles from where Joe was born in 1903, the son of a farmer and sometime sawmill worker.

My whole family was musical. My grandfather, Bert Logan, accordion player, one of the greatest. He could play guitar, too. My grandmother, Liza Logan, she's a songster, choir singer. Most church people, you know, usually they'd do their little Saturday night dirt, then get on their knees Sunday. But she was an all-time Christian, I can say that much, while she's sleeping in her grave. Not no wrong things did I seed her do, my grandmother.

My grandfather was pretty nice, too, but then he was kind of devilish. I took after him. He cuss some, then pray some, then sang the hymns some. He say he serve both God and mammon 'cause he didn't know which hand he's going to fall into. That's just the way he used to carry on foolishness 'cause he was a deacon with the church.

My grandmother didn't fancy going to the Saturday night suppers, but my grandfather would have a big one every once in a while, and she taken it mighty well. She'd enjoy seeing people dance, Charleston, strut, shimmy-she-wobble—that's when they would get on the floor with two together and they just shake like somebody having a chill, just stand there and tremble like a leaf from their head to the feet; they'd rear back and just tremble. They'd shimmy by the guitar and they'd shimmy by the hands, just anything that you could give a double knock for, just double slap with your hands, and they'd go to shimmying.

They'd kill a couple of shoats, you know, hogs, and barbecue them, have about a couple a hundred tater and custard pies, lots of little sticks of candy. They'd have corn whisky and home brew, some kind of beer they used to made. It was clear; called it California beer.

Usually somebody played the guitar. I beat the bucket when I's 'round about seven or eight years old. Gallon water bucket, put one hand in the bucket and rap on the outside. I could make that bucket talk. See, they danced by that; it was something like a drum. They used to fiddle sometimes, fiddle and banjo, but it's mostly guitar and French harp. Usually hear about "Rabbit on the Log" and "Old Joe

Turner." Them was really blues back in them days, real deep-down blues.

They'd have a apple biting sometime, have a apple swinging at the top of the house. Have what you call the shoo fly, stealing partners; I grabs you, he grab the next one, turn you a-loose, grab another one. Oh, it was just lots of fun, slapping the hands and sweating and I'm telling you, it was just hard day's work but nice.

People don't have the good time that they used to have back in those days. They be at your house tonight, tomorrow night they go to the next neighbor house and dance and play all night long, go to the field the next day just like they hadn't did anything. But today peoples can't take it. If they stay up all night now, they miss a day's work; but, then, we didn't pay it no attention. We'd walk fifteen miles, twenty miles to the supper, be all night getting back home, go get something to eat, and go right on to the field, go on to the jobs. Today's generation can't take what the old ones taken.

What the old ones took didn't suit Joe either, who "didn't want to plow, didn't want to chop cotton." He got his chance for a different kind of life when still a youngster, about nine. A minstrel show came to town—dancers, a jug band, a comedian, a blues singer.

They was doing dances, they give contests, anyone was welcome to win a prize. Everybody, white and colored, knowed how good I was at dancing at nine years old. So they had this 'test up, I think it was around fifty dollars if one winned these dance shows. That's exactly how I got with them; I winned this prize, I left with 'em. My parents didn't know nothing about it. I left 'em. I stayed gone a long time, they thought I was dead. Pittsburgh, Pennsylvania, New York, back to Texas in winter. Everywhere, we went everywhere.

They had dancing, cracking jokes, blackface comedians—we all used to do that. Take flour and soot to make you dark; we had wigs we wore sometimes; we had them old high hats and them long slop [frock] coats and a walking cane and them button-type spats. That's what we wore.

I stayed with that show six or seven years. I learned everything to be done about that show. I even drive trucks, done everything. They had a stage—reckon about ten feet, and we'd run down when we'd do our acts, go out and sell medicine all through the streets.

It was just a crooked show; they'd sell water, everything, just get it bottled up.

There's no money to be made in a show, I can tell you that part. You supposed to make a dollar and a half a night. The only way you could get your money, you had to be slick like the show. What you do, if you supposed to sell twenty-five bottles, you take you forty bottles and them other dollars goes in your pocket. That's the only way you get your money. All of us do it just so we can get something. *You'd* have done it.

Once he left the "doctor" show, he started calling himself "Po' Joe Williams"—he was much thinner then—and went to hoboing in earnest in Atlanta, Tampa, Miami, Pensacola, Columbus, Mobile, and then into New Orleans.

I wanted to see the French Market. I had a guitar. So I hit Canal Street walking that way and passed this place, big bulldog in the window, you know, RCA Victor. This lady, she walked out, say, "Come here, come here, my man." [Joe mimicked her in falsetto.]

I come in there and she say, "You play the guitar? You play the guitar?" I said I do.

"Sit down and let me hear you play, anything you can play. Come on in here, don't be scared." I went in.

"Sit down, sit down. You ever make any records?"

"No, I haven't ever made a record," I say. I sing, "Baby, Please Don't Go."

She ask, "You hear this on the records?"

I say, "No, ain't no record. I made that up."

"We'll give you a hundred dollars, we'll give you a hundred dollars, you stay here and play for me, back in the back here." I thought a hundred dollars was a heap of money then. I went back in there, sung that "Baby, Please Don't Go." I got that hundred dollars and I hit that Highway 61. Long about three or four months, everywhere I'm going, I hear myself hollering, on the record, you know:

> Baby, please don't go back to New Orleans,
> 'Cause I loves you so,
> Turn your lamp down low.

And all that hundred dollars gone, and I done walked all the bottom out of my shoes. Didn't have a dime, and I hated to hear that record. I said, "Oh, what a fool I done made out of myself for a hundred dollars." It was a hit, you know. Next year I went back to New Orleans, says to myself I'm going back in there to see what can I do.

She say [he mimicked her again], "Come in here, we have a little piece of money for you." I went in, they give me about fifty dollars.

"You want to make any other records?" she say.

I say, "No, I don't want to make nair nuthern." I got wise now.

"We give you three hundred," she say.

I say, "Oh, no, you don't give no contract, no royalty fees."

She say, "We not big enough to do that."

"You ain't big enough to get me then!"

It was somewhere about that time that I landed in Memphis the first time. That Memphis Jug Band was real popular then, Son Brimmer [Will Shade] and Shakey Horton in Chicago; Shakey was 'round about eight or nine years old, he's playing harp in the jug band. Beale Street Park, that was the music center right then. I dropped in Memphis—'course I had recorded, but that bunch didn't even know it. There was guitars, harps, bands, everything out there in Beale Street Park. I run in there, and Memphis Jug Band's out there with them tubs and washboard, fiddle, Son Brimmer, Gus Cannon, and all them fellows. Robert Johnson was there, he's there, everybody's in that park. They's raising the devil out there, all kinds of music.

I was a real small fellow wearing a cap with the bill turned backwards, and I come in there—I didn't know nobody in Memphis, I's just hoboing there from New Orleans—so I stand to myself. So this guy says—one guy is always smart, you know—says, "Hey, buddy, where you from?"

I said: "I come from New Orleans here, man. I live in Saint Louis."

"Why don't you join these fellows out here?"

I says: "No, I ain't tickled about joining nobody. I'm just traveling along, man. I don't have no harp player, no buddy, nothing. Plays by myself."

He say, "I bet you can't do nothing with that guitar." He's trying to give me a good time, you know.

"Well, whatever you think about it, it's your business," I say.

He says, "I'm going to see can you play that thing. I'll give you a quarter to play me a piece."

So that record of mine had come out, "Baby, Please Don't Go," but they didn't know I's Po' Joe Williams. And they's raising sand out there, Memphis Jug Band. So I cut down on that number, "Baby,

Please Don't Go," and they commenced moving away from the jug band, and every crowd commenced moving over that way. I could hear 'em talking: "That young man done got that guitar talking. That's that man that made that record, too. That's that man that made that record sure as the world." Women coming over there, snuffbox in their apron, handkerchief 'round their head, "Mister, ain't your name Po' Joe Williams?" I says, "No, no, you got the wrong man." "Oh, mister, you ain't telling nothing. You sound just like that record. You that man sure as the world." I taken all that crowd from the Memphis Jug Band. Ask old Shakey Horton in Chicago, he'll tell you.

So when I run into Memphis from then on, I was known, Front Street to Beale Street, all over that town. Used to work in Memphis, on the streets. I played a couple of nightclubs, but they couldn't hire me no more than one night. I wouldn't stay no place no more than two nights for nothing. I kept moving. Never stop, just kept moving.

I didn't want no job, nothing but that guitar. I was offered a heap of jobs, I would start a heap of jobs, but I'd never end one. Probably I'd make about a couple of days, that's all I'd want to stay, that's all. 'Til that Saturday night, that's my job, that Saturday night, Saturday in the day and Saturday night.

Saint Louis was really my stomping grounds. And back in Mississippi. I made lots of money, working in Missouri and Mississippi. I was liking everywhere, but in them two places, whenever I hit there, I was never lonesome. I always had a crowd.

I stayed in Saint Louis close around thirty years, off and on. I played south Saint Louis, north Saint Louis, played for white, colored both. Played streetcars. In the wintertime, that's where I played, streetcars, mostly. All them motorists know me. Me and my washboard player, we'd get in the back, there's no charge. We'd hit up on something real fast, that washboard and guitar, then he'd walk through the streetcar with a kitty cap, catching 'em before they getting off. Some of 'em ride on by and leave their stop, ride on around 'til the end of the car line listening at us play. Sometimes we'd end up with a hundred dollars, more than a hundred.

I was always backwards and forwards to Crawford, just like I am now. I used to play in here on the street. I come in here on the freight train, when I hit that street, they say "Po' Joe here," white and colored be packed out there, soon I have six blocks of people. Nickels, dimes, quarters and half-dollars, pockets be loaded. I'd go for a year, two years, three years. Then I'd run right back in here, to Crawford, Starkville, Brooksville, and then gone again.

I went everywhere, east and west, California, everywhere, every place in my mind. During the panic, the times that was poor, Hoover days, I didn't do nothing but ride from one hobo jungle to the other, north, south, east, and west, hoboing, me and my guitar. Lots of money was in the jungles. I made it good with my guitar.

In all those years of wandering, Joe crossed paths both with the other rambling blues men who kept one foot in the road and the home towners who did little wandering. He worked medicine shows with Jim Jackson and Furry Lewis, played all-day picnics up at Brownsville with Sleepy John Estes, rambled through the Delta with Robert Johnson and Charley Patton and later with Muddy Waters, knocked about Saint Louis joints with Peetie Wheatstraw and Walter Davis, recorded in Chicago with Sonny Boy Williamson and Robert Lee McCoy, and encountered scores of others along the way.

Since Joe had become an experienced recording artist, Lester Melrose asked his help when he was about to record Arthur "Big Boy" Crudup for the first time.

At that time we worked by the red light-green light, recording. See, when they flashed on red, you get in position, blue light, you get ready to stop. So Big Boy's first recording, he's so green, he'd start but he wouldn't never stop, he'd just keep on playing. So Melrose told me, "Joe, when it get near 'bout one minute to the ending, you catch him in the back."

So I told him, "Arthur, when I get ready for you to stop, I'll grab you in the back. Now don't stop dead, you just put the ending to your song. Just put the ending to your record."

"All right, all right," he says.

He's making "Mean Old Frisco," that's when he made his great hit. He get to hollering, "mean old Frisco," and three minutes and a half rolled up, Arthur still hollering. I catch him and he still hollering. More I catch him, he holler more. And Melrose cussing and pulling his hair: "Joe, I told you to catch him!" I said, "Hell, I *done* cotch him. Hell, I catch him and he get worse." So finally you know how they cut this record? Between verses, like you cut a chain. But it made a good hit though.

On records, Joe teamed successfully with a number of outstanding blues men, including Sonny Boy Williamson ("I put him on records; first thing he recorded was with me"); Walter Davis ("Walter lived about half a block from me in Saint Louis, but I knew him before he ever came to Saint Louis; his real home was in Grenada, Mississippi"); Robert Lee McCoy; Yank Rachel; Henry Townsend. At times he was backed by the bass playing of Ransom Knowling, an accomplished musician, who once told his wife, "I got to get drunk, Vi—I'm going to play with Big Joe."[1]

Joe never lost his raw-edged Mississippi style in all his years of wandering and recording. Adding to his distinctive sound was his nine-string guitar.

> I had this uncle, he's a great guitar player, his name's Wolf, I learnt him. And I had some pretty nice guitars when I come back here. Everybody say, "Let me see your guitar." Rather than to hurt somebody's feelings, I say I'm going to add on one string, maybe that'll stop 'em. So I add on seven strings and I left, and I came back and my uncle done learned how to play that seventh string. He played it just as good as I would. I left and stayed about a year, and I come back and I had eight on it. I said, "You want to play some now, don't you?" He said yeah. He picked it up and said, "I'm going to get it." So when I come back again, he done learned that eighth. Everybody's talking, "Wolf's playing eight strings like Joe do." I said, "I'll fix him. I'll put that ninth string on there; I bet he won't never get it." I put that ninth string on and come back, that's two, three years. So he said, "I can get these others right, but I can't get this other one right." I said, "I knowed it; I fixed it thataway this time."
>
> He never could learn that. In fact, that's the reason I put nine strings on it. I have lots of white musicians try it, they can't do anything with it. One of them said, "I put nine strings on there but, hell, I had to take 'em off." I say, "What'd you take 'em off for?" He said, "Aw, that ninth string what gets you."

Big Joe and other blues men who had been successful recording artists in the 1930s and 1940s found that the 1950s brought hard times. In 1955, Joe hauled his hefty bulk and his guitar up the steep stairs at Bob Koester's Blue Note Record Shop in Saint

---

1. Karl Gert zur Heide, *Deep South Piano* (London, 1970), 87.

Louis. Koester was planning a series of LPs on the blues and Joe wanted to audition for the new label. He had no trouble getting Koester to record him—the trouble was that the records didn't sell and only two sides were released. In the early 1960s he recorded for Chris Strachwitz in California, played some blues dates there, and then returned to Chicago, where, in his customary far-from-modest fashion, he claimed to have opened up the North Side to blues.

Wasn't no blues on the North Side of Chicago up in those times. Bob Koester, Delmark Record Company—I built that company, he didn't have but a room like this here back in Saint Louis—I's on the West Coast and he sent for me back in Chicago. I took an ordinary guitar, go in jazz clubs where people say they never heard blues at, and do auditions amongst them kind of peoples. Some of them say, "Oh, I don't want to hear them country blues, I don't like them." So I really had it rough, but I didn't give up. After while the man says, "Let him sit around until the folk music and jazz guys go off, and then I let him run audition." When all that would go off, they would call me to the stage. People that hadn't been liking country blues, when I get through, they say, "Well, I ain't been liking any of this, but I likes that way *he* plays that."

I opened up a place called Blind Pig. Got so popular the name got all over the city—Big Joe at Blind Pig. They organized this club on North Avenue [Oxford Coffee House]. I'd bring one musician from South Side Chicago a week. I brought Memphis Slim first to play with me, and next week I'd bring Willie Dixon, next I'd bring Little Brother Montgomery, next I'd bring Johnny Temple, Junior Wells, Otis Rush—I just brought every musician in there. That's how they got to listen to blues in the North Side of Chicago.

I trained Mike Bloomfield [a white guitarist] there, I started Mike there. And give Mike his first job. I had to go to Milwaukee to play a coffee house, and I got him to play there, him and Charlie Musselwhite. Charlie was playing guitar when he come from Saint Louis, and I started him on the harp with Sonny Boy's style. He's great. But I trained all of them. Also Bobby Dylan.

See, the way I knew Bobby, he was very young and he had just run away from home. I was living in Minneapolis, living in the jungle. And he stayed with me and come to Saint Louis and lived with me. I didn't see him after he left Saint Louis until I was in New York playing at this place right off central Broadway, and he saw these bills of Big Joe Williams. So Bobby came there, came down to the dressing room—he called me Low Daddy—"I saw your sign, Low Daddy, I want to come on up." I said, "Well, bring your suitcase." That's how I got him known in New York. I got up in that club and I called him, I say, "I have a very personal friend that I treasure." And I announced him. I got up and played the harp behind him.

So, after that, on Spivey, Victoria Spivey's label, he recorded with me as Big Joe's buddy. I was singing lead voice, he's alto. Me and him made this song, one of them Mississippi Sheiks' songs, "Sitting on Top of the World"—"She's gone and I don't worry, I'm sitting on top of the world."

He altoes it. Then I made several more things with him on Spivey label, but he didn't put his name on there because he'd already signed a contract with London. He wanted to put it on there, but I knowed better. And so we made a gang of numbers together. I got 'em on tape now, the first recordings Bobby did in New York.

Dylan's debt to Williams has been noted by more than one reviewer, particularly on his second album, "The Freewheelin' Bob Dylan," and Dylan, in turn, played a large part in popularizing the blues form with young white listeners. As the blues became popular with young whites, particularly in Europe, Big Joe was one of those who took part in the black caravans that traveled Europe, beginning in the 1960s. He was on the American Folk Blues Festival tour of Europe in both 1963 and 1968 and took encore after encore.

Me and Muddy Waters, Lonnie Johnson, Victoria Spivey, John Lee Hooker, Willie Dixon, we packed London Stadium, had never been packed. That's a big stadium, London Stadium. I always wanted to go to the European countries. Way back, I used to see those pictures, the foreign peoples jumping and going on. I said I want to see them countries. I said I'd like to get in there one of these days with my guitar, wonder will I ever make it? So, I made it.

I never did go to school. I didn't want to go to school. Before I left home, they wanted me to go to school. I didn't—I wish I hadda— but I didn't. I didn't have it in mind. I had nothing in mind but just what I'm doing today. I listened to "Nearer, Oh, My God to Thee" and all that kind of stuff on the old round records and that was exactly what I wanted to do. And I wanted to go to European countries. The only thing I have desired when I was nine or five or six years old, I have did it. The Lord have been real good to me.

I has always liked to be on the go. I goes pretty regular now, but not as regular as I's used to going sometimes. When the calls don't come. . . It's a prison to stay still and look at the same ground.

Arthur "Big Boy" Crudup, who wrote the song that put Elvis Presley on the road to fame but who never shared in the rewards, in the 1970s. Courtesy of Dick Waterman

# 16 · Big Boy

At the time Elvis Presley was rocking to fame and fortune in the mid-1950s with such blues-rooted songs as Arthur Crudup's "That's All Right, Mama," Crudup was driving a farm tractor. In the fall of 1973, the same Big Boy Crudup was living in a patched-up, unpainted house down a gravel road from Exmore, Virginia, still waiting for the past-due royalties he felt could chase the blues from his door.

A big man, well over six feet tall with the heavy shoulders and muscular arms of a lifelong laborer, Crudup greeted us in the rutted yard outside the frame house. He suggested we talk in a building a few yards away, where he held country dances on occasion. We sat in one of the restaurant booths around the walls of the large room. Bare light bulbs dangling from the ceiling showed the paint peeling from the walls and the dust covering splintered board floors.

Patient and courteous, the man called the father of rock and roll repeated the story he had told countless blues buffs and reporters, the story that reflects the royalty-and-red-tape ripoffs that have befallen many of the old-time country blues men. As he talked, his frustration came through, at times with resignation, at other times with indignation. "Honey, you want me to tell you the truth, don't you? Sometimes I just feel like going down here to the bridge and get me a piece of cement block with them holes in it, tie it around my neck and get up on the tallest part of the bridge and jump off."

Crudup wrote and recorded "That's All Right, Mama" in 1940 after his discovery by talent hunter Lester Melrose on a Chicago street corner. In 1954 it became the first of the blue-suede-blues hits for Presley, who later came out with Crudup's "Who Been Fooling You" and "My Baby Left Me." Crudup's songs, these and a dozen others, turned up on records by such artists as Elton John, Rod Stewart, the Grease Band, Creedence Clearwater Revival, and Ike and Tina Turner. While they often drew big returns, Crudup himself never enjoyed the fruits of his success. Tied up in litigation and red tape, an estimated $100,000 in royalties had accumulated in his name, he said, but remained out of his reach.

Elton John, he made my numbers and they's paying that money right now. That money's just piling up there and they ain't giving it to me and so there you are. People ask me about Elvis Presley, how do I feel about him. Ought to be mad with him, they say. For what? I said I don't even know the man. I said I know he's from Memphis, Tennessee, all right enough, but I've never met him. I didn't give him the songs. And he didn't steal them because I didn't write them on paper. I realize that that man have paid his royalty statement that I was supposed to get whether I got it or not. All of this here money that I done made and you tell me, "It's yours, Arthur, you made it, it's yours," but it's hung up there and they won't pay me off.

It was apparent that the frustrations counterpointed the hardships which, in his estimation, paid his dues to sing the blues. It started back on the farm where he was born, about a mile from Forest, Mississippi. He grew up there with his mother's parents.

In a way of speaking, I don't have a father. My mother and father was not married. I saw my daddy when I was seven years old and I saw him again when I was twenty-one years old.

I been having the blues ever since I was born, and I reckon that's the reason I can sing the blues. In my ideas, the blues is just a way a person is treated. It's coming from the heart.

Every kid had something they wanted and I didn't have nothing. From the time that I was a year old up until we left Mississippi in

1916, the clothes that I wore was what a white boy wore first. My mother worked for his mother. When a piece would get too little for him, she would give it to my mother for me.

I never owned a bicycle until I was fourteen years old and then I found it on the dump, bought the tires and chains and fixed it up myself.

The way I started playing music, I found a ukulele on the dump with the head busted and I taken me a piece of plyboard and put a bottom in it. I learned how to play that.

Crudup, his mother, and sister moved to Indianapolis in 1916. When his mother became ill shortly thereafter, he left school to go to work. At thirteen he was dumping molds in a foundry; at fourteen he was carrying iron. "That hot iron, it was running like water," he recalled. His mother recovered and went back to work, but he had carried a man's load and felt grown, and he never returned to school.

The family moved back to Forest around 1926, and he started farming and got married. "The panic fell and I had a wife and one kid to work for, and I have to help my mother and sister some. I was working for fifty cents a day and one meal." Then he and his wife separated and he began "running up and down the highway." He hit the juke houses in the little Mississippi towns: Belzoni, Drew, Indianola, Sunflower, Yazoo City. He heard musicians like Charley Patton, drank moonshine whisky for thirty-five cents a half-pint, ate barbecue sandwiches, and danced till daylight.

Eventually the highway led upcountry again. He packed his clothes in a cardboard box and caught a midnight train to Chicago to join his girl friend. He moved in with the girl and her aunt, paid eighty dollars of his savings as two months' house rent, and started looking for a job. "I was there three weeks, and one morning I seen her aunt looking all sour. She say: 'You don't want no job. You just one of those kind wants a woman to take care of you. You get your little clothes and you get out of here.' The girl said to me: 'Arthur, you don't know nowhere to go. You don't know nobody. Where can you go?' I said, 'I can go somewhere. I'm a man. I'm not a tramp.' "

That night and for three weeks he slept in a pasteboard box stuffed in the opening underneath one of Chicago's elevated train stations. "I'd go there around twelve or one o'clock and I'd get out of there before day in the morning, before the police come along and found me in there."

Until then, Crudup's musical experience had been confined to singing in church and in gospel quartets. Even though he had patched up an old guitar with wire around the broken neck and taught himself to play, he was no blues singer. Like many another before him, though, he took his guitar and his natural blues to the street and sang for what he could get in the hat.

He was on the corner at Forty-third and Hawthorne when he first met Lester Melrose, who recruited talent for Vocalion, Bruns-wick-Balke-Collender's race recording label, as well as for RCA Victor's Bluebird. "A boy by the name of Doctor Clayton (Peter Clayton, a blues singer from Mississippi) come by and stood there and just let me play a piece," Crudup said. "Then he went and got Lester Melrose and Lester Melrose put a dollar in the hat. I played a couple of pieces for him."

That night Melrose took Crudup to play for a party at the home of Tampa Red (Hudson Whittaker), one of the most popular blues guitarists of the day. After Crudup played, Melrose introduced him to the people there: " 'This is Tampa Red. That's Lonnie Johnson [the guitarist whose successful career eventually spanned sixty years]. This is Memphis Slim. This is St. Louis Jimmy. This is Washboard Sam [Robert Brown, often called the strongest of the Chicago singers]. This is Big Maceo [Big Maceo Merriweather, boogie blues pianist from Texas]. This lady here is Lil Green [the singer for whom "Why Don't You Do Right," later a hit for Peggy Lee, was written]. This one over here is Memphis Minnie [Minnie Douglas McCoy, who played guitar like a man and was one of the best-known women blues singers].' I couldn't

play another tune. Why, just the idea, me sitting up there playing to those musicians that had been making records."

Melrose offered Crudup a chance to record but was interested
in original material, and Crudup had never written his own songs.
With Tampa Red's help, he began trying to write the next day.
Three days later, he recorded his first four sides. "That's All Right,
Mama," "Who Been Fooling You," "Death Valley Blues," and "If
I'd Git Lucky."

The first session paid sixty dollars. Subsequent ones paid com-
parably—never enough to live on. Jobs were hard to find. It cost
twenty dollars at the employment office to get a good job. "The
employment agent and the man that run the job was kinda in
cahoots," Crudup said. "They would let you work long enough to
make your money back and maybe a day or two over and then
they would lay you off and hire somebody else."

Crudup worked at various times in Chicago as a thirty-six-
year-old delivery "boy," as a tire capper at Firestone, and as a
night cook in a restaurant on the tough South Side. "You could
find bodies 'round in the alley, down in the garbage cans, killed
by unknown parties," he recalled. "Nobody know who done it."

Shortly after he started working in the restaurant, it was
robbed. The holdup man took the money in the cash register and
eighteen dollars from Crudup—this at a time when he was only
making sixteen dollars a week. He recognized the robber, who
lived in his building, but refused to identify him in a police line-
up. Later the man asked him why. Crudup replied: "What good
would it do me? That wouldn't get my money back. I already
know you is in the Black Hornet gang. I couldn't even come
downstairs to the liquor store without probably getting bumped
off. I wouldn't be doing nothing but letting the state make some
money." The robber gave Crudup's money back. "And I never
did have no more trouble with them kind of people and so it's
just the way you carry yourself," he said. "A man can learn to get
along anywhere."

In 1945, Crudup returned to Mississippi, went back to his

wife, and started farming again, making only occasional trips to record with Melrose in Chicago. Just as Crudup knew how to carry himself to get along in Chicago, he knew how to get along in Mississippi. He joked about what he called the "rules." "Three things a black person didn't do, he would mostly get along anywhere that he'd go. Don't touch a white woman, a white-faced cow, and a bale of cotton, and you'd be all right. Don't steal no cotton. Don't steal a white-faced cow. And be durn sure you don't touch a white woman. You could get along. People say, 'Well, I don't understand that.' I say, if that's your rule, that's your rule."

The double standard of justice was an ever-present rule to be reckoned with. "Any time that you go to jail for killing a colored person, most any white man would go your bond," Crudup said. "If you had just a little bitty proof that you killed him in self-defense, he could nearly about get you out. If the jury did give you any time, you wouldn't be there long before they'd have you out on parole. But if you killed a white man, you can just get ready to run from now on because it ain't no possible chance, regardless of what he's done. I don't care what he's done to you, don't you do nothing to him."

The influence some large landholders wielded with the law was a factor to be considered. "Some white people ruin some colored people," Crudup said. "Say I'm working for this man and he's got a big plantation. He will tell me if I stay out of the graveyard, he'll keep me out of jail. See, that ruins me."

Knowing that the boss man would keep them from going to jail made some men belligerent, he explained. Going to a party on a farm where the owner didn't allow the police on the place, "you'd have to be particular and stay scared," he said. "One of his hands liable to come in just looking for a disturbance. If he step on your foot and if he tell you to put your foot in your pocket, just say "yessir' and go ahead on if you don't want to kill him or get killed, because that's what he come there for."

Crudup's ability to adapt to the rules, to cope within the system, did not mean indifference to the injustices. As he told of being treated unfairly when he was sharecropping in the Delta in 1949, he was obviously just as rankled and resentful as if it had happened the day before instead of nearly twenty-five years earlier.

I taken my family and put them in the field and worked all the year, made a crop. The man sold $4,484.50 worth of cotton that we raised. I was working on halves—half of that money was mine. He told me, "If the plantation hadn't of come out in debt, Arthur, you would have cleared $1,700. But the plantation come out in debt and nobody cleared a penny. But I can give you $50 a month furnish [an advance on a sharecropper's earnings] until March. When March come, your regular $60 a month furnish start. But it's no money for Christmas."

As though to add the final straw to the injustice, the plantation owner told Crudup to take a dump truck to the river and pick up a load of baseball-size rocks. "His kid's learning how to play ball and wanted to learn how to bat, batting them rocks across the fields," Crudup said. "And my kids out there working, trying to help me make a living. I had three there barefooted, and I had just enough for them to eat in the house for that day. Now what I'm getting my kids Christmas with and getting them a pair of shoes with?"

Crudup moved his family back to Forest. He worked for the city, farmed some, played Saturday night dances—anything to take care of his wife and children. "I was still recording, but my recording wasn't paying me enough to do no good. I had a couple of boys that's old enough to farm, and them and my wife and the smaller kids would make a crop, and I would hire out all the time to take care of them."

It was during this time that rock and roll caught hold, and as Crudup heard Presley's version of "That's All Right, Mama" over and over on radio and jukebox, he began to wonder about royalties. He wrote Melrose but never was satisfied with the answers he received. "Finally I told him that he could hold the copyrights on me and my contract but he couldn't make me sing, and I quit.

I decided it's no need for me just keeping on and ain't getting nothing for what I done already done."

He moved to Florida in 1955, where he drove a tractor one season and then bought a truck to haul his family and some of the other itinerant workers to Birdnest, Virginia, near Exmore, where they harvested potatoes, beans, and cucumbers. Until his health failed, they continued to alternate between Florida and Virginia, six months each place, following the work. Except for one brief episode with a small, unsuccessful recording company around 1960, Crudup had little to do with the music business until Dick Waterman—a Massachusetts attorney, promoter, and friend of many blues men—talked him into taking a booking at the University of Chicago in 1968.

Waterman, who had never met Crudup, wasn't sure what to expect from his new old-timer. Even in his active days in the blues, Crudup had performed very little in front of an audience; when he did, it was before black audiences in juke houses and small nightclubs.

Dick thought it was going to go bad with me because he realized that was my first booking playing to them many white peoples. I bet you it wasn't over twenty-five colored in the place. I wanted something to drank and he give me one of these little bottles you get on the airplane. He says, "I'll give you another one when you get ready to go on the stage. Now I don't want you to get drunk." I says okay. My brother-in-law had a pint in his pocket.

I played that concert and so Dick thought it was mighty nice. He says, "Arthur, now you see if I'd given you some more whisky, you might have messed up." I said, "Well, I done already dranken a pint." From then on, he would tell anyone, "If you don't give Arthur some whisky, he ain't gonna play."

Like many another blues man, Crudup had learned early that booze blended well with the blues. In the days when he was recording for Bluebird, he would take a bottle of whisky and his guitar to the studio and write his songs there. "I could do it better," he said. "You could give me the whisky I wanted to drink and I could get to dranking, and the blues start to falling out the ceiling." Whisky or no, Crudup said, you can't sing the blues unless you've lived them.

Ain't no way in the world for you to do something you ain't never had, you see. Take a rich man. He can sang the blues. But, now, he's just sanging it from the lips and the thought of what he want to sang. A poor man, he's sanging it from the way that he's treated, and it's coming directly from the heart.

A white man can't sing the blues like a colored person because it's things that he wanted, some of them he got. I know several that was poor, right in Mississippi. They lived on a white man's farm. When school would be going on, those kids went to school every day until school was out. And the colored peoples that lived on that farm, when March come, them colored kids got to come out of school and go to cleaning up the fields.

And so, therefore, he wasn't treated like the colored. And he can't sing the blues like the colored. The blues is coming from the heart. That's where it's coming.

The blacks sang the blues during those years Crudup traveled the concert circuit, but they sang them for audiences that were overwhelmingly white. It was a far cry from other days Crudup recalled in the South.

A colored person couldn't play for a white person if he couldn't play instrumental music and love songs and waltzes and all of that. He couldn't play for white people because white people did not fancy the blues.

Now the white is going for the blues more than the black is. Look like you should have more colored there than you do whites. I played out there in Berkeley, that big university, and it's full of colored people. I bet you it was five thousand peoples there that night and you could fair nigh count the colored was there.

My suggestion of that is, "What's the use of me going up here to Exmore to see something that I done already seen? What's the use in my worrying about going to hear such-and-such-a-one play the blues and I done already had the blues all my life?"

After Waterman coaxed him back to the blues scene, Crudup traveled back and forth across the United States as well as to

Australia and to Europe. "I went to twenty-six different towns in Europe over there," he said. "He [Waterman] sent me by myself. And, honey, I had never been out of New York."

Whether appearing with other old blues men or with hard-rock youngsters borrowing on the blues, Crudup prided himself on fitting in easily. "If you can play, even if it ain't nothing but a juice harp, you can play with me," he said.

But touring took its toll. "Sometimes sitting on the bus all day, you know just about how I feel when I get there," he said. "I go up and take a hot shower and lay down and get ready for that night. It's no enjoyment for me. I'm just there working to try to make a living. The doctor don't allow me to work in the fields no more. I got to do something for a living."

The death of Melrose complicated Waterman's efforts to recover Crudup's royalties. Each promise of settlement was followed by more red tape and more delay, Crudup said.

What they holding it for? They want me to die? If they pay it off when I'm dead, I couldn't enjoy it; and I can't carry it with me, so let me enjoy a little of it while I'm here.

I ain't never wanted to be a rich man nohow. I just wanta live decent. I don't want no mansion. I would like a decent house to live in, one where when wintertime comes that I won't have to walk around in the house with a coat on to try to keep warm.

Now I don't care for no Cadillacs. I wouldn't want one of them. If I got a automobile, don't make no difference if it is a secondhanded car, let it be a decent secondhanded car.

And that's all I want. If I want to buy me something, I'd like to have money enough to get what I want and not have to ask will you let me have so-and-so and I'll pay you at such-and-such a time. [He lifted his head and smiled slightly.] I don't know if I'm going to get it. I can't ever get the right understanding.

I worry about it sometimes. Then again I just say forget it. Nothing from nothing leaves nothing. I come here with nothing. I ain't got nothing. And I ain't going away with nothing. And it's no need of worrying my life with it.

Arthur Crudup died on March 28, 1974, still unpaid but not unsung.

*Left*, Albert Luandrew, the cotton picker and "Dudlow picker" who won fame as Sunnyland Slim, in Japan in 1978. *Above*, Little Brother Montgomery, whose "Vicksburg Blues" became a piano standard, in Chicago in 1975.
Courtesy of Delmark Records

McKinley Morganfield, better known as Muddy Waters, one of the top modern-day blues singers, in the 1970s.
Courtesy of Chicago *Tribune*

# 17 · Upcountry

Youngsters skipping rope and jumping hopscotch chanted this bouncy ditty on Beale Street around World War I.

> Run tell your mama,
> Run tell your papa,
> Run tell your grandma, too,
> I'm goin' up the country,
> Goin' where they don't 'low you.

But it was more than just a catchy rhyme—it was an exuberant anthem of the black man on the move. From the depths of the Mississippi Valley had begun to flow a steady stream of sharecroppers and tenant farmers as the southern Negro pursued his dreams northward.

The North was the natural land of dreams, the longed-for Canaanland of freedom during slave days, the promised land of good jobs, big money, equal rights and respect. Upcountry was the upbeat future, down home the downtrodden past.

World War I supplied the catalyst. Young black men left home for the army and were never content to return. The war virtually stopped immigration, and factory jobs opened up for blacks. And Jim Crow laws in the South speeded the departures.

Throughout the South, the path of the migration followed the railroad track, heading straight for the cities in the most direct routes northward. And, from New Orleans, due north for a thousand miles, straight through the whole of the Delta blues country, ran the Illinois Central Railroad.

From Tennessee, Louisiana, Alabama, Arkansas, and especially Mississippi, they surged to the city that Mississippi blues
man Robert Johnson called "sweet home Chicago." Some stopped
along the way, in Memphis or Saint Louis, when they ran out of
money and had to lay over long enough to earn more. Many took
their families with them. Others traveled alone, planning to send
for the ones left behind once they found work.

But sooner or later the "Creole," the "Louisiane," or the
"Southern Express" pulled into the Illinois Central Station on
Twelfth Street in Chicago and out they poured, the men in worn
suits long out of style, wagging battered suitcases or cardboard
boxes tied up with string, the women shepherding barefooted,
ragged children. Bewildered, lost, intimidated, they searched for
a familiar face among the crowds that turned out to meet friends
or relatives or just to stare. In their naïvete and lack of education,
these country-bred newcomers made easy prey for the con men
who—for a fee—promised lodging or jobs and often produced
neither. The new arrivals ended up with the thousands who had
preceded them in the jammed tenement blocks of the South Side
and near West Side, living in numberless apartment houses, kitch-
enettes, and "hot-bed" apartments shared by several families on a
shift basis.

Homesick in the cold winds of Chicago, disillusioned in their
dreams, they sought release—and reminders of home—in the
blues. Prohibition went into effect, but the Volstead Act didn't
come close to shutting down the wide-open town of Chicago.
Gangs and local government worked together to quench the public's illegal and very profitable thirst.

Jazz was for the whites in the big cafes and dance halls. Blues
was for the blacks in the speakeasies and back-alley dives on the
South Side or at countless house-rent parties offering white lightning and the blues for a quarter a head at the door. There was an
abundance of blues men, searching for their own dreams of fame
and wealth, following the allure of the big-name musicians who

had already come to the city or perhaps had just touched down in Chicago for a few weeks in their roamings.

By 1930, Chicago was the home of 233,000 blacks, 38,000 of them from Mississippi. In fact, the city had more Mississippi residents than any town outside the state—and many more than most towns within it.[1] The depression closed the gates at northern factories and slowed the flood tide of migration to a trickle, for hard times were easier to cope with at home.

But, as the depression eased slightly in the late thirties, the tide began to swell again. Prohibition was repealed, boosting the club scene—already healthy and vigorous—even more. Older, established artists, like Big Bill Broonzy, Tampa Red, and Memphis Minnie, played regularly at the bigger night spots. Often they would lend a helping hand to new arrivals, letting them sit in on a session. There they could be heard, and perhaps hired, by the owner of one of the small joints—usually just a counter along one wall, tables on the other, with the band and what went for a dance floor squeezed in between. Five or six hours of work brought maybe three dollars each for the musicians.

If a blues man couldn't make that scene, he could go "scabbin' "—playing in a joint for the change he could pick up in tips. Or there was always the bottom of the barrel—playing on the street near the open-air Maxwell Street Market in the old immigrant area of Chicago known as Jew Town. Sooner or later all the newly arrived blues men hit Jew Town, the center of amateur blues in the city.

With the forties the tide flowed north like never before. From 1940 to 1950, the black population of Chicago increased 77 percent, from 277,000 to 492,000, with half the increase from Mississippi alone.[2] The biggest years for the blues were immediately after World War II, years of prosperity and pursuit of pleasure.

1. Mike Rowe, *Chicago Breakdown* (London, 1973), 35–36.
2. *Ibid.*, 35.

Chicago had the clubs, the talent, and the audience. The city drew blues men and their fans like a magnet.

The music of down home gradually changed as the new city dwellers reached for a more aggressive, harsher sound, a more vibrant beat to match the faster pace and abrasive life of the city, and for words to speak of the concerns of the city man—jobless-ness, hard-nosed cops, violence, bright-lights excitement. In the clubs of the South Side, this new sound was shaped, taking the Delta blues, heightening its naturally raucous, rough-voiced qual-ity, intensifying its beat, transforming it into the urban blues. Chicago was the spawning ground for the urban blues, which eventually became known as Chicago blues. Chicago was where it was.

It was in those years that three blues men were drawn by the magnet. Their stories speak for themselves and for all their blues brothers who journeyed to Sweet Home Chicago.

### Sunnyland Slim and Little Brother

"The blues," said Little Brother Montgomery, "was the lowest thing in the music when we was boys."

"Oh, yeah," said Sunnyland Slim, "it was the lowest. My father was a preacher and my folks didn't stand for us to sang no blues, no nothin' like that."

Little Brother continued: "It wasn't in a class with no other kind of music. See, blues come from the rough treatments that you had from somewhere, hoboing or some woman or something, you know. That's what kind of started the blues, jails and first one thing. And the people get down and worried and they'd play the blues. You get sad, don't feel right, that's where the blues came from."

The interview had been set up with Sunnyland Slim, Albert Luandrew, at his apartment on 179th Street. The apartment, up green-carpeted stairs above a tavern, abounded with bright-col-ored furniture, throw pillows, and small ornaments. Sunnyland, a big, genial, hospitable man, made a place for the tape recorder amid the flowers and figurines on the coffee table. He had just started to talk about his life when the doorbell rang. "That must be Brother," Sunnyland said and opened the door to admit a chunky man, nattily dressed in a blue paisley sport shirt and self-belted knit slacks.

Montgomery, called by many the grand old man of jazz and blues pianists in Chicago, took a chair by the coffee table and found an ashtray for his ever-constant cigarette. Mainly content to let Sunny tell of his experiences, he occasionally joined in to supply a name, insert an opinion, or talk about the blues.

Luandrew went on with his story, telling how he had been born in 1907 on his grandfather's farm out from Vance, Mississippi, and grew up there until he was about ten.

I was a lover to the minstrel shows, and to hear music—organ, guitar —kind of did me in and look like it would stay on my mind. I'd cut up all your wood and kindlin' to get a chance to play your organ. A boy called Jeff, he showed me a little bit. And I'd get a shoebox top and draw the keys, hold my hand there the way I'd hear the sound it hit. [Here he held out one hand, immense, with long, slender, supple fingers that would easily span an octave and a half.]

Well, my mother died, and this next marriage of my father, it wasn't comfortable. Me and my stepmother didn't get along, and my stepmother was so mean to me and when I was about twelve, I started to running away. I'd run away to my uncle and I'd run away to my cousins. They'd come get me, but I'd run away again. Finally, I told my grandfather I just couldn't stay there and he give me five dollars and so I left for good.

He hired out doing odd jobs, tending to livestock, catching fish, picking blackberries for sale, and, at harvest time, picking cotton.

I always was a good cotton picker, pick a lot of cotton. I have picked high as seven hundred a day. [Top field hands would average between four hundred and five hundred pounds of cotton a day.] It was fifty cents a hundred, the best you could get. After I run off from home, I'd go out there and pick four hundred a day, or four hundred and fifty. They'd pay me. Well, I got to give some of that for my keep, where I'm sleeping, but sleeping is very cheap then.

So I'd go to the Saturday night thing—this was along about twenty, twenty-one. I run up on this piano player at a joint—he had a kind of pot gut and they called him Dough Belly. He could play a lot of "da-wang-wang-wang-da-da-da," you know, what all that stuff was then. Well, I come in there with my little money. I wasn't drinking; I'd just buy a quart or half-pint, pass it to him, say, "How you do that?" He'd show me. Then I'd get off by myself and learn a little bit, little bit, so finally I's playin', secret to myself.

Up to this time Luandrew had stuck close to home, even though he wasn't living with his family, but now he took to rambling. He got tied up with "a one-legged piano player, could play one piece good, but he was a good card sharp." The card shark owned an Essex he had bought after cleaning up in a high-stakes game, and because Luandrew was handy with cars, he took the youngster along to do the driving. They struck out for Greenwood, Mississippi, where a run-in with the local police cut short their stay, then headed on for Pickens, Canton, and a couple of other small towns. When the car broke down beyond Luandrew's ability to repair it, the association dissolved and Luandrew headed back north to Lambert.

Though he had picked up some pointers in his wanderings, he was still no great shakes as a pianist. But he was good enough to get along playing at country shindigs around Lambert for fifty cents a night, free barbecue, and all the corn whisky he could drink. "I's just doin' whatsomever I's doin'," he admitted. "I wasn't doing but one key." It was a step up when he was hired by the local motion picture show operator for a dollar and a half per night—the whites downstairs, the blacks upstairs, and Luandrew and the piano in the back with the man who changed the reels.

Not much later, he moved up to Memphis where he took a job with the railroad. But, "to make sure everything balance," he got a small loan, acquired some bottles, bought some malt, and started making beer. With his job and his sideline, he supported himself and began running with some of the lesser-known musicians like Van Hooks and P. R. Gibson. The big names he viewed from afar—Jim Jackson; Barbecue Bob (Robert Hicks); Blind Arthur Blake, who was often in Memphis; Memphis Minnie, who was back and forth between Memphis and Chicago. "It was a lot of peoples in Memphis then, I mean all the sporting class—Cab Calloway, Duke Ellington—everybody was coming to play the Palace Theater, the Daisy Theater."

Beale Street was living up to its reputation for fast living. "Them joints was wide open then; things was jumping. You could hear tell of somebody getting killed near 'bout like nothin'. The ambulance keep busy running to the hospital.

"I started to messing around with the average musicians. P. R. started showing me some A chords. I tried to play—I didn't play nothing, I ain't goin' to tell no lie too much, I couldn't play but in three keys, you know. But I could keep a house, could make you sell some fish and whisky, and keep sangin' the blues. I used to sang a lot."

Here Brother broke in: "Sunnyland is one of the greatest out there for singing. He can sing the blues. Now, the greatest blues singer of the females of all times is Bessie Smith. I played on her show at Jackson, Mississippi, and she'd walk out on one of them stages and light up that theater. She didn't have no mikes or nothing. Sunnyland can sang like that. I tell him—talk and tell him in front of his face and behind his back—if he would take time to rhyme his words good as he can sang, he'd be the Bessie Smith of the men. He got some of the best lungs you ever heard."

Sunnyland added: "Bessie Smith was, you know, diverse. She could sang blues, and then she went with the big bands, with Count Basie or Duke. Wasn't like Ma Rainey. See, Ma Rainey couldn't do none of Bessie's style.

"Ma Rainey come through Memphis about the time I was talking about. Georgia Tom [Thomas A. Dorsey], Ma's regular piano player, had quit her. So she hired me. We went to Portageville, Missouri, had nothing but a piano, guitar, and drums—no amps. And the first thing she stepped out on, the first thing she did, she said 'B flat,' she patted her foot to the guitar, and when she started out, she wasn't in the key of the guitar *or* me. All I could do was hit that one key and I didn't know how to change the pace, you know. So I goes back to P. R. then, I carries a quart of corn whisky, and ask him to show me them other keys. He show me a D chord with each hand, he stayed there with me and drank my whisky and showed me that. And the next thing I learned, E natural. Well, there wasn't nothing to it.

"But like Memphis Slim [Peter Chatman], he played for years and years, he didn't ever get no farther than C and G. Whenever he see me or Brother or somebody coming going to be sanging something in B flat or some other key, he talk just a little bit, 'Come on, Brother,' that way he got something to hide behind because he could not play in those keys. Play a little in F and C. I know. I know about him. I played for his daddy. His daddy an old-time hustler. He's going to them picnics out there from Memphis [big, all-day gatherings in West Tennessee and North Mississippi that drew many of the musicians in the area]. He carried me 'round with him 'cause he called me a 'dudlow,' a piano player, say I draw the crowd. Back then they didn't call it a piano player, what they used to call it down South was a 'dudlow picker.' "

Brother commented: "The number 'Dudlow Joe' is the boogie-woogie, it was a boogie. Everybody who could play that, could play 'Dudlow Joe,' they'd call you 'dudlow pickers.' Clarence 'Pine Top' Smith, around 1925, made 'Pine Top's Boogie-Woogie.' He named it boogie-woogie and soon everybody went to callin' it boogie-woogie."

Sunnyland continued: "So Old Man Chatman would carry me around, he'd give me what he want, maybe a dollar—better not say I'm hungry too much, you know." He chuckled at the remembrance. "Pete was just trying to play then. I didn't know him at that time, but later he come around through Memphis."

In the fifteen years that Luandrew lived in Memphis, he

played on Beale—at the Midway, the Wagonyard, the Hole in the Ground, but mostly at the Harlem Inn on Florida. He also rambled the area, to the picnics, to the joints, over in Arkansas and up in Missouri. "Me and that old albino fellow, Speckled Red [Rufus Perryman] what sang the 'Dirty Dozens,' we run through all the best, lively joints in Missouri—Caruthersville, Portageville, New Madrid, Sikeston, Cairo. All them best piano players was running up and down them roads, to them joints. I'd go up to Missouri every year and mess around in harvest times. That makes the times good, you know. And so a piano player had a pretty nice way to go. He'd get him a girl everywhere he went and he could holler. So we had it very nice, I think.

"And I'd play in Arkansas—Pine Bluff, Hughes, Wilson—at the majority of the best houses. That's when I got my name. See, was this train running from Memphis to Saint Louis on the Frisco, they called it the Sunnyland. It killed my uncle and it killed my cousin and it killed a gang of peoples. And then peoples started to say, 'Why don't you write a song?' I sang that song through Arkansas, all through Terrell, all through Wilson, anywhere I play. You could hear people goin' through the field plowing mules, mocking me. After I sang it so good, all the people started calling me Sunnyland."

West Memphis, Arkansas, just across the river from Memphis, once merely a wide spot in a gumbo road, began to open up about this time. "When I first come to West Memphis," Sunnyland recalled, "crawfish would be standing on Eighth Street—which is the lead street—standing down there right off the highway. You had to put on hip boots to get down to some of them places. Then Memphis got closed and West Memphis started to opening up. The towns got the joints, that's where the piano players is. Why, some of them places in West Memphis, they'd have two shifts of piano players.

"There was a lot of good players around. Roosevelt Sykes start to hanging 'round about thirty-four; he come through and he started playing behind us. Memphis Slim was around; he would get drunk and shoot his money off with those craps. Walter Lewis and little old Zack Moore—they playing over at the levee camp, Clark's Camp, in Arkansas—they drift through there."

Brother chimed in: "I lived in Memphis at the Bluff City Hotel on Third and Beale, and then I lived on Texas Avenue 'round nineteen thirty-three. I played up at Harlem Inn, that joint where Van Hooks and all of us used to play at."

Sunnyland said: "Yeah, that's where a whole lot of 'em got bumped off in there. Well, you see, I come up to Chicago in thirty-three, but I didn't stay here no time. I didn't want to stay here 'cause the cotch games and the gamblin' is wide open down South. That's what I likes to be around. All the joints was wide open and just anywhere they said Sunnyland, *blam*, 'Yeah, he's back, he's here!' If a man would pay somebody three dollars, I could get five dollars, 'cause I was known, get five dollars a night and my board.

"And it was hard in those days to go in joints and get a job in Chicago. The peoples I was with the week I was up there didn't know their way around too much, and I didn't know anybody much. If I hadda been the man that Little Brother is today, perhaps I could have stayed. I could have played for the white folks as well as I could get through to the colored.

"Brother can play any kinda popular songs, play for any party. Brother can play in a class with Teddy Wilson or anybody you want. Brother can play. But I'm just a boogie and blues player. And the blues really wasn't taking off in Chicago like it was in Arkansas, Mississippi and Florida and Georgia and them places. See, well, I had already made it, you understand. That's why I wouldn't want to give up, what I say, something for nothing. Perhaps I'd been a bigger man today than I am."

The hard times of the thirties in Chicago that kept Sunnyland from moving up drove many musicians back South, including Eurreal "Little Brother" Montgomery. Brought up in a sawmill town in Louisiana, where his father ran a barrelhouse, Brother left home at eleven to play piano in other sawmill towns, in tur-

pentine camps, brothels, and juke joints. His path led him in and
out of New Orleans, into contact with some of the top jazzmen
of the day and on the road with Clarence Desdune's Joyland Rev-
elers. "Jazz come from blues, you know," he said at one point,
talking about the difference in the two musical forms. "If you
can't play blues good, you ain't gone never play jazz. Jazz is a
feeling within a person. Music comes from within a person anyway, not the notes. Notes is only mathematics. That ain't no
music. That just sound like arithmetic. But the music come from
within you."

In 1928, Brother tried his luck in Chicago, playing for rent
parties on the South Side. He made a few recordings for Paramount, but just as he was becoming known, the depression hit
and he went South to his former home in Jackson, Mississippi. He
organized a swing band, the Southland Troubadours, and did
some recording in New Orleans and some wandering on his own,
playing the sawmill and levee camp circuit as well as the joints
on Beale. The band broke up in 1939, and by the start of World
War II, he was ready to try Chicago again.[3]

Luandrew had moved to Chicago in 1941, and when the recording industry began to pick up in the days following the war,
both men were on hand to try to capitalize on the boom. Chicago
was seeing a revival of Dixieland jazz, and Brother joined other
old-time jazz musicians in recording and playing the New Orleans
themes, including a Carnegie Hall concert in 1948 with the Kid
Ory band.[4]

Sunnyland, on the other hand, was struggling to make it with
the blues alone. He had moved into a basement apartment on
East Thirty-first, and many of the Chicago musicians used the
apartment for a rehearsal hall. "That's where you catch all of
them," Sunny continued, "Otis Spann, Big Bill Broonzy, Brother
Montgomery, Tampa Red. They's rehearsing there at my house,
just like you can do out there now." He pointed to the small,

3. Zur Heide, *Deep South Piano*, 45–53.
4. *Ibid.*, 55.

yellow-brick building behind his apartment, where a rehearsal was scheduled for later in the day.

Small independent labels were popping up, trying to cash in on the success of the Chicago name, and Luandrew pursued success with many of them. He recorded on thirteen different labels up to the sixties, at times even hawking the records from his car, and played on countless other sessions as an accompanist.

"Everybody in Chicago, after they found out what they could do with the blues, this one and that one open a little tin-pan-alley record company," Sunnyland said. "And they say, 'Man, we can do something for you.' Then you try to get some money out of a company, they go broke, they's broke. They went around the corner and they changed names, you understand what I mean. It was just like these churches where every storefront you could get to is a church. It's a racket."

Brother joined in: "All those big record companies, that's how they get to be billionaires and the artists don't have nothing. See, they take everything. Them musicians made them rich, they didn't make theirselves rich; but they take it all, don't pay 'em no royalties or nothing on their numbers. But they didn't make it theyselves, they taken it from the musicians.

"Whoever gets to the recording station first with it, it don't have to be they number, it's theirs. I composed 'Forty-four Blues,' me and Friday Ford and Dehlco Robert. Roosevelt Sykes and Lee Green, after I taught it to 'em, they beat us up to Saint Louis and made it so they got the name of it. So I changed it to 'Vicksburg Blues' and made it myself. And it's one of the biggest that's out there, and I ain't ever got a hundred dollars out of it. Everybody made it—I don't know one guy ain't ever made that—they don't pay me for it. It's they 'Vicksburg Blues.' "

Sunnyland lamented: "I got eight records in there on two companies. I didn't get nothing out of them, not a penny. And when I did 'Brown-Skinned Woman' in forty-nine or fifty, they give me around a thousand dollars. That's the most I ever get out of any record. I thought that's a lot of money. I didn't know."

Brother declared: "I got sense enough to didn't get out there too much now, but I used to. I thought everybody was fair. But they ain't. Music is a brutal business."

## Muddy

Scott Cameron, wearing blue jeans and T-shirt and driving an older-model Cadillac, met the train at the commuter depot in Westmont, Illinois, as promised.

Cameron, Muddy Waters' manager, had set up the interview. As he drove to Muddy's house, he repeated what he had said earlier on the telephone: "Don't expect to talk to Muddy more than thirty minutes and probably not that long. He gets tired. And don't ask him how he got his name." The prospects sounded vaguely discouraging, particularly after an hour's ride on a commuter train from Chicago.

The house itself was white frame, located on a small corner lot, and surrounded by middle-class, equally unpretentious homes. "Muddy moved here recently," Cameron said, parking his Cadillac across the street. "He wanted to move away from the South Side before, but his wife didn't want to leave." He later said that Muddy's wife had died a few months before, of cancer.

Cameron led the way into the house through the kitchen, where several young people, including Muddy's son, were frying chicken and fixing lunch. Muddy's two small granddaughters sat on the floor in front of the television set in the living room with their grandfather, a small, very dark man with broad features and wide-spaced cheekbones. He looked younger than his years—he was born in 1915—but the effects of the 1969 car wreck that killed his driver and the young couple in the other car were still apparent. Muddy spent three months in the hospital, nine weeks of that in traction. It was a year before he began playing again, and several more years before he quit using a cane. He rose with difficulty for introductions, and the few steps he made were stiff and slow.

But there was nothing slow about his hospitality. "Can I offer you a drink, some wine, champagne?" he asked. "Open that bottle of Mateus," he shouted to the crowd in the kitchen, "and bring some glasses. Now, babies," he told the little girls, "you go on in the back and turn on the TV back there. Here," he said to the young man who brought the wine, "take these children in the back.

"Now," he said, settling back in his red velvet wing chair, "where did you say you're from?"

"We both live in Memphis now, but I'm from Friars Point, Mississippi" was the answer.

"Friars Point? You say Friars Point? Well, that's close to my home. I'm from Stovall, grew up there, lived there all my life 'til I came to Chicago. Do you know the Stovalls? Did you know Mr. Howard Stovall?" he asked.

"Yes, I know the family."

"And what's your name? McKee? Your father John McKee? I knew him, yeah, I knew who he was. He had a plantation down there at Friars Point. And you his daughter? Is that so?" he said.

"Yes, I grew up in Friars Point. And we wanted to talk a little bit about Mississippi, about what it was like when you grew up around Stovall."

"Well," he answered, "I just have to tell the truth about it. You know. You're from down that way. I grew up hard. But I grew up with a good boss and that was Mr. Howard Stovall and I love him today. He's dead, but I love him today for that particular thing." (A few months before, Stovall's youngest son, Robert, who lived in Chicago, had brought his niece and nephew from Mississippi to a club where Muddy was playing. When Muddy found out they were there, he asked them to stand up and introduced them to the crowd at the nightclub. "These are my people," he said.)

"My grandmother raised me," Muddy continued. "She taken me when I was a baby." Muddy was born in Rolling Fork, Mississippi. His mother, Berta, died when he was very young, and he was reared by his maternal grandmother, Della Jones. Named McKinley Morganfield, he had been called Muddy Waters since he was a boy, because, the usual story goes, he liked to play in the muddy bayou that ran behind his grandmother's house on the Stovall plantation. (Per instructions, we didn't ask him how he got his name.)

My grandmother was a woman, and she didn't know how to get out there and hustle as good as some men, but she did the best she could do. But I grew up real poor. I grew up without money and the little money I's gettin' at that time wasn't enough to even say I had money. I worked for fifty cents a day from sun to sun. That means like fifteen or sixteen hours a day.

But, on the sideline, I loved my guitar so well, I would get out at night and do that guitar. I had started with the harmonica when I was seven, at nine I was doing pretty good, thirteen I was extra. But then I started with that guitar and when I's gettin' pretty good, I go and play for parties. If you can remember what I'm talking about, when they started pickin' cotton, they started having parties, hustling them little nickels and dimes.

They would have the parties just where they lived at. If they had a little single house—which you know what I'm talking about, that mean a little room to sleep in, the kitchen to cook in—they would take the beds out, that's if it wasn't raining, and put them on the outside and have the whole little room to do their dancing in. We had pretty dances then. We was black bottoming, Charleston, two-step, waltz, and one-step. Them dances nowdays, somebody standing still, killing the girl, guy standing in one place, the girl's runnin' all 'round. We had nice dances, then, real nice.

And they would pull up a cotton house, you know—I'm talking to peoples understanding me now—they'd pull up a cotton house and that's they little gambling shed. [Small frame sheds at the edge of the fields stored the cotton until the wagons took it to the cotton gin.] Mostly dice, but they played coon-can, they played pitty-pat, and they played Georgia skin, that was a big game. Few peoples play at a little poker, few. All them big Memphis gamblers, they would play cotch and poker, stuff like that. We nickeled and dimed, see. I shot dice all night long for a penny. That was our thing; we couldn't get no higher than a penny.

And the way we make lights, take coal oil—I'm talking for home now, you know, I don't dig kerosene, I dig the name coal oil—put it in a bottle, take the rope, the plow line that you plow the mule with, stick it all the way in the bottle and put a little wet on top and light it. They had their lamps hanging all 'round like that.

Well, they'd come get me on time for parties, but they wouldn't bring me back on time. And like lot of mornings I get home and change my little ironed blue jeans and put on my cotton-picking clothes and go to the field and work. Done picked cotton all day, play all night long, then pick cotton all day the next day before I could get a chance to sleep.

But that was fun to me. Them parties was real fun. That's the best part of my life, good experience and fun. I'm trying to learn what I know now, and I think that was a good way for me to learn it, was to go through that. That cure me, knock me down.

Before Muddy played for parties himself, he listened to some of the best blues men of the day—Charley Patton, Big Joe Williams, the Mississippi Sheiks.

I just a young boy, but I loved it so well, anytime they in my vicinity I was there. Walk. Catch a ride on a wagon. Steal the mule out of the lot. I was there. Son House, he played on the Belmont part of Stovall's plantation. You know, there was Prairie, West End, and Belmont. He was there like a month in a row every Saturday night. I was playing harmonica then, and I sat there and I watched that man's fingers. Look like to me I never heard a man could play guitar like that in my life. I said, "Can't nobody touch this man." That man was just so good he was unlimited, to me.

Clarksdale, the largest town close by, would have been the logical gathering spot for musicians except that Clarksdale had a twelve o'clock closing hour. "Twelve o'clock, you better be out of there, get off the streets. That great big police come down Sunflower Street with that big cap on, man, waving that stick, you'd better get out of there, boy. I'm telling you. That's why all this country stuff, people go to the country. Friars Point'd go up to four o'clock in the morning, sometimes all night."

Beckoning seventy miles to the north was the biggest city in four hundred miles.

Memphis, Memphis, M–E–M–P–H–I–S. The biggest city I ever seen in my life. Clarksdale, it wasn't saying a word. Biggest city I'd ever seen in my life.

Memphis, like I say, was up north. And Beale Street was the street. Black man's street. More slickers come off Beale Street than come out of New York. So many slick people came from down that way, learnt how to gamble, learnt how to con, how to cheat, from down in that part of the country. And Beale Street was the main line.

Couple of us what plays, like me and Son Sims, sometimes we'd go up to Memphis just to come back for the big word, "We's in Memphis last night." That was a big word, you see. Sometimes you go on a bus, sometime you go on a train, sometime you drive up there if you had a good enough car 'cause people thought it was so far, didn't think a car could go a hundred and forty miles. That was sort of like you was goin' almost to California. You get in a car goin' to Memphis, you wouldn't be that tired, but you think you'd be that tired, you'd change drivers. "You drive some, I'm tired."

I'd go out in that little park up there on Beale. Everybody on a Saturday evening out there, somebody over here playing guitar, somebody singing gospel, like Maxwell Street used to be in Jew Town. This Walter Horton that's up here now, he's out there blowing the harp, and Honey Boy [David] Edwards, used to play guitar, and little midget, Buddy Doyle, he could sing good.

I didn't never meet none of the big ones like Jim Jackson. I didn't have time to stay that long. I'd go up like on Saturday, come back Saturday night, come back Sunday. Get back home, you'd catch that mule Monday morning. Early. Get on that tractor, sharpen a hoe before you go so your wife could chop cotton.

Even more impressive than a trip to Memphis was an appearance on King Biscuit Time with Sonny Boy Williamson II (Rice Miller) over radio station KFFA in Helena, Arkansas. The daily fifteen-minute broadcast was lengthened to thirty minutes on Saturday, and musicians competed for guest spots. It meant catching ɪe ferry at Delta Landing to cross the river, but Muddy and others headed for Helena nearly every weekend after the show went on the air in the late thirties. "If you get a chance to be on the air, your peoples back home could hear you. If we got a chance to set in and do a couple of songs, man, when we got back on

Stovall, that was the whole talk. Everybody that's heard it on the radio was runnin', tellin' all the people all on the plantation, 'I hear them, man, I hear them, they on it!'"

Along with working on the plantation and playing parties for blacks and sometimes for whites, Muddy had an additional source of income. He made ditch-bank whisky.

We'd get back there in them little canal ditches and them little woods, hid off the highways. So we'd get back there, get one of them fifty-gallon oil drums, that's what you cook it in. You got to get the copper pipe, make your coil. Get one of them big wooden barrels, that's your cooling barrel. Get that flour dough and cinch up where your pipe go through so no steam come out.

You start the fire. And you set there. It's a baby, you got to nurse it. You can't rush the fire. You got to set there. It start to doing its thing and you can hear the pipe start making a little funny noise. Pop. Pop. Pop. Pop. Pop-pop-pop-pop-pop. There it is.

All of the South was dry then, it was dry. The people so thirsty for it, you make it, you sell it. No ageing, no nothing. Sell.

This illegal sideline made Muddy suspicious when folklorist Alan Lomax first came to record him on a field trip for the Library of Congress in 1941.

I didn't know how to take this man. You know, 'cause we from the same place. See, I couldn't handle this white man goin' to put me in his car and drive me 'round, goin' into my house. I thought 'cause I was bootlegging corn whisky, I say, "Uh-huh, revenue man trying to get into me." I say, "He don't talk like my peoples, he musta not live here because he got a different accent."

So he kept saying he wanted a drink of water, and I didn't have no ice so I go to the pump and pump him off a cool'n. Same cup I drink out of, he drinks out of that, too. I said, "Not a white man doin' this!" No, no, this was too much, he goin' too far, you know. But my mind still thinkin', "Oh, he'd do anything to see can he bust you."

And when he brought his machine, he got his old guitar and he started playin', and he said: "Well, I came down to see Robert Johnson. I heard Robert Johnson's dead and I heard you's almost as good or just as good, and I want you to do something for me. Will you let me record some of your songs, and I'll play them back and let you listen to them? I want to take it to the Library of Congress." And I didn't know bit more what did he mean by Library of Congress. What you talkin' about I don't know.

I ain't never heard my voice in my life. I'm so glad to hear my voice, and I played like from eleven until about six o'clock that afternoon, 'cause I had to go and play my little midnight joints, you know. And he sent me twenty bucks and two copies of the song I made. And it would have taken me, well, how long to make twenty dollars if I worked five days for three dollars and seventy-five cents? That's good money, twenty dollars, and, boy, I really appreciated that. And I say, one day people goin' to hear me on record, like I hear other peoples like John Lee Williamson, Sonny Boy. And Robert Johnson. He had passed but his records strong.

I been listening to blues records all my life as I can remember what the blues was. We didn't have record players then; we had gramophones. You wind them up, but it wasn't too many of them. If I want to hear something, I could go a couple of miles across the fields to where somebody had one.

Barbecue Bob and Blind Lemon Jefferson and Blind Blake, Roosevelt Sykes—they was my thing to listen to. Roosevelt Sykes been playing at "Forty-four Blues" on the piano. I thought that's the best I ever heard. And then here come Little Brother Montgomery with "Vicksburg Blues," and I say, "Goodgodamighty, these cats goin' wild, ain't they."

I pictured so many people from the records. I knowed their color. I knowed their size. When I sees 'em, I was all disappointed. Charley Patton, he had that big voice. I thought the dude weighed two hundred fifty, you know, and he's big and black, much blacker'n I am. When I seen him, he was brown-skinned and neat. I said, "It can't be." He's a little man, pretty, yellow-skinned. Say, "Hey, this man can't be doing this."

Lomax was so impressed with Muddy that he recorded him on a second field trip into Coahoma County the next year as well. "We see one another ever once in a while now," Muddy said. "But the man did a lot for blues people. He discovered Big Bill Boonzy. I think he give him a big hand. He give Son House a hand, he give me a hand, he give Robert Johnson a hand. The man just did a lot for blues."

Not too long after Lomax's second trip to Stovall, Howard Stovall left the plantation for the army, leaving a manager in charge. Muddy explained why he left Stovall for Chicago in 1943.

The manager and I had just a little run-in. I was gettin' twenty-two-and-a-half cents an hour. So I asked him for a little raise and he blew all to pieces.

He says I'm the only man ever ask him for a raise and if I don't want to work for what I'm workin' for, get down off his tractor—his tractor, now whose tractor it is is Howard Stovall's tractor—leave it settin' in the road, don't take it to the barn, don't take to the shop. He came on like that three times, and when he was comin' on, my mind was making up like this: "Ain't but one thing to do—he'd never like me no more and I'd never like him no more—kiss him goodbye."

Chicago, here I come. That big empty city, here I am, little lost black boy in it. I had some people there, but I didn't know where they was. I didn't know nothing. I looked up a address of some boys that we's raised up together and I came to their house and I stayed there. I got here on a Saturday, got a job on a Saturday working at a paper factory, making containers. I was working Monday.

Work there eight hours a day—I never did that before—my paycheck was forty-something bucks or fifty-something bucks a week. You got to be kiddin', you know. Soon I put in some overtime, worked twelve hours a day and I brought a hundred-and-something bring-home pay. I said, "Goodgodamighty, look at the money I got. I have picked that cotton all the year, chop cotton all year, and I didn't draw a hundred dollars. Goodgodamighty, look at the money I got in my pocket."

I got here on a Saturday and my [induction] papers was here Monday morning. I'm so dumb, see, before I left, I go by Coahoma, tell this man at the board I got to go to Chicago to take care of a little business. You know they's calling 'em into the army fast then. I say, "If you should need me in a couple of weeks, send the papers to Chicago." He gets on the phone, calls the manager at Stovall, and the manager says, "We done had this falling out," and *bam*, the papers was there Monday morning.

I don't know what to do now. I ain't got no money to go back to Camp Shelby [the induction center in Mississippi] with. So this boy take me over to this little branch board up here and I told 'em my story and the man there says, "Don't worry. You got a job?"

"Yeah, yeah, I'm workin' now," I tell him.

"Go on to your work," he said. "Don't do nothing 'til you hear from us. Forget these papers."

This is in May. I heard from that draft board in Mississippi in September again. They saying I left a defense job. So help me God, plantation a defense job. Well, I guess it was defense. The cotton was selling to the army, like making shell wadding and making paper. Anyway, I smoothed out a little bit and didn't hear no more.

After he got settled in Chicago, first living with some cousins on the West Side and then in his own apartment nearby, Muddy began playing house parties. "I go to them pay-your-rent things and get me like ten or twelve bucks a night, and I was makin' twenty something some good nights with tips." He started meeting the established blues men of the city—Tampa Red, Big Maceo, Lonnie Johnson, Sonny Boy, Lee Brown—but the one he remembered best was Big Bill Broonzy. "It's hard to get on records then," he recalled. "And you in, you done made hits, and you got a big name—the little fellow ain't nothin'. But Big Bill, he don't care where you from; he didn't look over you 'cause he been on records a long time. 'Do your thing, stay with it, man; if you stay with it, you goin' to make it.' That's what Big Bill told me. Mostly I try to be like him."

Muddy started playing in neighborhood bars, "mostly on weekends, but I have played seven nights a week, worked five days, sometimes six days," he said. "I was makin' five dollars a night playin'; my paycheck was thirty-five dollars a week. I never did go get good jobs. I'd get them little old cheap jobs because I didn't ever keep one too long, and that thirty-five dollars was a good extra side money for me."

In the late years of the war and after, blues hit their heyday in Chicago. "Hey, yeah, when they started World War Two, blues people came up to Chicago like mad from down South," Muddy said. "That's what made Chicago such a big blues city. When I came in there and got myself settled down, it was the biggest blues city there was in the books. You want to hear blues, come to Chicago. This was all over the world."

With the burgeoning recording industry in Chicago after the

war, it was only a matter of time before Muddy became a part of it. "Chess was a company just trying to get off the ground and they was lookin' for talent. They had a black dude out, Sammy Goldberg, hustling up blues talent. And he found me right away." Muddy made "I Feel Like Goin' Home" and "I Can't Be Satisfied," using the same melodies he had recorded for Lomax as "Country Blues" and "I Be's Troubled," and Chess had an overnight sensation on its hands. Muddy and his down-home blues were what the newcomers from the South wanted to hear. They bought his records and went to hear him at the Boogie Woogie Inn, the Du Drop Inn, and the Club Zanzibar.

Now when he went back to the home place at Stovall, he had taken on new status. "I went back in forty-nine. Mr. Stovall, Mr. Howard Stovall, he had some of the congressmen, three, four of 'em, over there. He said, 'This is my boy, he's raised right here.' I'm on my way to Helena to broadcastin'. He say, 'You don't go nowhere. You got to play, play and play.' He give us, like seven dollars or eight dollars apiece and a whole good fifth of whisky. Well, when I was there living, you know, I couldn't make but a dollar and fifty cents there, you know."

And now on trips to Memphis, he was no longer just a country musician playing in the park but the star attraction at the Hippodrome Nightclub. He laughed about the change. "After I made records and everything, I became a big shot then," he said. "They'd hire me from Chicago and go down there. I became a big shot. I played a couple of times at the Hippodrome since I made big shot."

Then, very serious, he said: "Now I'm just kidding about that big shot. I've never been a big shot and I will never be one. I'm just plain Muddy Waters from Clarksdale, Mississippi. We got the headquarters from Stovall. That's me. The big shot, I don't know what you talkin' about. I's just having fun with you."

In the early fifties, Muddy's music began moving away from the down-home pattern, toward an up-tempo, raucous Chicago style.

They started putting a beat to the blues in the fifties. Rhythm and blues started in fifty-two, people started to leaving the real slow stuff and got to pushing it up a little bit. Between blues and rock, that's when the rhythm and blues came in. But to me, I called it slow blues, fast blues. I don't know about all that rhythm and blues. You just play the blues fast, pep it up, that's the onliest difference.

But the best records I made were in the old days back then. That Mississippi sound, that Delta sound is in them old records. You can hear it all the way through.

His hit record, "Hoochie Coochie Man," came out in 1954, the band made a four-month nationwide tour ending in Los Angeles that year, and Muddy was number seven in the annual Cash Box Best R and B artist poll.

And it was in the fifties that Muddy and his group became one of the first black bands to play at the University of Mississippi at Oxford.

That's before the black boy [James Meredith] went to school there. And the twist was out, you can dig what I'm saying? And none of them girls ain't studying about no color, you know. We's playin' that music, they's getting down there doing the twist. Them girls down doing and their little white panties showing, they just twist down there. I'm scared to look *any* way. I had my head over, looking like a pump handle.

So help me Jesus Christ, they put them lights out! If I'm lying, I don't want even to say another word to you—they put them lights out! And they put us out in the rain. I's trying to work to get my check, and the man bring it out to the car. They put us out in the rain, pouring-down rain. Wouldn't even let me stay in the kitchen for to get my check.

It's the black man and the white woman, the ones they jealous of. You don't look up. I don't look up. But a black woman could work for a white man all day long, that's fine, nice. And now you know I'm telling the truth. That's the way it was.

I think it's much different now. But me, I don't care where I am, I'm still black, you know. If I want to get a white wife and she don't want to marry me, what I'm going to say, "Come on, I'm goin' rape you." Get on away from there, that's crazy stuff.

I think they'll probably learn. About forty thousand years from now, maybe they'll learn better. They know more now, true, I believe it. I been down there. It's so much different. I been to Georgia, I been to Florida, I been to all those southern places, so much different, so much different. You could stay in most any hotel you wants. But, see, peoples like me is not gonna go in no place with no kinda disturbance with nobody. You'd be surprised how some people treat me now. I was in Tennessee—Murfreesboro—last week. Man, seem like it not no Tennessee—seem like Chicago."

Muddy's travels took him not only all over the South but all over the world. He began touring Europe in 1958, when he played a circuit with Otis Spann. "I've been there so many times, it just seems at home when I get there, I'm back to Chicago, you know," he said. Ironically, it was his popularity in Europe that introduced him to the young white audience at home. The English rock group, the Rolling Stones, took their name from one of his tunes. When the Beatles first came to the States, the two people they asked to see were rock and roller Bo Diddley and Muddy Waters.[5]

On the walls of his living room, along with pictures of Martin Luther King, Robert and John Kennedy, and a drawing of himself, hung two Grammy awards, two nominations for Grammys, a *Downbeat* magazine plaque, and a plaque from a *Playboy* magazine poll. As Little Brother Montgomery had said: "Muddy Waters wins everything from down there in Nashville. Them Grammys, Muddy Waters win it every year for the last three, four, five, or six years. Muddy Waters a good blues man."

The blues was always Muddy's music. "How I play other music?" he asked. "I don't know how, don't know how. When they goin' to play other music, I just set back and look. My style, it's changed a little bit because you learn a little more, you learn a little more tricks. But it's still the blues."

Like most southern blues men, Muddy grew up hearing churchgoers call the blues "devil music."

5. Bruce Cook, *Listen to the Blues* (New York, 1973), 181.

My grandmother, she say I shouldn't be playing the blues, I should go to church, she'd tell me. Finally I say, "I'm goin' do this, I'm goin' do it." And she got where she didn't bother me about it. But to this day I never figured out why people say that you sinning, devil gonna get you, if you play the blues. Yeah, call it the devil's music.

I had a certain friend of mine say that he don't play no more blues 'cause it's the devil's music. And he was my real buddy 'til he said that. The devil's music [Muddy said, disgustedly]. I don't feel no more it's the devil's music than you playing sweet jazz. You talking about devil's playing, you can do just as much devil harm playing sweet jazz as you will playing my kind of blues.

My blues is something that makes people happy with, to pick you up, tell you what done happen to you. My blues get you up. But my blues is not to set there and smoke that grass and say, "Hey, jam, jam, jam, jam, jam!"

[Why do you think Mississippi produced so many outstanding blues men? he was asked.] So much of hard times was down there. We had nothing to do but go from house to house and try to get a half a pint, a pint, of that moonshine and learn how to play them guitars and try to make ourselves enjoy ourselves. That's the onliest way we could give over. Everybody had the blues in the blacks. It's the late years when blacks don't have no blues. After World War Two, they seen things, eyes came open, they woke up and we don't have no more blues. But every black had blues then.

I think Mississippi was the hardest time of all. Arkansas people doing fairly good. They was eatin'. I know I got up one Christmas morning and we didn't have nothing to eat. We didn't have a apple, we didn't have a orange, we didn't have a cake, we didn't have nothing. I came up hard. Days passed, months passed, I didn't have a nickel in my pocket, and I'm growin' up to be a big-sized boy. I'd be hungry and go by a store and couldn't buy a nickel's worth of bologna. That's how poor I was. I says, "Um, do I have a curse on me? Why everybody got something but me?"

Like I said, I've paid my dues. There's a lot of these kids you see 'round here playing, call themselves playing blues; they don't know anything. Just learn how to play the guitar a little bit and get a hundred-thousand-dollar contract. Me, poor me, I never had nothing, never will. Just thank God I'm living. I'm fifty-eight years old. I just feel good, you know, and love peoples. I love peoples.

Well, I did my thing and I feel good and I feel great for doing it. I'm so thankful I lived long enough to do it, to get it over. And there's so many white kids—not the people come to see me, I mean musicians—is doing things behind me, that just love my thing. Sometime I gets shaky, you know. I must have set a place for something.

It was time to go. The train back to Chicago was due, and the interview had been going on for more than an hour. Muddy gave us a copy of his latest album, shook hands, and asked to be remembered to the Stovall family. Driving to the station, Cameron said, "I've never seen Muddy talk so much."

Albert King. He helped urbanize the blues.
Courtesy of Memphis *Press-Scimitar*

Bobby Blue Bland, *left*, and B. B. King. They've come a long way from their days as Beale Streeters.
Courtesy of Associated Booking Corporation

# 18 · B. B., Bobby, and Big Albert

There is a ritual that unfolds at a blues show, unplanned and unrehearsed—a kind of ritual of spontaneity much like that which is an unwritten but integral part of the program at fundamentalist black church services. This is ironical, considering the eternal conflict between many church people and blues people, but understandable, too, because so much in the blues—the fervor, the outpouring of *feeling*—springs from experiences in the church. Numerous blues singers refer to the audience as the "congregation." The music and the message from the stage draw a response not unlike that which the measured, emotional cadence from the pulpit brings from the amen corner. And while the church has produced many a blues singer, the blues have been the training ground for untold numbers of preachers.

For B. B. King, the ritual involves far more than mere performance or the time he spends onstage. In an era when "total performance" has become a catch phrase in entertainment, he concentrates on total *appearance*. Night after night, year after year, in an incredible pace, which he maintains even after having become the world's premiere blues man, he makes it a point to show up early for his engagements, whether on the chitlin' circuit, which he continues to travel, or in the champagne settings to which he has won entrée. Lesser entertainers than he yearn for privacy and complain of a too-demanding public; he meets his willingly. He has paid his dues, but he still feels certain obligations.

For this concert at the Mid-South Coliseum in Memphis, he arrives at 9 P.M., knowing full well that as the performer with the top billing it will be at least midnight before he takes the stage. The show, which has drawn a capacity attendance of almost twelve thousand, is in its second hour, but a hundred or so waiting for a glimpse of him remain crowded around the entrance for entertainers. There would be many more than that, but Sunbeam Mitchell, an early Beale Street sponsor of B. B. and a cosponsor of this show, has shooed them away. Those remaining, mostly young and mostly black, include another old friend, Rufus Thomas, who calls himself the world's oldest teenager. B. B. hugs him and Sunbeam, exchanging pleasantries, then turns his attention to the young attention seekers. Perspiring but smiling, he stands among them for a half-hour, signing autographs and accepting an occasional hug or kiss from admiring young black women, before someone brings him a chair. He puffs on an unfilled, unlighted white pipe with an elaborate, curved stem. He'll change later into ruffled stage attire of many colors, which will set off oohs and ahhs, but even now his baby-blue business-cut suit brings a compliment. It's his cue to repeat one of his favorite lines: "Everybody thinks you got to wear torn clothes, scratch yourself all over, and not know your ABC's to sing the blues." He laughs, but he knows that everybody knows it once was no laughing matter, that his dreams once were as tattered as his jeans. Prompted by his audience, he again traces the long, long road from Itta Bena, Mississippi, to Beale Street and then to Chicago, New York, Las Vegas, and around the world.

Even in such an informal gathering, a kind of call-and-response byplay is evident. "Right on, brother," a woman murmurs. "You the greatest, B.," a man says. B. B. shakes his head slowly.

Some people, they tell me "Man, you're just the greatest there is when it comes to blues," but I don't let it give me no big head. I know my limitations. I know there are things I'd like to do that I can't do. I know there are people who can sing and play better than me—people that nobody know. Every night, every show, I'm still trying to learn, still scuffling. You know, I scuffle just as hard now as back when I started. Because when you get there, you know, you want to stay there, and that means you still got to scuffle.

And then comes his message, as a sort of defender of the faith, for his followers to go forth and spread the word that there's nothing bad about the blues, that they should be proud of them, not ashamed. "Some young people dig us, but do you know that most of them are *white*? The blues belong to *us*. Lots of our young people think the blues is low down and obscene. They ought to be proud of the blues, because that's the one thing Negroes have that nobody in the world can equal. Nobody nowhere, no way. I saw this singer in Vienna, a Chinaman, singing the blues, and he sang them OK, but not like the Negro. Nobody can do the blues like black people do the blues."

B. B. finally excuses himself and heads for his dressing room, where he'll go over the same ground again in an interview with a television newsman before going on stage. Rufus Thomas, grinning, shakes his head.

He's come a long way from that old raggedy guitar. B.'s come a long way from Beale Street Amateur Nights. And like they say, the more things change the more they stay the same. B., back when he was just starting out at WDIA, used to do this singing commercial for Pepticon. Now he's doing these television commercials for Pepsi Cola and Colgate and AT&T.

Amateur Nights on Beale, that's where B. B. King got started, right there on Beale. See, at one time we had contestants come up to perform, and then after everybody performed, they'd all come back on stage and the audience would applaud for first prize, which was five dollars, and three dollars for second, and two dollars for third. B. B. would be in that line. Then it got so that they cut that out, and everybody that come up would get a dollar. And B. B. was happy to come up and get that dollar. Now he knew that I knew that he needed it, and I would put him on anytime he came down there to the Palace Theater. He would play old raggedy guitar and sing the blues good and he was a good entertainer even at that time. I mean, the potentials were good, and I'd put him on there so he could get that dollar. And that was the extent of it, one dollar and one dollar only. One dollar. No soles on his shoes and a raggedy guitar.

When he first came on WDIA, which Nat D. Williams and I arranged that, he used to have a fifteen-minute segmented program. And I'd just turn my radio off. *Off.* B. B. sounded so bad it hurt your feeling. I mean it hurt your whole heart, mind, soul and body. But B. B.'s such a beautiful man. . . . People told him how bad he sounded, and he kept digging. It only goes to show you that if you keep digging, you going to reach it. And B. B. kept on, kept on, and started making "Three O'Clock in the Morning," first big record, and other songs. And he's still keeping on. B.'s beautiful.

The words are echoed by Bobby Blue Bland in the tiny dressing room adjoining B. B.'s. "B. and I, we started out on Beale Street right after Jackie Robinson broke into big league baseball," he says slowly. "Well, B. is the same thing in blues as Jackie Robinson was to baseball. I'll tell you what: B. didn't just go up there by himself; he opened the door for a lot more of us. He's the father of black music. And he's, well, he's a perfect gentleman. Nice guy. Very humble."

Bland, too, has come a long way from their scuffling days on Beale, but he has remained ever in B. B.'s shadow. He had arrived a few minutes before B. B., unnoticed except by Sunbeam Mitchell. Bland, sipping from a can of beer, shared it with Sunbeam. They talked about the days twenty-five years earlier when B. B. and Bobby, as well as other Beale Street singers, performed at Mitchell's Club Handy for five dollars a night and all the chili they could eat.

Those were the days, too, when Bobby jockeyed cars for fifteen hours a day in a parking lot at the foot of Beale, then did his gigs. It was as a driver, in fact, that he became associated not only with B. B. but with Roscoe Gordon and the late Johnny Ace. Later he became a member of their group, the Beale Streeters, as a singer. Unlike most blues men, he plays no instrument.

He hadn't even intended to become a blues singer when, still a teenager, he moved to Memphis after World War II from the nearby farming community of Rosemark, Tennessee.

I've always been concerned with singing, first spirituals and then white country blues—you know, what they call hillbilly. There used to be a morning radio show here in Memphis, Gene Steele, the Singing Salesman, and when I listened to him sing "Take That Night Train to Memphis," I got interested in hillbilly music and in coming to Memphis. Then I started listening to the Grand Ole Opry and singing hillbilly songs at the store there in Rosemark. That was kind of unusual, a black kid singing white songs. I made me some nickels and dimes.

When I moved to Memphis, it was very, very tough. Not many places blacks could venture into. It was the wrong time and the wrong place for a black singer to make it singing white country blues. So. . . .

He shrugs. There's no apparent bitterness that he didn't become the Jackie Robinson of white country music, a role that was to be filled fifteen years later by another professional baseball player, Charley Pride.

Just as the radio show at WDIA served as the launching pad for B. B., it helped Bobby get his career off the ground. "B. B. had me on one Saturday morning, and I sang a song I wrote, 'Army Blues,' about not wanting to go to the army," he says, grinning. "Well, I guess I wasn't the only one who didn't want to go to Korea. People started calling in to request the song, and it became my first recording."

He did go to the army, and by the time of his discharge in 1955 Duke Records, which had signed him to a contract, had transferred from Memphis to Houston. "I remember the bus fare to Houston was $13.80," he says. "They sent me $15."

The hard times, though, were behind him. His records since then have sold consistently well, often making the rhythm and blues charts, and he commands top billing unless, as in this concert, B. B. King happens to be on hand. And regardless of billing, it probably is unfair to compare the two: Their material, their style, their interpretation of blues remain in stark contrast.

I like the soft touch [says Bobby]. I don't like the harsh. I listened to a lot of Perry Como, Tony Bennett, Nat King Cole for diction, for delivery. And I still know more hillbilly tunes than I do blues. Hank Snow, Hank Williams, Eddy Arnold—so much feeling, so much sadness. The only thing I can relate to is songs that tell a story. True lyrics, true story. You know, a lot of people fail to listen—that's why they make fun of hillbilly music. I listen to "Hee Haw." Buck Owens, he has a lot of Baptist in his songs.

Maybe what's happening to the blues will happen to hillbilly music, too. Blues is getting its proper chance, proper respect. It's not a bad word any more. The young generation is changing things. White people are listening now. You can sit down and be yourself.

Big Albert King lumbers into the dressing room, clenching a pipe with exaggerated curved stem between his teeth, mopping at a face glistening with sweat. He has just finished his act and the applause goes on. There are no encores because of the top-heavy program.

"Hey, man, you coming to my birthday party at Sunbeam's?" he says to Bland. Bobby grins. "I don't know, baby. You making it mighty hard on us out there," he says, motioning toward the stage. "Listen to that. You going to be a tough act to follow. Your blues getting to be as big as you."

He's huge: six-four, 260 pounds. It's true, too, that his blues are very big at the moment—rivaling, perhaps, those of half-brother B. B. Most of his lyrics may epitomize the country blues, such as "Drowning on Dry Land," but there's an urban element in Albert King, as surely as in B. B.

If B. B. is regarded as the greater guitarist, his praises sung and his style emulated by legions of young people, Albert King is one of the unsung heroes in the instrumental urbanizing of the blues. As with so many others, it began with twanging a wire plucked from the barnyard fence during his boyhood in Indianola, Mississippi, and Forrest City, Arkansas.

You nail the wire up with a bottle at the top and a brick at the bottom and you pick the one string. It gives you a Hawaiian sound, a beautiful sound if you use small wire.

My first guitar I paid out a dollar and twenty-five cents. This boy wanted to go to the movies with his girl. He wanted a big soda called a belly washer and one of these big stageplank cakes. I was a little richer than him and I said, "Man, ain't but one way I can let you have the money, that's to get the guitar." I worked with that thing day and night.

The more he worked with the wailing and whining sound of Mississippi Delta bottleneckers, the more he merged it with that of the Hawaiian steel guitar—and then he electrified the combination. He and others like him are to the blues, in short, what REA was to the country. Blues purists may complain, just as some country people fought rural electrification, but the fact remains that Big Albert helped to inject into the country blues a sound-of-the-city power that was to reverberate two decades later in the music of a Stax recording colleague in Memphis, Isaac Hayes.

Back when I started playing, most of the great blues men played my part of the country at one time or another—Son House, Howling Wolf [Chester Burnett], Muddy Waters, the second Sonny Boy Williamson, Lonnie Johnson—they didn't know A from Z, no chord changes, no different keys. I never taken a music lesson in my life. I can read music now, learned by listening to other fellows and watching them read. I'm pretty equipped to handle it now. I learned the hard way.

Nowadays we got kind of a modern way of doing the blues. But we're saying the same thing. It all means somebody has been mistreated through life, somewhere along the line. Or they are fixing to get up and get let down. A lot of people give modern words to it. It all adds up to the same thing.

When I was real small, I had to slip off and go to the after-hours places. People would play a while, half of the night, get drunk and go to sleep and wake up and start again. It looked like everybody was in the country then. People was more together then. They didn't have too much, but they lived.

Living is a little bit easier now, for the body, but not for the mind.

You got something on your mind. You got to keep yourself on the ball. It's not really easy.

Big Albert left Memphis, where he was night manager of a garage for four years, about the same time the younger B. B. arrived in the late 1940s. By 1956, long after B. B. had established himself as a full-time music man, Albert was still working in construction, playing with his band on weekends in Osceola, Arkansas, and rehearsing on rainy days.

I had scuffled and bought me an old forty-six Chevy coupe—and I had it paid for. I had my guitar and an amplifier. I had one pair of summer pants, about three, four white shirts, one sports shirt, and my coveralls, of course.

I had made a trip to Saint Louis, and a friend of mine taken me around to two or three places where the bands was playing. The crowds was nice, you know, big crowds, really getting together. I said, "Jesus Christ, all this work. I should be up here. I should be able to get in with somebody." I went on to Saint Louis.

I sat in with two or three bands, did my little thing, you know. Then I sat in with a band at the Lakeside Club in East Saint Louis. The man heard me play the blues, and he hired me right away at nine dollars a night. In the meantime, this friend was a little shadetree mechanic; I would help him around.

I did that for a year and a half. Then I started my own three-piece group, working at a tavern in Kemlock, Missouri. You were just likely to get shot at. They was really rough. I was getting all the gate. If I didn't draw nobody, I didn't have nothing. But they liked the way I was playing and singing. People went to hiring me. Things got to going real good.

I bought a fifty-eight red Ford station wagon and put my name on the side in white letters—Albert "Blues Boy" King. I tell you I was really getting together.

Still, another decade was to pass before Albert would enjoy the wide success that had been B. B.'s for years. In 1968, he was booked by rock entrepreneur Bill Graham for the Fillmore West in San Francisco on the same bill with Jimi Hendrix and Big Brother and the Holding Company. They packed the place for four nights, and Big Albert had earned himself a place in the hearts of the record-buying youth market. The admiration worked both ways.

The kids got tired of all this rock 'n' roll. The blues is a different sound. It's pure. The kids are very understanding. They know what you are doing long before you get there. They're very smart. You have to be clean with them, you have to be straight. Either you give a good show, either you are for real or they drop you like a hot potato if you are phony. This I appreciate them for. They are the best bunch of people I ever played for in all my life. When I quit playing for them, I'll quit playing.

• • •

Now it's past midnight. Bobby Bland and B. B. King still haven't taken their turns on the stage, but the master of ceremonies appears to be in no hurry. Amid one of his toilet-humor tales, Bland's musicians—nine of them, two horns included—march onto the stage and begin tuning their instruments. "You just hold your horses," the emcee barks at them. "It's not time for God yet."

Part of his resentment can be explained, perhaps, by the fact that Bland's is the only act of the evening not to be introduced by the emcee. Mel Jackson, Bland's tiny trumpeter and manager, makes a low-key introduction contrasting sharply with the high-pitched intensity of the others. Bobby ambles to center stage, sings one line softly into the microphone, tosses a falsetto holler over the shoulder—a stylistic gesture he repeats at least once in each of his numbers—and then waits for the congregation's churchlike reaction to subside. The call-and-response encouragement, of course, comes from the middle-aged-and-up part of the audience; from the younger generation, there is a torrent of shrieking not unlike that at an Elvis Presley concert or, in another day, the frenzy of the bobby-sox fans of Frank Sinatra. He finishes his first song, says it's nice to be back performing for home folks including his mother, who has come up from Rosemark for the show. He asks for and receives a round of applause for her.

It's quickly obvious that Bland has become more a balladeer than blues man in the pure sense of the word. The lyrics are

more important than the music licks. This may be personal pref-
erence to some degree, but probably a stronger reason is that,
unlike most male blues singers, he plays no instrument. There's
at least one advantage: he enjoys a freedom of movement that
most others lack. Surprisingly graceful for a man of his size, he
strolls about the stage continuously, flipping the microphone cord
this way and that, using his voice itself as an instrument; now it
is Nat King Cole velvet, now Perry Como lazy smoothness, now
Dinah Washington torchiness, now even—with that over-the-
shoulder growl—B. B. King bluesiness. But his songs—"Driftin'
and Driftin'," "The Feeling Is Gone," "Gone for Good"—generally are more tender, less assertive than the gut-level blues.

As he has done for more than two decades, Bland closes his
show with the same song, "Stormy Monday," in the same manner,
getting down on his knees to sing beseechingly: "Lord have
mercy, Lord have mercy on me." Call it stylistic or call it gim-
mickry—but call it effective. The applause goes on for a full ten
minutes after he has left the stage. Still the policy of no encores
prevails. It's now approaching 1 A.M. It's time for the main man.

In contrast to Bland, B. B. King starts his show with an instrumental solo on Lucille, his electric guitar. Whereas Bland uses
his voice as an instrument, B. B. uses Lucille not merely as an
instrument but as a voice in itself. Indeed, as soon as he straps
Lucille on, there are calls from the audience to "Let Lucille talk,
B.,—let Lucille sing." He *does* let the guitar do the talking quite
often as he tries to think of a new line to toss at the audience.
Lucille responds with a bottleneck vibrato even though B. B.
uses no bottleneck; he was never able to master the slide that
cousin Booker White had tried to teach him to use, but he man-
aged to duplicate the sound—master the technique, in fact—with
trilling fingers. Others before B. B. had developed a style of
"bending" notes, but he perfected it.

For all his excellence and innovative improvisation on the
guitar, however, it's not really what most of his audience came to
hear. As many old-time blues musicians—friends of his included

—have been muttering, maybe he and his band are indulging in too much innovation, too much jazz, too much bop, too much swing, too much *white* (though his back-up musicians are all black) to suit most blues people. What he sings, how he sings, stirs the crowd more than the music accompanying the message. And mostly what he sings—with classic moan, groan, and blues holler—are songs built around the classic theme of the bare-bones blues: man and woman and their relationship, especially their sexual relationship. His blues, perhaps because of the affluence they have brought him, are more authoritative than most. He lays down the law to his woman as he sings about "Paying the Cost to Be the Boss" and "I Got Some Help I Don't Need." There is no Bobby Blue Bland-ness in his finale, either, his theme song, "Why I Sing the Blues," in which the quintessential blues man gets down to the essence of the blues bred aboard the slave ships and lashed into life by the white man's whip.

He's besieged backstage again after the show ends at 1:30 A.M. He'll spend another half-hour or so signing autographs and chatting. After that, there's the party at Sunbeam's place. They'll be there until dawn helping Big Albert celebrate his birthday, swapping memories of old Beale Street and singing its blues.

# Bibliography

Adkins, Walter P. "Beale Street Goes to the Polls." M.A. thesis, Ohio State University, 1935.

*The Blue Light District of Beale Street.* Nashville: Architect-Engineer Associates, 1974.

Bridges, G. C. *Memphis in Pictures.* Memphis: George C. Bridges, 1940.

Church, Annette E., and Roberta Church. *The Robert R. Churches of Memphis.* Ann Arbor: Annette E. Church and Roberta Church, 1974.

Cook, Bruce. *Listen to the Blues.* New York: Charles Scribner's Sons, 1973.

Coppock, Paul R. *Memphis Sketches.* Memphis: Friends of Memphis and Shelby County Libraries, 1976.

Daniels, Jonathan. "He Suits Memphis." *Saturday Evening Post,* June 10, 1939, pp. 22–23, 46–55.

Dixon, R. M. W., and J. Godrich. *Reporting the Blues.* London: Studio Vista, 1970.

Federal Writers' Project. *Tennessee: A Guide to the State.* New York: Viking Press, 1939.

Ferris, William, Jr. *Blues from the Delta.* London: Studio Vista, 1970.

Fox, Jesse W. "Beale Street and the Blues." *West Tennessee Historical Society Papers,* XIII (1959), 128–47.

Fuller, T. O. *Pictorial History of the American Negro.* Memphis: Pictorial History, 1933.

————. *Twenty Years in Public Life.* Nashville: National Baptist Publishing Board, 1910.

Fulling, Virgil. "Amateur Night on Beale Street." *Scribner's Magazine* CI (May, 1937), 59–61.

Groom, Bob. *The Blues Revival.* London: Studio Vista, 1970.

Hamilton, G. P. *The Bright Side of Memphis.* Memphis: G. P. Hamilton, 1908.

Handy, W. C. *Father of the Blues.* New York: MacMillan, 1941.

Hornsby, Alton, Jr. *In The Cage*. Chicago: Quadrangle Books, 1971.

Hughes, Langston. *The Big Sea*. New York: Alfred A. Knopf, 1940.

Hutchins, Fred. "Beale Street As It Was." *West Tennessee Historical Society Papers*, XXVI (1972), 56–63.

Hutchins, Fred L. *What Happened in Memphis*. Kingsport, Tenn.: Fred L. Hutchins, 1965.

Jones, LeRoi. *Blues People*. New York: William Morrow, 1963.

Keil, Charles. *Urban Blues*. Chicago: University of Chicago Press, 1966.

King, Woodie, and Earl Anthony, eds. *Black Poets and Prophets*. New York: New American Library, 1972.

Lamon, Lester C. "Negroes in Tennessee, 1900–1930." Ph.D. dissertation, University of North Carolina, 1971.

Lee, George W. *Beale Street: Where the Blues Began*. College Park, Md.: McGrath, 1934.

———. "Poetic Memories of Beale Street." *West Tennessee Historical Society Papers*, XXVI (1972), 64–73.

McIlwaine, Shields. *Memphis Down in Dixie*. New York: E. P. Dutton, 1948.

Miller, William D. *Mr. Crump of Memphis*. Baton Rouge: Louisiana State University Press, 1964.

Oliver, Paul. *The Story of the Blues*. New York: Chilton, 1969.

Olsson, Bengt. *Memphis Blues*. London: Studio Vista, 1970.

Petrie, John Clarence. "Demand Justice for Negroes." *Christian Century*, LI, (July 4, 1934), 910.

Phillips, Virginia. "Rowlett Paine, Mayor of Memphis, 1920–24," *West Tennessee Historical Society Papers*, XXVI (1972).

Powdermaker, Hortense. *After Freedom*. New York: Viking, 1939.

Puckett, Newbell Niles. *The Magic and Folk Beliefs of the Southern Negro*. New York: Dover Publications, 1969.

Rowe, Mike. *Chicago Breakdown*. London: Eddison Press, 1973.

Russell, Tony. *Blacks, Whites and Blues*. New York: Stein and Day, 1970.

Terrell, Mary Church. *A Colored Woman in a White World*. Washington, D.C.: Ransdell, 1940.

Tucker, David M. *Black Pastors and Leaders: Memphis, 1819–1972*. Memphis: Memphis State University Press, 1975.

———. *Lieutenant Lee of Beale Street*. Nashville: Vanderbilt University Press, 1971.

Weathers, Ed. "Carnival Knowledge." *City of Memphis Magazine*, (April, 1977), 34.

Zur Heide, Karl Gert. *Deep South Piano*. London: Studio Vista, 1970.

# Index